ACCELERATED PROFICIENCY FOR ACCELERATED TIMES

ACCELERATED PROFICIENCY FOR ACCELERATED TIMES

A REVIEW OF KEY CONCEPTS AND METHODS
TO SPEED UP PERFORMANCE

Dr. Raman K. Attri

Copyrights © 2018 Speed To Proficiency Research: S2Pro©

All rights reserved. No part of this publication may be reproduced, distributed, or transmitted in any form or by any means, including photocopying, recording, or other electronic or mechanical methods, without the prior written permission of the publisher, except in the case of brief quotations embodied in critical reviews and certain other noncommercial uses permitted by copyright law.

ISBN: 978-981-14-6276-4 (e-book)
ISBN: 978-981-14-6275-7 (paperback)
ISBN: 978-981-14-6274-0 (hardcover)

Published at Singapore
Printed in the United States of America

https://www.speedtoproficiency.com
info@speedtoproficiency.com

National Library Board, Singapore Cataloguing in Publication Data

Names: Attri, Raman K., 1973-
Title: Accelerated proficiency for accelerated times : a review of key concepts and methods to speed up performance / Dr. Raman K. Attri.
Description: Singapore : Speed To Proficiency Research, [2020] | Includes bibliographic references and index.
Identifiers: OCN 1154810008 | ISBN 978-981-146275-7 (paperback) | 978-981-14-6274-0 (hardcover) | 978-981-14-6276-4
Subjects: LCSH: Core competencies. | Executive ability. | Employees--Training of.
Classification: DDC 658.3124--dc23

To a great friend, Pal,

for being there for me,

despite the speed of life

"When you shorten the time it takes for workers to become proficient, the capital and resources required to introduce a new product, maintain operations and infrastructure, and perform a service are also proportionally reduced. I call this *speed to proficiency*."

Charles Fred (2002, p. 16)
Breakaway

CONTENTS

PREFACE xiii

1   INTRODUCTION 1

2   JOB PERFORMANCE: ASPECTS AND DIMENSIONS 7
    2.1 Performance Improvement   8
        2.1.1   Human resource development   8
        2.1.2   Learning paradigm of HRD   10
        2.1.3   Performance paradigm of HRD   11
    2.2 Dimensions of Job Performance   18
        2.2.1   Value of individual performance   19
        2.2.2   Job performance   19
        2.2.3   Dimensions of job performance   20
        2.2.4   Complex nature of job performance   22
    2.3 Perspectives on job performance   22
        2.3.1   Behavioral vs outcome performance   23
        2.3.2   Task vs contextual performance   27
        2.3.3   Individual vs team performance   29
        2.3.4   Multidimensionality of job performance   31
    2.4 Learning and Performance   32
        2.4.1   Abilities, knowledge and skills   32
        2.4.2   Central role of learning   34
    2.5 Acquiring Skilled Job Performance   37
        2.5.1   Fitts and Posner's three-stage skill acquisition   38
        2.5.2   Anderson's three-stage learning model   40
        2.5.3   Ackerman's three-stage model   42

2.5.4	Langan-Fox's skill acquisition model	44
2.6 Summary		48

3 PROFICIENT PERFORMANCE: JOURNEY AND TRANSITION ...49

3.1 Novice-to-Expert Progression		50
3.1.1	Novice to expert progression as stages	51
3.1.2	Problem-solving approaches as an indicator of stages	52
3.1.3	Tasks performance as an indicator of stages	53
3.1.4	Measurable attributes as an indicator of stages	53
3.1.5	Novice to expert transition as a process	54
3.1.6	Implications	55
3.2 Stages of Proficiency Acquisition		55
3.3 Proficiency Scaling		62
3.3.1	Hoffman's proficiency scaling	63
3.3.2	Jacobs' taxonomy of human competence	66
3.3.3	Implications of proficiency scaling	66
3.4 Proficient Performance		69
3.4.1	Role of proficiency in performance	69
3.4.2	Development of proficient performers	70
3.4.3	Characteristics of proficient performers	71
3.4.4	Measuring proficient performance	76
3.4.5	Importance of proficient performance	77
3.5 Expert Performance		78
3.5.1	Attributes of expertise	78
3.5.2	A holistic view of expertise	82
3.5.3	Construct of expert performance	83
3.5.4	Deliberate practice mechanism	84
3.5.5	Time to expertise	86
3.5.6	Relevance of expert performance	86
3.6 Expert vs Proficient		89
3.7 Summary		90

4 ACCELERATED PROFICIENCY: MEANING AND DRIVERS 93

4.1 Accelerating Proficiency		94
4.1.1	Time to Proficiency Metrics	97

4.1.2	Studies on time to proficiency	100
4.1.3	How long is time to proficiency	103

4.2 Accelerating Learning vs Proficiency ... 105
4.3 Business Drivers for Speed ... 108
4.4 Theory of Accelerated Proficiency ... 114

4.4.1	Theoretical aspects	114
4.4.2	CTT as Basis of Accelerated Proficiency	115
4.4.3	CFT as Basis of Accelerated Proficiency	117
4.4.4	Unified Theory to Explain Accelerated Proficiency	119

4.5 Summary ... 120

5 METHODS TO ACCELERATE PROFICIENCY ... 123

5.1 Thematic Categories of Methods ... 124
5.2 Cognitive task analysis (CTA) methods ... 126

5.2.1	Using CTA to design training	128
5.2.2	Complimenting CTA with other methods	132
5.2.3	Challenges and benefits	134
5.2.4	Cogntive work analysis	134

5.3 Simulations-based Training methods ... 135

5.3.1	Time compression	135
5.3.2	Expert-based simulation	137
5.3.3	Above Real-time Training	137
5.3.4	Gamification	139
5.3.5	Virtual or synthetic environments	142
5.3.6	Immersive strategies	142
5.3.7	Operational simulation	143
5.3.8	Benefits	145

5.4 Scenario-based Training methods ... 146

5.4.1	Scenario-based training	146
5.4.2	Desirable difficulties	147
5.4.3	Tough case time compression	148
5.4.4	Conceptual skills	152

5.5 Part-task Based Methods ... 154
5.6 Workplace Activities-based Methods ... 157

5.6.1	Informal and social learning	157
5.6.2	Experiential and action learning	158
5.6.3	Structured workplace activities	159

5.6.4	Cognitive apprenticeship	161
5.6.5	Structured on-the-job training	165
5.6.6	Deliberate practice at work	167
5.6.7	Deliberate performance through action learning	168
5.6.8	Learning organizations	169

5.7 Technology-based methods 172
    5.7.1 Expert-based systems 172
    5.7.2 Tutoring systems 172
    5.7.3 Performance support systems 173
    5.7.4 Knowledge capture systems 174
    5.7.5 Personalised learning systems 175

5.8 Summary 179

6 CHALLENGE TO ACCELERATE PROFICIENCY 181

6.1 Challenges to Accelerate Proficiency 182
6.2 Issues with Training Methods 184
6.3 Issues with Workplace Methods 190
6.4 Applying Lessons from this book 193
6.5 Final Words 198

RELEVANT PUBLICATIONS 203
REFERENCES 205
INDEX 257
THE AUTHOR 259

ACCELERATED PROFICIENCY FOR ACCELERATED TIMES

PREFACE

I wrote this book to pioneer a growing area of research on *Accelerated Proficiency* in organizational and business literature. The business world is not only changing at a high pace, but it is also becoming overly complex. The skills and knowledge acquired today become irrelevant or obsolete quickly. There are instances when merely one day of delay in launching a product could cost a company millions of dollars. This business reality of cut-throat competition between global organizations is everlasting. In that kind of dynamics, it is indeed not viable for businesses to wait for their employees to become proficient in the critical skills required to support the business, customers, and to address the competition.

That's where the concepts of accelerated proficiency, time to proficiency, and speed to proficiency are making rounds in business conversations and literature. The organizations are now shifting their focus on how they can shorten time to proficiency of employees and bring them up to speed to the required performance.

However, it is easier said than done. Most organizations have been struggling to bring their employees up to speed on job-related skills. They have to wait sometimes for months or years for their employees to come up to the desired level of performance. The last five decades' research on performance and allied areas has revealed some processes, methodologies, and methods to effectively reduce the time it takes for an employee to deliver consistent performance. The reality is that even today, despite the extensive research, there is a lack of proven knowledge-base in the training industry as a whole. The key gap is the lack of effective or result-giving mechanisms to accelerate the proficiency of employees.

Time is money and a reduction in time should be the first goal of any training program or any other employee development initiative. That is the pretext this book. This book is developed out of extensive literature review I conducted during my doctorate research at Southern Cross University.

To develop a condensed and coherent knowledge-base on *Accelerated Proficiency,* this book is organized around reviews of studies on performance and proficiency from several different disciplines spanning over five decades. The book explores concepts, themes, nature, and challenges associated with the process of accelerating proficiency.

In particular, this book is designed to explore some questions - What is the nature of the proficiency in the organization? What is the meaning and goal of accelerating proficiency? Whether or not proficiency and performance of employees can be accelerated? What kind of methods has been researched and proven to accelerate proficiency?

ACCELERATED PROFICIENCY FOR ACCELERATED TIMES

It is imperative to clarify that the intent of this book is not to develop or converge to any framework on accelerated proficiency. The discussion in this book is limited to literature review while the findings, models, and framework that came out of my doctorate research are covered elsewhere. Readers are encouraged to read my other books to read about proposed models or frameworks: *Modelling accelerated proficiency in organisations: practices and strategies to shorten time-to-proficiency of the workforce – Doctorate thesis (2018)*. *Designing Training to Shorten Time To Proficiency: Online, Classroom and On-the-job Learning Strategies from Research* (2019), *Speed to Proficiency in Organizations: A Research Report on Model, Practices and Strategies to Shorten Time to Proficiency (2019)*, *Models of Skill Acquisition and Expertise Development: A Quick Reference of Summaries (2019)* and *Accelerate Time to Proficiency: Model, Process and Strategies (forthcoming)*.

I encourage new and seasoned researchers to join hands to develop and extend this budding research area. Contact me for any joint research work.

Dr Raman K Attri

May 2020

1

INTRODUCTION

During the last half a century, researchers and scholars have tried to unlock the mysteries of human learning, identify the process of developing people to the higher level of competence and improving overall performance at work and in other areas. 'Proficiency is critical to performance in complex work contexts' (Hoffman, Feltovich, et al. 2010, p. 250). In a work context, proficiency has been defined as a level where a practitioner is able to perform reliably and consistently (Kuchenbrod 2016). It is crucial for the sustainable existence of any company to develop their employees' knowledge, skills, and performance to the desired level of proficiency (Bruck 2015).

INTRODUCTION

This book addresses a critical challenge in modern organizations: the workforce generally takes a significant amount of time to reach full proficiency in several job roles, which in turn puts market and financial pressures on organizations. The literature review presented in this book aims to explore this relatively new research topic. Specifically, the focus of the review is on how organizations view the concept and process of accelerating proficiency, and the methods/approaches organizations have used successfully to decrease the time to proficiency of the workforce.

The literature review is based on the general premise that knowledge and skills play vital parts in delivering desired performance at the job. As people gain more proficiency and expertise in the job, their performance level increases. Accelerating the pace with which people acquire proficiency thus sits at intersections of job performance, skill acquisition, and proficiency development. The literature review approaches the topics of performance, knowledge and skill acquisition, expertise, and proficiency from a historical perspective first before reviewing the emergence of the concept of accelerated proficiency and methods to accelerate proficiency.

The general theories underlying the concept of proficiency (and thus that of accelerated proficiency) are grounded in seminal and classic works conducted during fiver decades between the 1960s and 2010s by leading theorists such as Murphy (1989), Campbell (Campbell 1990; Campbell, McHenry & Wise 1990; Campbell et al. 1993), Borman and Motowidlo (Borman & Motowidlo 1993; Motowidlo, Borman & Schmit 1997; Motowidlo & Van Scotter 1994), Dreyfus and Dreyfus (Dreyfus & Dreyfus 1986, 2004, 2005),

Fitt (Fitt 1964; Fitt & Posner 1967), Anderson (1981, 1982, 2000), Ackerman (1988, 1992), Chi (Chi 1982; Chi 2006; Chi, Glaser & Rees 1982; Chi, Glaser & Farr 1988; Chi, Glaser & Rees 1981; Glaser & Chi 1988), Ericsson (Ericsson 2000, 2002, 2003, 2004, 2006a, 2007, 2008, 2009a, 2009b, 2009c; Ericsson et al. 1993; Ericsson & Charness 1994; Ericsson, Prietula & Cokely 2007; Ericsson & Towne 2010; Ericsson & Ward 2007), Spiro (Spiro & Jehng 1990; Spiro et al. 1987; Spiro et al. 1990; Spiro et al. 2003) and Klein (Klein 1993, 1997, 1998, 2003; Klein & Baxter 2009; Klien & Borders 2016; Klien, Hintze & Saab 2013; Klein et al. 1997), among others. The work of these theorists is thoroughly reviewed, alongside recent developments in the literature.

The review presented in this book takes forward the conceptualization of *accelerated proficiency* and *accelerated expertise* proposed in experimental research conducted by Hoffman (Hoffman et al. 2008, 2009, 2014; Hoffman, Andrews & Feltovich 2012; Hoffman & Andrews 2012; Hoffman, Andrews, et al. 2010; Hoffman, Feltovich, et al. 2010, 2010) and Fadde (Fadde & Klein 2010, 2012; Fadde 2007, 2009a, 2009b, 2009c, 2012, 2013, 2016). Their work reflects recent advances on the topic of accelerating proficiency of people in training and work settings. In their studies, they have identified several theoretical issues and gaps. In particular, the gaps such as lack of good understanding of the concept, process, and methods of accelerated proficiency have served to conduct this literature review in the organizational and workplace context.

The chapters in this book dive into the literature review of various aspects and dimensions of the concept of accelerated

INTRODUCTION

proficiency and build a concise knowledge-base on the business challenge of shortening time to proficiency. This book is organized as follows:

Chapter 2 introduces major themes on performance from historical and classical studies as it leads to the concept of proficiency. The broader perspectives from studies and advances in human resource development (HRD) and performance improvement are reviewed. The chapter discusses the studies that characterized dimensions of job performance. The classic, seminal, and historical work of significance, such as theories of stages of skill acquisition are reviewed in this chapter.

Chapter 3 presents the definition and nature of proficiency. The literature on proficiency is reviewed as it relates to the topics of performance, knowledge/skill acquisition, and expertise acquisition. Key studies on novice-to-expert transition and the concept of proficiency scaling are reviewed.

Chapter 4 presents the imperatives in the literature that assert the need for accelerating proficiency. The historical and current work on accelerated proficiency is reviewed. Then the theoretical aspects of accelerating proficiency are explored.

Chapter 5 explores studies on various methods proposed by researchers for accelerating proficiency of people or personnel in various settings. The methods are reviewed for their implications and evidence towards the acceleration of proficiency.

Chapter 6 enumerates the gaps highlighted in previous chapters in regards to the nature and attainment of accelerated proficiency. The role and challenges of using training interventions to accelerate proficiency in organizations are also discussed. The chapter concludes the book by appealing for further research in broader methods to accelerate proficiency.

2

JOB PERFORMANCE: ASPECTS AND DIMENSIONS

This chapter presents a review of the broader topic of job performance. Most of the work on modeling of performance is grounded in seminal and classic studies, while modern researchers have extended those studies further. The major studies on job performance from historical and classic research are presented in this chapter. The chapter introduces the broader field of human resource development (HRD) as it relates to performance improvement at the workplace. The studies that characterized various dimensions of job performance are explored. A linkage is established between learning and performance before discussing major themes on the acquisition of skilled performance from the classic and seminal studies.

2.1 PERFORMANCE IMPROVEMENT

2.1.1 Human resource development

Human resources make the heart of any organizations. The business success of an organization depends on the skills, capabilities, potential, and expertise of its people primarily among other resources (Jacobs 2003). The discipline of human resource development (HRD) has long been investigated for a range of issues related to human performance in organizational contexts. Most commonly, HRD is defined as 'a process for developing and unleashing human expertise through organization development and personnel training and development for the purpose of improving performance' (Swanson & Holton III 2001, p. 4). Traditionally, HRD has been associated with training and development (T&D) interventions. Training and development include workplace interventions to enhance the learning of the employees towards developing their capabilities and expertise. However, lately in the last two decades, researchers such as Swanson & Holton III (2001) proposed that HRD processes focus on organizational development (OD) as well as training and development (T&D). Organization development includes the processes to enhance the effectiveness of the organization as well as care for employees(Werner & DeSimone 2009). According to Swanson & Holton III (2001) the OD is 'process of systematically unleashing human expertise to implement organizational change for the purpose of improving performance'.

Thus, OD activities are central to any organizations towards preparing employees for changes and indeed requires or affected by HRD activities (Cummings & Worley 2001; Rothwell & Sullivan 2005). Nevertheless, the purpose of HRD processes and interventions is probably unquestionable towards improving performance and developing the expertise of employees and organizations as a whole: 'HRD should exist for the purpose of improving performance; it must be performance focused, considering the relationship of HRD to the organizational system it serves' (Swanson & Arnold 1996, p. 17).

Various studies attempted to explore different aspects of HRD, emphasizing the key goals of HRD such as training and development (McLagan 1989a, 1989b), facilitating organizational change through learning (Chalofsky & Lincoln 1983), increasing human potential (Nadler, Wiggs & Smith 1988), delivering organizational performance (Jacobs 1989), improving work-related learning capacity (Watkins 1989), performance improvement (Gilley, England & Wesley 1998), performance and productivity improvement (Smith 1990), and unleashing human expertise through organizational development (Swanson 1995). It is seen that HRD exhibits considerable overlaps in theory and practice with other domains such as career development, organizational and process effectiveness, performance improvement, strategic organizational planning, human resource management and human resources (Swanson & Holton III 2001, p. 12). Researchers most commonly divided studies on HRD into two separate paradigms: learning paradigm and performance paradigm (Swanson & Holton III 2001, p. 12).

2.1.2 Learning paradigm of HRD

The learning paradigm of HRD is dominated by three perspectives on learning – 1) individual learning which considered individual's learning as the outcome of various instructional and training interventions (Gagne & Briggs 1974); 2) performance-based learning that focused on individual performance resulting from learning (Holton, Bates & Ruona 2000); and 3) whole systems learning which encompassed enhancing team and organizational performance through learning in addition to individual performance (Watkins & Marsick 1993). According to this paradigm, developing expertise of employees resides at the heart of any HRD intervention. In an organizational context, 'expertise almost always refers to the ability to use knowledge and skills to achieve outcomes that have value to someone else' (Jacobs 2003, p. 5). Towards that, Jones (1981, p. 188) asserted HRD as a 'systematic expansion of people's work-related abilities' (as cited in Swanson & Holton III 2001, p. 5).

Training and development have been considered as one critical part of the HRD processes in this paradigm. Classic research studies in HRD are almost all focused on training and development function from the angle of workplace learning and employee education. Swanson & Arnold (1996, p. 17) highlighted the intersection of HRD and adult education at the workplace: 'First, the context is organizations. Second, the dependent variable, or desired outcome, is performance, which will directly affect the goals of the organizations. Third, the intersection includes education and training interventions'. Swanson (2007) proposed that employees need skills not only to maintain the system but also to change the system, later being significantly different from the former. Early studies on training and development focused on competence development of employees. Employee competence was defined as the use of a specific set of knowledge or skills (Jacobs 1997).

However, some early studies argued that competence or employee abilities have a direct relationship with performance (Morf 1986) which in turn can be measured at the organization, process or individual level (Swanson 1999). It has also been reconciled in some studies that '[t]he primary outcome of HRD is not just learning but also performance' (Swanson & Holton III 2001, p. 139). This aspect is reviewed in the performance paradigm section.

2.1.3 Performance paradigm of HRD

The second paradigm of HRD is the performance paradigm, which focused on enhancing total individual performance through nonlinear as well as learning interventions. In an organizational context, researchers have argued that competence is a limited construct (focusing on acquiring skills and knowledge only) which does not convey true goals of HRD interventions (Swanson & Holton III 2001). In a study conducted by Evers et al. (2011), they noted several organizational and tasks factors that influenced the professional development of teachers and in turn, the occupational expertise. While performance has been linked to the knowledge, skills, and abilities of an individual (Clark 2008), improving performance at the workplace requires focusing on more than just human competencies. This school of thought represented the second paradigm of HRD, performance paradigm, which is dominated by two perspectives on performance – 1) individual performance improvement focuses on individual level performance systems; and 2) whole systems performance improvement or just called *performance improvement,* is a broader focus on performance improvement at multiple levels. The former approaches include *human performance technology* (HPT) (Gilbert 1978; Stolovitch & Keeps 1992) while later approaches include *performance improvement* or *performance consulting* (Holton III 1999; Robinson & Robinson 1995; Rummler & Brache 1995)

A comprehensive literature review indicated that there are over 50 different performance improvement models falling under individual, organizational and societal categories (Gok & Law 2017; Schaffer 2000). The studies on performance improvement are based on the premise of improving performance with or without a human lens (Swanson 1999). Considering that performance of an individual in the organization is not a singular function, researchers suggested taking a system view to HRD that encompassed looking at different parts of the HRD as system elements which interact with each other through various processes (Jacobs 1989, 2014a; Swanson 2001; Yawson 2013). General system theory describes any performance improvement process that uses a simple thinking model of inputs, processes, outputs, and a feedback loop (Swanson 1999). System theory also emphasized improving performance based on measurements: 'Performance improvement can only be manifest through outputs and change in outputs can only be assessed through some form of measurement' (Swanson 1999, p. 7).

An important implication of this line of thought was to investigate the role and impact of organizational development on how human expertise was developed, and performance was improved in the workplace. In a direction-changing publication using a multidisciplinary approach based on their consulting engagements, Rummler & Brache (1995) proposed that there were three performance levels: organization performance being the first level, process performance as the second level and individual performance as the last level. Their model fundamentally changed the way performance improvement was viewed in organizations. Extending Rummler & Brache (1995) work further, Swanson (1994, 2007) proposed performance diagnosis matrix that included organization, process, an individual level performance which is impacted by performance variables such as mission/goal, system design, capacity, motivation, and expertise. Integrated taxonomy of performance domains proposed by Holton III (1999) suggested four domains of performance: mission, process, social sub-system and individual.

Behavior Engineering Model (BEM)

Among seminal studies that investigated the performance paradigm in HRD, Gilbert (1978) coined a term *worthy performance* to communicate the return on investment on performance. He proposed a *behavior engineering model* (BEM) which distinguished between a person's behaviors and the environment support that encourages or impedes the performance. This model suggested that there was more than an individual's capability to produce a worthy performance (Gilbert 1978). In his work, he indicated that two sets of factors that influenced performance: (1) environmental factors, which included information, resources and incentives; and (2) individual factors, which included knowledge, capacity, and motives. While the environmental factors support or impede performance, the individual factors contribute towards a performance at the individual level (Gilbert 2013). Extending that work, Chevalier (2003) elaborated that information element in BEM model was about the role and performance clarity, relevant and frequent feedback about performance, description of expectations of performance and clear guides for performance. Resources element included tools, material, processes, procedures, and overall physical and psychological work environment and work conditions required to perform the job. Incentives element included adequate financial and nonfinancial incentives given to performers, enriched job designs, and positive work environment allowing further career opportunities.

On the other hand, knowledge represented the skills, knowledge, behaviors, and experience to match the requirement of performance. Motives represented people's motivations and desire to work. Lastly, capacity represented the adaptation, flexibility, capacity to learn, which is free from emotional limitation. Chevalier (2003) postulated that final performance depended on push-pull forces exerted by environmental factors and individual factors.

The major application of Gilbert's model is seen in identifying the barriers to the expected performance (King Jr & Cennamo 2016). Some studies specifically used Gilbert's BEM model to evaluate performance improvement (Wooderson, Cuskelly & Meyer 2017); design safety interventions to improve performance (Crossman, Crossman & Lovely 2009); and justify the investment in human performance interventions (Humphress & Berge 2006).

There have been several implications of the studies using Gilbert's BEM model in HRD. One of them being that performance improvement requires several environment support systems in place, apart from skills, knowledge, and behaviors possessed by an individual (Chevalier 2003). The second implication being that performance can be improved with or without training, with the latter being more prevalent (Dean 2016). The third implication is that accomplishments and outcomes should be the way to measure performance instead of behaviors, as they are just the means to achieve accomplishments (Binder 2017).

Human Performance Technology (HPT)

While the influence of environment and organizational factors on performance cannot be denied, it was seen that organizations suffer more from performance issues related to organizational factors. For instance, in a meta-analysis of 327 performance improvement projects completed between 1986 and 2012, Hartt, Quiram & Marken (2016) noted that 65% to 74% performance issues targeted organizational or environmental factors, whereas 26% to 35% of the performance issues focused on individual performance factors only. This study indicated that causes related to an individual's performance issues could be a small percentage of overall performance causes at the organizational level. Researchers contended that when there are performance issues, the diagnosis needs to be done at the organization, process, team, and individual level (Swanson 2007). Such a performance analysis of organizational and environmental factors is the foundation of *human performance technology* (HPT), a framework developed from BEM to address the performance problems in the organizations systematically (Pershing 2006; Van Tiem, Moseley & Dessinger 2004, 2012). HPT was defined as:

> A systemic and systematic set of processes for assessing and analysing performance gaps and opportunities; planning improvements in performance; designing and developing efficient, effective, and ethically justifiable interventions to close performance gaps or capitalize on opportunities; implementing the interventions; and evaluating all levels of results. (Guerra-Lopez 2016, p. 3)

Pershing (2006, p. 6) defined HPT as 'the study and ethical practice of improving productivity in organizations by designing and developing effective interventions that are results-oriented, comprehensive, and systemic'. Conceptually HPT is similar to organizational development because it is an applied behavioral science and is based on systems theory (Cho & Yoon 2010; Jacobs 1989; Pershing 2006). Both OD and HPT are concerned with improving organizational performance (Stolovitch 2007). The core of the HPT philosophy is a combination of three processes – performance analysis, cause analysis, and intervention selection (Van Tiem, Moseley & Dessinger 2012). HPT model emphasizes heavily on analysis of possible performance issues and causes across different levels surrounding the worker. This includes analysis of mission, vision, and goals of the organization (organizational analysis); analysis of the environment surrounding the job (environment analysis); analysis of difference between desired performance and actual performance (gap analysis); and analysis of causes of the gap between actual and desired performance (cause analysis) (Van Tiem, Moseley & Dessinger 2012, 2012). On similar lines, Rothwell et al. (2000) presented a *human performance improvement* (HPI) model developed for American Society for

Training and Development (ASTD) based on key processes of performance analysis, cause analysis and intervention selection. This model was represented as a change management system in which performance is continuously measured and evaluated. In a study, Deterline & Rosenberg (1992) contended to perform the mission, strategy, and goal analysis, as well as analysis of work, organization and competitive environment, as part of the organizational analysis. They argued that one should assess several causes that may be leading to the performance gap. The cause analysis may include looking at consequences, incentives and rewards; data and information; resources, tools and environmental support; individual capacity; motives and expectations; and skills and knowledge.

Researchers have positioned the scholarly appeal and theory-driven practice value of HPT and attempted the development of theory from implications of HPT (Cho & Yoon 2010; Pershing, Abaci & Symonette 2016; Pershing, Lee & Cheng 2008). Implications of studies on HPI/HPT is in its particular focus on a holistic understanding of processes, procedures, and models used specifically towards improving workplace performance. A characteristics premise of HPI/HPT is that training is not the only solution to improve performance (Stolovitch & Keeps 1999). Consequently, performance interventions are not always entirely training related. Deterline & Rosenberg (1992) indicated that interventions may include but are not limited to coaching, compensation, cultural change, documentation, environmental engineering, health/wellness, job aids, job/work design, leadership/supervision, performance management, performance support, staffing, team building, and training/education.

In recent studies, it was found that HPT practices described performance improvement processes followed by the practitioners to a reasonable degree (Kang 2017; Pershing, Lee & Cheng 2008). Nevertheless, the studies of performance and performance improvement are now widespread into several sub-disciplines. Performance is an important concept in HRD which encompasses both learning and organizational performance: 'HRD will only be perceived as having strategic value to the organization if it has the capability to connect the unique value of employee expertise with the strategic goals of the organization' (Swanson & Holton III 2001, p. 147).

Performance of employees at the job that is job performance is an important aspect connected with developing employee skills, proficiency, and expertise. The studies revealing this relationship are reviewed in the next sections.

2.2 DIMENSIONS OF JOB PERFORMANCE

Effective performance from employees in any job is a key business expectation that fuels business operations, profit, and competitive advantage (Sonnentag & Frese 2002). The poor performance of an individual at the job may have far-reaching effects on the team performance, as well as an organization's performance.

2.2.1 Value of individual performance

In the literature, business performance of an organization is believed to be the result of collective forces of resources, strategies, technology, and people: 'Organisations perform well and create value when they implement strategies that respond to market opportunities by exploiting their internal resources and capabilities' (Afiouni 2007, pp. 127–128). Researchers recognized skilled people in an organization as one of the key contributors to business performance and organizational competitiveness (Afiouni 2007; Huselid & Becker 2011). The critical value of the individual performance of people in organizations was widely recognized: 'Organisations need highly performing individuals in order to meet their goals, to deliver the products and services they specialised in, and finally to achieve competitive advantage' (Sonnentag & Frese 2002, p. 4).

2.2.2 Job performance

Despite its importance, the term *performance* does not seem to have one universal definition because there are several perspectives through which performance is viewed, defined, and measured. Though numerous studies have been conducted in the field of individual performance, various disciplines have focused on different aspects of performance. The *Oxford English Dictionary* defines performance as 'the action or process of performing a task or a function'[1]. More generally, when an individual exhibits skill to

---

[1] https://en.oxforddictionaries.com/definition/performance

desired standards to get the job done, this is what determines performance.

For a long period, task performance and job performance have been differentiated in the literature. While task performance indicates whether something was done to the desired specification or not, job performance indicates whether the job achieved the stated business outcomes. Job performance is viewed as the result of several cognitive, psychomotor tasks or abilities working together. Murphy (1989, p. 185) explained the distinction as:

> Job performance is certainly a function of the individual's performance on the specific tasks that comprise standard job descriptions but is also affected by variables such as success in maintaining good interpersonal relations, absenteeism and withdrawal behaviors, substance abuse, and other behaviors that increase hazards in the workplace ...

Thus, to produce overall job performance, several other things are required, such as teamwork, self-development, and personal attributes like perseverance, interpersonal and communication skills. Seconding Murphy's (1989) assertion, other studies also maintained similar view: 'Total [job] performance is much more than specific task or technical proficiency' (Campbell, McHenry & Wise 1990, p. 214). Viswesvaran & Ones (2000, p. 218) observed that several classic studies in the 1980s and 1990s had recognized that 'job performance entails more than just task performance'.

2.2.3 Dimensions of job performance

During the last several decades, the literature has generated a range of dimensions that characterized job performance. In the review of performance-related studies spanning the last few decades,

Viswesvaran (1993) and Viswesvaran & Ones (2000) observed 486 different performance dimensions across various occupations which were reported in the literature prior to 2000. They classified these dimensions into ten groups: (1) overall job performance; (2) job performance or productivity; (3) effort; (4) job knowledge; (5) interpersonal competence; (6) administrative competence; (7) quality; (8) communication competence; (9) leadership; and (10) compliance with rules (Viswesvaran & Ones 2000). However, they found that there was not one dimension that could fully explain the dynamics of job performance and that each dimension was complexely interrelated:

> The existing research in this area [individual job performance] appears to be that each performance dimension is complexly determined (jointly by ability and personality) and that it is impossible to specify a sole cause or antecedent of a particular dimension of job performance. (Viswesvaran & Ones 2000, p. 224)

More recently, Koopmans et al. (2011) conducted a comprehensive meta-analysis across 107 studies related to individual performance framework published until 2010 in four major databases. They found that performance had several different dimensions, which may be similar across several jobs and each of those dimensions could be measured with some indicators, varying from job to job. They reasoned that it was difficult to say if these measures captured the complexity of performance at work. Alongside the dimensions of job performance, the measures of job performance also showed the similar diversity that there was not one single measurement prevailing across occupations.

2.2.4 Complex nature of job performance

The complexity of job performance was discussed in the literature with reference to factors that impact performance as well. In a meta-analysis, Sonnentag & Frese (2002) found that there were two kinds of studies on the effects of situated work factors of on-the-job performance. They noticed that one set of studies indicated job characteristics such as job design interventions (e.g., meaningful tasks), control at work and group-work enhanced the job performance, while another set of studies showed factors such as role ambiguity, role conflict, and work environment stressors inhibit performance. This showed that the job environment, as well as job design, impact job performance. Among others, team performance plays an important role in the successful attainment of organizational goals within the team (or group). The interplay of such factors makes job performance a complex phenomenon.

In a study conducted by Campbell, McHenry & Wise (1990, p. 314), the authors elaborated on the complex nature of job performance as: 'There is not one outcome, one factor, or one anything that can be pointed to and labeled as job performance. Job performance really is multidimensional'. Swanson (1999) maintained the same view.

2.3 PERSPECTIVES ON JOB PERFORMANCE

Historically, literature has suggested several different perspectives to explain performance: task vs. contextual performance (Borman & Motowidlo 1993); behavioural vs. outcome performance (Campbell et al. 1993); task vs. job performance (Kanfer & Kantrowitz 2002);

individual vs. team performance (Sonnentag & Frese 2002), and job vs. organizational performance (Griffin, Neal & Parker 2007; Sudnickas 2016). Collectively, the literature suggests a range of dimensions, major ones being behavioral performance, task performance, outcome performance, contextual performance, individual and team performance. These dimensions are reviewed next.

2.3.1   Behavioral vs outcome performance

Sonnentag & Frese (2002) stated that performance has two different aspects that represent extremes - behavioral or action aspect (what an individual does) and an outcome aspect (what the consequence or result of the action is).

Behavioral performance

Behavioral performance was one of the key dimensions found in the classic studies of Campbell (1990) and Murphy (1989). Murphy (1989) pioneered the work performance theory in which he emphasized behavior as performance. Apart from task-related skills and behaviors, the contribution of other skills and attitudes affected overall task performance. Murphy (1989) believed that task performance is about the accomplishment of duties and tasks written in job descriptions. He theorized that work performance has four dimensions: (1) task behaviors; (2) interpersonal behaviors; (3) downtime behaviors (related to work avoidance); and (4) destructive/hazardous behaviors (related to noncompliance, violence, etc.).

Building on the work of Murphy (1989), Campbell (1990) considered not only task-related behaviors but also performance behaviors not directly related to the task. He acknowledged that performance is not just about job-specific task proficiency. Rather, an individual's proficiency in several non-job-specific tasks as well, such as perseverance and discipline that is required to obtain reasonable performance. Campbell (1990) included eight dimensions to the work performance: (1) job-specific task proficiency; (2) non-job-specific task proficiency; (3) written and oral communications; (4) demonstrating effort; (5) maintaining personal discipline; (6) facilitating peer and team performance; (7) supervision; and (8) management and administration.

Studies by Campbell (1990), Campbell, McHenry & Wise (1990) and Campbell et al. (1993) led to an important demarcation and characterization of job performance, in particular, the conceptual differences between behavioral performance versus outcome performance. Campbell (1990) and Campbell, McHenry & Wise (1990) maintained that only actions which are measured and those which lead to organizational goals count towards individual performance. Emphasizing the behavioral view, Campbell & Wiernik (2015, p. 48) maintained that 'individual job performance should be defined as things that people actually do, actions they take, that contribute to the organisation's goals'. Campbell et al. (1993) defined performance as behaviors or actions that are relevant to the goals of the organization. This view implied that the outcome of the work such as the number of parts made, the number of sales made, among other metrics, was a result of individual behavior. However, this view maintained that measuring an individual's performance in terms of job outcomes was problematic. Motowidlo, Borman & Schmit (1997) strongly made the argument that a performance model should not include results but should focus on behaviors only. They reasoned that results are a function of not only an individual's performance but also several other factors. Unless these factors are isolated, results do not represent an individual's contribution to the organization's goals (Motowidlo, Borman & Schmit 1997, p. 73).

Outcome performance

In contrast, the second view suggests that the outcomes and results of the behaviors are equally important indicators of work performance. The supporters of the outcome view have positioned an argument that business organizations value performance in terms of accomplishments (Gilbert 1978, 2013). Accomplishments can be work outputs or things such as decisions made, strategies identified or end results (such as sales improvement). Binder (2017, p. 20) stated 'the value delivered by human performance is in the *accomplishments* it produces and that the behavior needed for producing those accomplishments is costly, not valuable for its own sake'. The supporters of this view reasoned that the value of human performance is in the accomplishments it produces. This view also considered behaviors to produce those accomplishments were costly and not valuable in itself. Besides, there are challenges in defining performance only in behavioral terms too, because not every action or behavior is measurable. Unless someone focuses on results, it is difficult to identify the behaviors that are strongly correlated to produce the desired outcomes or results.

Reconciling behavior to outcomes

To reconcile these two aspects, Viswesvaran & Ones (2000) suggested a middle ground based on their analysis of over four hundred different dimensions they found in the last several decades' studies on work performance. Viswesvaran & Ones (2000) defined work performance as 'scalable actions, behavior and outcomes that employees engage in or bring about that are linked with and contribute to organisational goals'. This view combined behavioral aspects, as well as outcome aspects of job performance. Supporting this combined view, Moon, Kim & You (2013, p. 227) insisted on considering performance as an 'outcome and product in addition to behaviour or process in human resource development'. Several studies compared the strategies of behavior-based versus outcome-based performance management systems (Oliver & Anderson 1994; Piercy, Cravens & Morgan 1998, 1999). However, studies exploring empirical relationships between the individual's behavior aspects and outcome aspects are scarce. Yet, the implications of how performance is measured (at the behavior level or outcome level) have a bearing on how one views the process of acquiring performance. For example, Farrington-Darby & Wilson (2006, p. 27) believed that '[d]isciplines that favour studying expertise [or performance] from an output perspective will look to the decision rather than the decision-making, the solution more than the process of problem solving ...'

Nevertheless, whichever way performance is defined or measured, individual performance is still shown to be one of the most critical workforce metrics in organizations. Moreover, studies have indicated that individual performance was an important component of work and organizational success (Sonnentag & Frese 2002). Maximizing individual performance, therefore, is critical to the health of the organization.

2.3.2 Task vs contextual performance

Campbell (1990) model of eight dimensions of work performance, like Murphy's (1989), included task-related proficiency as one of the key dimensions that determine work performance. Borman & Motowidlo (1993, p. 73) proposed that task performance was 'the proficiency with which incumbents perform activities that are formally recognised as part of their jobs; activities that contribute to the organisation's technical core'. Other researchers defined task performance using terms like *job-specific task proficiency, technical proficiency* or *in-role performance*. For example, job-specific task proficiency was defined as the 'degree to which the individual can perform the core substantive or technical tasks that are central to a job and distinguish one job from another' (Viswesvaran & Ones 2000, p. 32). Early research suggested that task proficiency of an individual was the major source of variation in task performance (Borman & Motowidlo 1993). Thus, task proficiency represented one key element of task performance. However, task performance was shown to encompass many other aspects as well. Campbell's (1990's) and Murphy (1989) acknowledged that performance was not just about job-specific task proficiency, but organizations looked for an individual's proficiency in several non-job-specific tasks, such as perseverance and discipline to achieve reasonable performance.

Borman & Motowidlo (1993) suggested dividing these aspects into two distinct categories of performance behaviors related to tasks, such as (1) job-specific task proficiency, which contributes to organizational effectiveness; and (2) performance behaviors such as non-job-specific task proficiency, written and oral communication, demonstrating effort, maintaining personal discipline, facilitating team and peer performance, supervision and leadership, and management and administration, which lead to organizational effectiveness in other ways. Based on that distinction, they developed the construct of task performance and non-task performance and called the latter as *contextual performance*. Contextual performance comprised of those activities which contributed indirectly and 'maintain the broader organisational, social, and psychological environment in which technical core must function' (Motowidlo, Borman & Schmit 1997, p. 75). Most of the contextual performance was believed to be behavioral-related competencies, social behavior, and personality traits. (Borman & Motowidlo 1993) identified five categories of contextual performance: (1) volunteering to carry out tasks activities that are not formally part of the job; (2) persistence to complete a task successfully; (3) helping others; (4) following organizational compliance norms; and (5) supporting and defending organizational objectives.

Also, contextual performance was not considered mandatory but 'discretionary' (Motowidlo & Van Scotter 1994, p. 476). For instance, Motowidlo & Van Scotter (1994) postulated that knowledge, skills, abilities, and experience are more correlated to task performance than contextual performance. However, personality traits such as interpersonal skills and motivations affected contextual performance. They also noted that task performance and contextual performance each contributed in its own way and independently to overall job performance. Further, Motowidlo, Borman & Schmit (1997) asserted that because the performance was assessed through supervisory ratings, motivation was associated with both task performance and contextual performance.

Research suggests that performance could not be fully explained using this distinction of task vs. contextual performance. For instance, Bott et al. (2003) conducted a personality survey on 356 employees in a manufacturing organization across a wide range of jobs and suggested that task performance and contextual performance demonstrated weak to moderate correlation. Similarly, at an Australian public sector agency, Bish & Kabanoff (2014) found by surveying 100 mid-level managers that managerial competencies of star performers, while most were categorized as task performance and contextual performance, there were several competencies like self-direction and willingness to lead that could not be contained in this model. This evidence indicated that there is more to the job performance of an individual beyond the task and contextual performance.

2.3.3   Individual vs team performance

The literature suggests that while on one side, task performance alone did not define success in the job, at the same time, individual performance alone was not the sole contributor towards business outcomes. Individual performance and group performance intertwined together due to changes in work arrangements in modern organizations because people are working with others to meet stated business goals (Lynn, Skov & Abel 1999). Some studies proposed that the term performance should have an aspect of collective business results (Parker & Turner 2002). However, task-related skills at the individual level vs at the group level are not the same. Sonnentag & Frese (2002, p. 7) maintained from their analysis that 'task-related skills and knowledge are not sufficient when accomplishing tasks in a team-work setting'. Further, since the work is performed in teams, the social aspect is also an important determinant of job performance. To lessen this divide, Griffin, Neal & Parker (2007) modeled work performance to be measured at three levels. That is, organization level, group level, and individual level.

Though there are several factors, known and unknown to the literature, the social aspect, team interactions, and conflicts are some of the variables which make job performance in the organizational settings a highly complex phenomenon. How teams are structured, organized and interact with each other has a determining effect on an individual's job performance. In a study involving 525 individuals in 54 teams, Tims et al. (2013) noticed that structuring the job for the team has a direct impact on an individual's job performance. Lynn & Kalay (2015) also found that if a team has strong clarity on its vision, it would positively influence the team's ability to succeed. Furthermore, in an analysis of 28 studies, Schmutz & Manser (2013) found that team behaviors, such as teamwork or coordination, affect overall business outcomes. These studies showed that the social aspect of an individual's job performance could not be ignored.

At a team and organizational level, job performance is also impacted by employee engagement with management, their peers and overall organizational goals. Anitha (2014) conducted 383 questionnaires with employees from middle and lower management levels from small-scale organizations. The author noted that employee engagement had a significant impact on employee performance. Working environment and team and co-worker relationships were determining factors on employee engagement. Similarly, based on 110 questionnaires from front-line hotel staff in Romania, Karatepe (2013) established that employee engagement fully mediated the job performance of the employee, as well their extra efforts towards customer service. Employee engagement as a key factor to job performance, as well as a key determinant of organizational competitiveness, has been identified in recent studies (Albrecht et al. 2015; Bedarkar & Pandita 2014).

2.3.4 Multidimensionality of job performance

Recently, in a meta-analysis of 107 studies published until 2010 in four major databases, Koopmans et al. (2011) noticed a prominent trend toward measuring individual job performance as task performance or task proficiency. However, task performance is just one dimension of the overall job performance: 'There is not one outcome, one factor, or one anything that can be pointed to and labelled as job performance. Job performance really is multidimensional' (Campbell, McHenry & Wise 1990, p. 314).

The above review of the literature on performance indicates that while organizational business performance is a much larger domain, job performance is more than just an individual's task-related performance. Both behavior and outcomes are important for producing the performance for the job, among several other aspects. Contemporary research studies have recognized that developing individuals in the workplace to produce such overall encompassing performance is a challenge and been addressed by contemporary research studies (Campbell & Wiernik 2015; Dumas & Hanchane 2010; Houger 2006; Kanfer & Kantrowitz 2002; Khan, Khan & Khan 2011; Quartey 2012; Wallace 2006).

Irrespective of how performance is measured, an individual's job performance is a critical determinant of an organization's performance and competitiveness. In this book, the term *performance* refers to job performance an individual must demonstrate to meet organizational goals.

2.4 LEARNING AND PERFORMANCE

2.4.1 Abilities, knowledge and skills

Task performance and job performance are direct functions of abilities or skills acquired by an individual. In a seminal study based on 3,000 cases, Hunter (1986) reported that abilities influenced job knowledge and work samples, which in turn affected the supervisory rating of performance. He noted that abilities of the individual did not directly affect the supervisory ratings, but job knowledge and work samples produced by an individual correlated well with the supervisory ratings. His model supports that knowledge and skills are mediating variables when determining an individual's performance. Subsequently, other classic studies established that the knowledge, skills, and abilities one acquires as a result of job experience or training are the primary determinants of performance of any job (McDaniel, Schmidt & Hunter 1988; Qui'nones, Ford & Teachout 1995).

Motowidlo, Borman & Schmit (1997) theorized that intervening variables to performance are knowledge, skills and work habits that are basically learned through experience. They postulated that task knowledge (procedures, judgment, heuristics, rules, and decisions), task skills (using technical information, solving problems, and making judgments) and task work habits (pattern of behaviors, tendencies, choices one makes in a situation, motivational aspects, persistence, and planning) affect task performance. Similarly, other sets of contextual knowledge (knowledge about effective actions in situations that call for volunteering, helping, supporting, persisting, and defending), contextual skills (carrying out actions deemed effective in a situation) and contextual work habits (ways of handling conflicts, tendencies, and interpersonal styles) also affect contextual performance. These skills and knowledge possessed by an individual manifest themselves in the form of differences in job performance among workers performing the same job.

The literature indicated that the nature of knowledge and skills possessed by an individual also determined performance. Campbell (1990) explained that job performance could be predicted from one person to another with the help of three direct determinants: declarative knowledge (i.e., knowledge of facts, principles, and procedures), procedural knowledge and skill (i.e., knowing what to do and actually doing the task), and motivation (i.e., choice to exert effort, how much and how long). The level of training, education, experience, the range of skills and amount of practice, etc.

determined the level of declarative and procedural knowledge or skills someone exhibited. This model supported the linkage of knowledge, skills, abilities, and experience towards individual performance. Recent studies have suggested a strong linkage between providing appropriate knowledge and skills to employees through training and job performance (Dumas & Hanchane 2010; Khan, Khan & Khan 2011; Niazi 2011, 2011; Quartey 2012). Thus, the review indicates that performance is considered as a function of knowledge, skills, and abilities of an individual, though performance is not solely attributable to these characteristics alone.

2.4.2 Central role of learning

Several studies have proposed that learning has a central role in the performance concept and is a central underlying mechanism to acquire knowledge and skills (Campbell 1990; Hesketh & Neal 1999; London & Mone 1999). Learning has been viewed as a long-term behavioral change, which should positively affect performance. Historically, some classic work has shown that individual performance improved with learning in terms of time spent on the job (Avolio, Waldman & McDaniel 1990; McDaniel, Schmidt & Hunter 1988; Qui'nones, Ford & Teachout 1995). An employee's willingness and cognitive ability to learn task requirements were shown to be an important determinant of job performance. Sonnentag & Frese (2002) scanned 146 meta-analyses published in 20 years in twelve major journals of the workplace and organizational psychology and discovered that most researchers believed that there was 'an underlying mechanism of cognitive ability' that helped an individual acquire job knowledge and skills to impact job performance positively. No two individuals may have the same cognitive ability. Thus variation in learning and job performance are inherent. Based on the analysis of several studies, Kanfer & Kantrowitz (2002, p. 32) observed that 'individual differences in general cognitive ability may account for more variance in performance when performance is defined in terms of skill acquisition or job proficiency'.

Learning a task or skill leads to eventual performance, whether it is behavioral, a task, an outcome or job performance. Thus, learning is considered to be a major dimension of performance. Though the role of learning in improving performance is well understood, the nature of the relationship has been debated extensively. The relationship between performance and learning is reversed during training versus after the training. During any training intervention, learning is contended as more important than in-training performance, while after the training, at the job performance is contended to be more important than learning. In a study, Bjork (2009, p. 313) expressed that performance during a training event may not be the right indicator:

> Performance during training is often an unreliable guide to whether the desired learning has actually happened. Considerable learning can happen across periods when performance is not improving and, conversely, little or no learning can happen across periods when performance is improving markedly.

From this perspective, learning becomes more important than performance during training. Soderstrom & Bjork (2015, p. 193) termed learning as 'the relatively permanent changes in behavior or knowledge that support long-term retention and transfer' while they termed performance during training as 'the temporary fluctuations in behavior or knowledge that are observed and measured during training or instruction or immediately thereafter'. Furthermore, the performance within a training intervention may not be the desired performance required at the job. However, what matters is the job performance of an individual after training. Bjork (2009, p. 319) highlights a challenge as: 'The problem for a training organisation is to maximise performance when it matters, that is, *after* training and, specially, when individuals are deployed'. The corollary to this assertion is that accelerating performance within training may have very short-term effects as 'expediting acquisition performance today does not necessarily translate into the type of learning that will be evident tomorrow' (Soderstrom & Bjork 2015, p. 193). However, at the job, the performance (i.e., outcomes and behaviors) matters more than learning. Sonnentag & Frese (2002, p. 6) suggested that as:

> One might argue that what ultimately counts for an organisation is the individuals' performance and not their learning—although learning might help to perform well. This line of reasoning stresses that learning is a highly relevant predictor of performance but is not performance itself.

In general, the review of the literature indicates that learning is one of the key determinants of performance. Knowledge and skill acquisition appear to be inseparable parts of job performance. In their study about pilots tackling direct problems, Dreyfus & Dreyfus (2005) noted that as an individual acquired experience, he passed through five stages: novice, advanced beginner, competent, proficient and expert. Such representation assumed that performance or skill proficiency was a continuum in which the novice was on the one end of the continuum, while the expert was on the other end. As such, the overall goal of knowledge and skill acquisition is to develop a higher level of competence, proficiency or expertise of an individual, which is then translated into performance through behaviors/actions or results.

2.5 ACQUIRING SKILLED JOB PERFORMANCE

An individual's knowledge and skills are an inseparable part of job performance. Campbell (1990) explained that job performance could be predicted with the help of three direct determinants—declarative knowledge (i.e., knowledge of facts, principles, and procedures); procedural knowledge and skills (i.e., knowing what to do and actually doing the task), and motivation (i.e., willfully exerting effort, extent and length). 'An underlying mechanism of cognitive ability' helps an individual acquire job knowledge and skills, which positively influences job performance (Sonnentag & Frese 2002, p. 10). Thus, learning plays a central role in skill acquisition. To deliver a performance to certain standards, one needs to acquire skills to a certain level of mastery. In general, the goal of acquiring skills is to perform the task to desired standards or produce outcomes as per desired organizational goals.

Most of the skill acquisition studies are either approached from a learning standpoint or expertise development standpoint. Since the 1980s an immense amount of research has been conducted to understand the nature of expertise (cf. Cambridge Handbook of Expertise and Expert Performance by Ericsson et al. 2006). The classic scholarly works have suggested that experts are highly skilled individuals who think remarkably in a different way than novices (Anderson 1981). From that perspective, expertise can be defined as 'the possession of a large body of knowledge and procedural skills' (Chi, Glaser & Rees 1982). Ericsson et al. (1993) explained that the mechanism of attaining expertise in certain closed domains such as sports, chess, music was to engage in highly intense and focused practice on domain-specific activities under a coach, termed as deliberate practice. Chi (2006, p. 23) made an argument that expertise is acquired and is an outcome of skill acquisition as 'presumably the more skilled person became expert-like from having acquired knowledge about a domain, that is, from learning and studying and from deliberate practice'. Charness & Tuffiash (2008) viewed expertise as a superior performance, which is achieved through a combination of high-level skills and domain-specific knowledge and skilled memory.

In the literature, skill acquisition has been explained from different viewpoints. Knowledge and skill acquisition have been grounded in well-regarded classic and seminal work conducted in the 1960s, 1970s and 1980s such as Fitts & Posner (1967), Anderson (1981, 1982), Ackerman (1988) and Shiffrin & Schneider (1977). Some researchers, in more recent times, such as Langan-Fox et al. (2002), have extended these theories further. For several decades, one of the most common trends was describing skill acquisition in terms of stages in which performance or the proficiency of skills was improved as individuals gained more practice and experience.

2.5.1 Fitts and Posner's three-stage skill acquisition

Some of the earliest explanations of how an individual progressed towards skilled performance were the notions of practice and automaticity. For several decades, the practice has been accepted as the most fundamental mechanism of skill acquisition towards mastery of skills. Fitts (1964) and Fitts (1964; 1967) suggested that perceptual-motor skill acquisition occurs in three stages: *cognitive stage, associative stage,* and *autonomous stage,* which support progression from conscious to a less conscious form of practice. Anderson (1981, 1982, 2000) proposed a general theory of cognition called Adaptive Control of Thought-Rational (ACT-R), which described learning progression in three stages: *declarative knowledge stage; knowledge compilation stage; and procedural knowledge stage.* Ackerman (1988) supported that skill acquisition followed similar stages, as indicated by the above theories.

In Fitts and Posner's (1967) version, the first stage was termed as a *cognitive stage*. In this stage, learners are still trying to get accustomed to the task, understanding the instructions and trying to develop strategies to perform the task. A performer at this stage tends to develop 'basic factual understandings, the broad outline, the essential nature of each of the steps and the order in which these must be performed' (Cornford & Athanasou (1995, p. 12). This stage is characterized by the learner's attempt to understand the demands of the task and then 'distinguish between important and unimportant aspects of the task' (Schneider 1993, p. 316). The goal of this stage is to acquire declarative knowledge about the task.

Then the learner progresses to the next stage called a*ssociative (practice fixation stage)*. At this stage, repetition of skill and involvement with reality increases the depth of understanding, and the steps and sequence of skill performance are imprinted in permanent memory. Performance strategies are also refined at this stage. Prior learning is leveraged to develop strategies in new situations. Associations are developed by the learners between clues and responses for 'making the cognitive processes more efficient to allow rapid retrieval, thus transforming declarative knowledge into procedural forms' (Schneider 1993, p. 316).

Finally, with practice, an individual reaches a stage called *autonomous stage*. At this stage, skills can be subconsciously executed, and the action becomes very automatic. The nature of skills at this stage is sometimes called *automaticity*. The learner is becoming skilled on the task to a level where s/he does not need many resources. More cognitive resources are available to process other activities. Problem-solving is usually done with the conscious mind. At this stage, accuracy, as well as speed, are improved. However, the rate of improvement will hit a plateau after a certain amount of practice.

2.5.2 Anderson's three-stage learning model

The major implication of Fitts and Posner's (1967) learning model towards proficiency/expertise development was to layout the instructional activities in stages. This model described the sequence of events proposed for the development of skill and provided the mechanism and guidance for instructional events by which the automaticity is achieved (Clavarelli, Platte & Powers 2009). While Fitts and Posner's (1967) learning model appeared to explain the mechanism of psychomotor skills, it did not explain how the learning actually took place. To explain the learning mechanism, Anderson (1981, 1982, 2000) proposed a three-stage learning model, Adaptive Control of Thought-Rational (ACT-R). This model described learning progression in the form of three stages. The first stage is declarative knowledge stage. Declarative knowledge stored in declarative memory refers to facts, processes, principles, concepts, and information, etc. The learner receives information, background, generation instructions, etc. about the topic of skill. For performing any skill, the knowledge relevant to or required to do so is learned in declarative form. Declarative memory mainly links the propositions, images, and sequences by associations. In the next stage of knowledge compilation, the knowledge about a skill is converted gradually from declarative to new procedures, which can be applied without much attention. Inferences are drawn from pre-existing factual knowledge in the declarative memory, and this leads to the learning of procedural knowledge, which is the third stage. Procedural memory, also called long-term memory, stores information in the form of representations in what Anderson (1981, 1982) called *productions*. ACT-R theory described three types of learning processes: (1) generalization, which refers to productions becoming broader in application; (2) discrimination, which refers to productions becoming narrow in application; and (3) strengthening, which refers to the more frequent use of certain productions. New productions are formed by associating, disassociating or in terms of combining or un-combining existing productions. This stage involved domain-specific *proceduralization* and *composition*. The *proceduralization* involves creating domain-specific productions during the interpretation of declarative knowledge. The *composition* is combining several steps or adjacent procedures into one. The number of steps is reduced on each iteration of the procedure. The reduction in steps thus leads to improved learning in initial phases of practice. However, as one's speed increases with practice, learning does not appear to improve at the same rate that was in the initial phases of the practice. In the last stage, *procedural knowledge* is developed. This refers to a representation of what needs to be done in a given situation. Practice refines appropriate procedures. Responses become more generalized and automatic. With continuous use over time, the productions become automatic and part of the unconscious mind. The practice is essential for developing learned procedures into automaticity of expertise in any field (Ge & Hardré 2010). ACT-R theory indicated that both declarative and procedural knowledge resides in separate long-term memory systems. A major implication of ACT-R theory was that cognitive processes were involved in developing automaticity. The ACT-R theory incorporated several learning mechanisms which have been translated into instructional strategies (Oyewole et al. 2011). To implement ACT-R theory in skill acquisition training, Clark (2010) suggested instructional techniques like goal and reasons, overview, connection to prior knowledge, new knowledge, demonstrated the procedure, practice, and feedback.

2.5.3 Ackerman's three-stage model

One limitation of Fitts and Posner's (1967) three-stage learning theory and ACT-R theory is that they do not explain the influence of task characteristics and task instructions on skill acquisition. To address this deficiency, Ackerman (1988) presented an integrated theory that was based on an analysis of measures of ability, nature of the information processing and nature of skill acquisition. On the skill portion, he supported that skill acquisition follows similar phases, as proposed by Fitts & Posner (1967), Anderson (1982) and

Shiffrin & Schneider (1977). He stated that abilities are structured based on three components: complexity processing, the content of information (figural, verbal, numerical content) and speediness of processing. He described how one develops ability structures as s/he passes through stages of skill acquisition. He reasoned that ability-performance relations are a function of three task characteristics: consistency of information processing demands, task complexity and degree of task practice. He proposed that in tasks characterized by consistent information processing components, general ability, and broad content ability determines the performance during the cognitive phase. However, for inconsistent tasks, general and content ability determined the performance across all three phases. At the cognitive stage, demand is the most attentional resource based on the task characteristics because the learner is trying to understand the task instructions, goals and 'formulating the strategies for task accomplishment' (Ackerman (1992, p. 599). In the associative phase, performance is determined by perceptual speed abilities, while psychomotor abilities determine performance in autonomous phases. Ackerman (1988) reasoned that to go beyond this stage to the autonomous stage, a learner needed first to develop consistent information processing characteristics. Similar to the account given by Fitts & Posner (1967) and Anderson (1982), (Ackerman 1992, p. 599) explained the nature of performance at this stage: 'Performance at this phase of skill acquisition is typically highly speeded and highly accurate'. At this stage, the learner needs little or no attentional effort.

2.5.4 Langan-Fox's skill acquisition model

From the expertise building perspective, a major implication of this model was the proposition that more cognitive resources are required in the first two stages, which slows down the speed of performance. This happens more prominently on the novel, complex and inconsistent tasks. Therefore, based on this model, it was inferred that the sequence of tasks based on task characteristics might be an important determinant of expertise development. Subsequent research studies identified a few flaws in this model. Langan-Fox et al. (2002, pp. 104–105) mentioned that Ackerman's theories 'largely ignore the experiences and internal processes of a person (e.g., how they feel, what strategies they are using, the role of the external environment)'.

The popular three-staged models of Ackerman (1988), Fitts & Posner (1967), Shiffrin & Schneider (1977) and Anderson (1982) explain the mechanism of skill acquisition but do not provide any way to know where one may be in the process of skill acquisition. As one practice, not only cognitive ability varies, but also the task characteristics change over time and environment in which one performs the job also changes. Langan-Fox et al. (2002) contended that skill acquisition should be considered as a process that assumes the influence of other variables, internal to human, as well as external on to performance. They proposed an integrated process model for skilled performance based on learning in general during skill acquisition. They considered two sets of factors that influenced skilled performance: internal influences and external influences. Among internal influences, Langan-Fox et al. (2002) believed several factors like changing levels of consciousness, automaticity, motivation, emotion, metacognition, and memory influenced skill acquisition. Changing level of consciousness was based on Rasmussen, Pejtersen & Goodstein (1994) observations that a performer may be conscious about when to choose between three types of behaviors: skill-based, rule-based and knowledge-based, depending on the task characteristics. The amount of practice determined how soon the individual would achieve automaticity or automatic processing (Shiffrin & Schneider 1977). However, inconsistent tasks demand a higher level of practice than consistent tasks (Ackerman 1988). Langan-Fox et al. (2002) believed that motivation in the form of difficult goals, as suggested by Ackerman (1988), influenced acquiring complex skills. Self-regulatory processes and metacognition were assumed to impact skill acquisition in terms of how people perceived their skills in relation to task difficulty. This observation indicated that performers were always able to monitor their state and change their cognitive strategies during skill acquisition. Langan-Fox et al. (2002) also postulated that emotions have a great impact on skilled performance, a factor previously missing from the skill acquisition theories but 'most central and pervasive aspects of human experience' (id. 109). Emotions may also have a positive or disruptive effect on performance depending on the affective state of the performer.

Memory is another component that influences skill acquisition profoundly, as explained by Anderson (1982). Langan-Fox et al. (2002, p. 111) contended that in stage one of skill acquisition, in which demand for attentional resources is high, working memory is most predictive of task performance. In stage two of skill acquisition, the associative memory is likely to be more predictive than in stage one, and procedural memory could predict higher performance in stage three of skill acquisition. Lastly, retention factors have a strong influence on skill acquisition because retention leads to 'improved capacity to draw an association between new and established information' (id. 112). All of these factors, to varying degrees, influence how someone progressed through skill acquisition, and demonstrated skilled performance. Among external influences, Langan-Fox et al. (2002) noted that interruptions, goals, practice format and task characteristics influenced how someone acquired skilled performance. They indicated that spaced or continuous practice format may determine how soon the state of automaticity is achieved. The interval between practice sessions may markedly affect performance. Workplace interruptions and expectations to handle two or more incompatible tasks at the same time may adversely affect stage one and stage two of skill acquisition. Nature of task, whether it is novel, complex or familiar, has a similar implication of using cognitive resources and may impair performance (Ackerman 1988).

The major implication of Langan-Fox et al. (2002) skilled performance learning model is it views skill acquisition and proficiency development as a process in which several factors influence how soon an individual can achieve a skilled performance state. This model might also suggest that in addition to task characteristics and practice amount, several other internal and external factors must be addressed to accelerate skill acquisition.

These skill acquisition theories provided congruent accounts of the final state of automaticity of performance expressed as *autonomous performance* (Fitts & Posner 1967) or *procedural performance* (Anderson 1982). This final stage is characterized by speed and accuracy, as indicated in Ackerman (1988). Langan-Fox et al. (2002) termed this state as *skilled performance*. Cognitive literature views automaticity as one of the characteristics exhibited by highly proficient workers and experts who are considered the individuals who deliver superior skilled performance (Dreyfus 2004).

There are several other skill acquisitions models, all of which are not reviewed here. For a detailed discussion on over twenty-three different skill acquisition models, readers are encouraged to refer to author's other book *Models of Skill Acquisition and Expertise Development* (Attri 2019a) which provides a detailed taxonomy of skill acquisition models, as shown in table 1.

Table 1: Taxonomy of major skill acquisition/expertise development models (Attri 2019a)

Basis	Theory or Model
Stage-based models	Conscious Competence Theory
	Learning Stage Model by Fitts & Posner (1967)
	ACT-R Theory of Cognition by Anderson (1982)
	Theory of Ability Determinants of Skill Acquisition by Ackerman (1988)
	Cognitive Skill Acquisition Theory by VanLehn (1996)
	Theory of Skill Retention by Kim et al. (2013)
	Vygtosky (1978) Zone of Proximal Development
	Staged Skill Acquisition Model by Dreyfus & Dreyfus (1986)
	Model of Domain Learning by Alexander (1997)
	Proficiency Scale by Hoffman (1998)
	Levels of Human Competence by Jacobs (1997)
	Novice to Expert Transition by Rosenberg (2013)
	Mastery Learning Model by Blooms (1968)

JOB PERFORMANCE

Practice, time or task-based models	4-Component Model of Complex Learning by van Merriënboer (1992)
	Deliberate Practice Model of Expert Performance by Ericsson et al. (1993)
	Recognition-Primed Decision (RPD) Model by Klein (1993)
Factor-based models	Model of Intelligence as Expertise Development by Sternberg (1999)
	Skilled Performance Theory by Langan-Fox et al. (2002)
Expert modeling-based models	Cognitive Apprenticeship Model by Collins (1989)
	Cognitive Task Analysis (CTA) Approach to Model Expertise
	The trajectories of Expertise by Lajoie (2003)
	Zone of Proximal Development by Vygotsky (1978)
Cognition-based models	Cognitive Flexibility Theory by Spiro et al. (1990)
	Cognitive Transformation Theory by Klein & Baxter (2oo9)
	ACT-R Theory of Cognition by Anderson (1982)

Source: adapted from Attri (2019a)

2.6 SUMMARY

In this chapter, the concepts and dimensions of job performance were reviewed from a human resource perspective, learning, and skill acquisition. Learning, knowledge acquisition, and skill acquisition are undeniable ingredients to develop performance. However, certain aspects of performance like proficiency are key goals of employee development at the workplace. The next chapter dives into studies on defining and developing the proficient performance of the employees.

3

PROFICIENT PERFORMANCE: JOURNEY AND TRANSITION

The literature on proficiency is reviewed in this chapter as it relates to the construct of performance, knowledge and skill acquisition and expertise acquisition. The existing literature on proficiency is mainly derived from classic expertise theories or skill acquisition theories such as those proposed by Dreyfus and Dreyfus (Dreyfus & Dreyfus 1986, 2004, 2005), Ericsson (Ericsson 2000, 2002, 2003, 2004, 2006a, 2007, 2008, 2009c; Ericsson et al. 1993; Ericsson & Charness 1994; Ericsson, Prietula & Cokely 2007), Benner (1984, 2004), Chi (Chi 2006; Chi, Glaser & Rees 1982; Chi, Glaser & Farr

1988; Chi, Glaser & Rees 1981, 1982; Glaser & Chi 1988), and Hoffman (Hoffman et al. 2008, 2009, 2014; Hoffman & Andrews 2012; Hoffman, Andrews & Feltovich 2012; Hoffman, Andrews, et al. 2010; Hoffman, Feltovich, et al. 2010), among others.

Key studies on novice-to-expert transition and the concept of proficiency scaling are reviewed at the beginning of the chapter. Then this chapter presents the review of allied concepts upon which the definition and nature of proficiency are established. This includes the concept of progression towards proficiency and proficiency scaling. The review then develops the dimensions of proficient performance as characterized by several classic studies. The chapter also reviews the studies on expertise and expert performance as there is considerable overlap between the literature on expertise and proficiency. This chapter is foundational to the concept of accelerating proficiency which is discussed in the next chapter.

3.1 NOVICE-TO-EXPERT PROGRESSION

Performance development literature emphasizes heavily on the process and nature of novice to expert transition. This transition is basically how a novice develops and transition towards becoming an expert. Several researchers have maintained that expertise is not an end state, rather it is a journey that is characterized by progressively increasing skills, experience and intuition (Benner (2001; 2005; 2004; 2019).

3.1.1 Novice to expert progression as stages

A review of the literature suggests that novice-to-expert transition could be viewed as staged progression. This view reports a level-like shift in qualitative characteristics of the individual, thus giving the notion of stages one passes through towards a higher level of skill mastery or higher performance. While the basic idea of such transition is that experts are relative to the novice, the goal of such an approach is 'to understand how we can enable less skilled or experienced persons to become more skilled...' (Chi 2006, p. 23).

Classic studies defined stage-like progressions towards automaticity of skills (Fitts & Posner 1967; Anderson 1982; Ackerman 1988). Later researchers have developed more refined details of the stages towards proficiency. Among them, Shuell (1986, p. 364) noticed that 'as an individual acquires knowledge, his or her knowledge structure gradually evolves in qualitative as well as quantitative ways'. Subsequently, classic studies indicated a qualitative shift in traits as novice learners moved towards higher proficiency (Benner 1984; Dreyfus & Dreyfus 1986). Similarly, Hoffman (1998, p. 84) supported this qualitative shifts: 'The distinction between "novice" versus "expert" implies that development can involve both qualitative shifts and stabilizations in knowledge and performance'. This implies that the novice-to-expert transition process could be viewed as being made up of several stages.

Theorists have used different development parameters for qualifying level-like shifts, for example, the transformation of skills as second nature (automaticity), as well as implicit knowledge

(Alexander 2003a; Spiro et al. 2003). Some studies have established that it is possible to qualitatively define proficiency levels in terms of skills and knowledge exhibited by professionals on-the-job.

3.1.2 Problem-solving approaches as an indicator of stages

The most significant studies in this regard were carried out by Dreyfus and Dreyfus (Dreyfus & Dreyfus 1986, 2004, 2005), popularly known as *Dreyfus and Dreyfus model*. Dreyfus & Dreyfus (2005; 2004) suggested a progression in terms of how a performer handles a situation. They suggested that an individual acquires an intuitive grasp on situations and problems while passing through five stages—novice, advanced beginner, competent, proficient and expert. As one progresses through the stages, the approach in solving problems become more intuitive. This staged model could explain the progression towards expertise reasonably well in nursing and medicine professions (Benner 2004). Benner (2004) attempted to define levels of proficiency on the Dreyfus and Dreyfus model in terms of certain attributes of expected performance at each level in the context of nursing professions, demonstrating that progression could be reasonably explained using stages specified by the Dreyfus and Dreyfus model. Peña (2010) and Khan & Ramachandran (2012) applied the Dreyfus and Dreyfus model in the context of clinical and healthcare jobs and asserted that there is a level-like progression which can be demarcated qualitatively in terms of job attributes.

3.1.3 Tasks performance as an indicator of stages

Some researchers maintained that task performance could be an indicator of different stages (Chi 2006; Merrill 2006; Schreiber et al. 2009). According to this premise, the novice completes simple versions of tasks during training, and as skill levels increase, s/he can move to more complex tasks. Progressively, s/he becomes skillful at relatively more complex tasks. The learner could address several cues at the same time. The literature indicates that measurement of task performance must reflect this gradual acquisition of skill. Merrill (2006, p. 269) stated that proficiency measurement requires one to 'detect increments in performance demonstrating gradually increased skill in completing a whole complex task or solving a problem'.

3.1.4 Measurable attributes as an indicator of stages

Another group of researchers took a measurement approach to define proficiency levels in terms of some measurable attributes of jobs. For example, Chi (2006) proposed that proficiency levels could be roughly measured using inputs such as academic qualification, years of experience in the task, peer feedback or even profession-related tests. Schreiber et al. (2009) developed metrics for measurement of pilot proficiency using simulators and postulated that it is possible to develop an objective measure of performance in complex jobs that require a range of judgment and meta-skills. Recently, Kim (2012, 2015) proposed a different approach: measurement in terms of knowledge structures across different levels of learning progress. The author defined a set of measures indicating the levels of the features of knowledge structure. Relations between the measures and the features of knowledge structures were determined based on theoretical assumptions, as well as empirical evidence. A similar approach was suggested by Dörfler, Baracskai & Velencei (2009), who used knowledge as the demarcation for levels to explain the stages or levels of expertise.

3.1.5 Novice to expert transition as a process

The notion of stages conveys the idea of progression being a process. Both foundational and more recent research studies support the view that developing a higher level of performance to proficiency and expertise can be viewed as a process. Studies by Lajoie (2003) focused on transitions and trajectories to increase expertise. In characterizing this progression, Lajoie (2003, p. 22) noted that 'becoming an expert is a transitional process'. At the same time, researchers have maintained that expertise is not the ultimate goal rather it is a 'nonlinear process state' (Moon, Kim & You 2013, p. 228). A certain amount of quantity of knowledge, skills or behavior does not mean expertise. Bransford et al. (2004) also maintained that expertise is not a finished product; rather it is a continuing process. Expertise is not a defined stage; rather expertise grows out of interactions with the environment. The literature has viewed expertise as a continuous process of adjusting knowledge, re-learning, changing mental representation as one interacts with situations, reflects upon it, and use pattern recognition and correct one's way of thinking (Alexander 2003a). In terms of the continuous process towards adjustments, Sternberg (1999, p. 359) contended that developing expertise involves 'the ongoing process of the acquisition and consolidation of a set of skills needed for a high level of mastery in one or more domains of life performance'. In a dynamic world, abilities are not always static. Alexander (2003b, p. 12) asserted that 'the journey toward expertise is unceasing. Even those who have attained the knowledge, strategic abilities, and interests indicative of expertise cannot sit idly by as the domain shifts under their feet'. Thus, it is reasonable to infer that expertise involves a constant evaluation of one's progress towards mastery.

3.1.6 Implications

While most of the staged model gave a theoretical framework on progression towards expertise, the staged view did not explain the actual mechanisms or methods of developing an individual to the next level of performance (Dall'Alba & Sandberg 2006; Peña 2010). The issue is that the actual mechanism of acquiring proficiency is not elaborated upon in the current expertise literature the way it could be applied or used in organizations. Moon, Kim & You (2013, p. 226) stated the limitation in expertise literature: 'Most studies can't explain how the expertise reaches to a specific level or stage by multiple mechanisms. Accordingly we have to develop specific and realistic model for how expertise develops'. Therefore, the basic issue that arises is the lack of understanding of the concept and process of proficiency in organizations.

3.2 STAGES OF PROFICIENCY ACQUISITION

The discussion on proficiency acquisition is incomplete without a separate review of Dreyfus & Dreyfus's model, which has seen its place in several classic studies. Dreyfus & Dreyfus (1986) observed numerous performers, mostly aircrew emergency staff and jet pilots to understand how they tackle direct problems. They proposed a model that was based on the premise that skill acquisition is a continuous process in which skills are transformed into performance by experience and mastery (proficiency). Dreyfus & Dreyfus (1986) observed that only experience with concrete situations produced higher levels of performance. They discovered that during skill acquisition, a learner passed through five levels of proficiency: novice, advanced beginner, competence, proficiency, and expertise.

They identified few characteristics that varied gradually from one stage to the next, how they perceived the elements of the situations (components), how they recognized which part of the situation to pay attention to (perspective), how they made decisions to act in a particular way (decision), and finally, how much they were committed or involved with the task (commitment) (Dreyfus & Dreyfus 1986, 2004, 2005). They observed that perception shifted from context-free understanding of facts to more situational understanding. In terms of the progression of these characteristics, as someone moved up from the novice stage, knowledge began to be treated in the context of the situation. Further, with experience, an individual became more selective in what elements of the situation were considered more important. In the beginning, novices were not able to recognize the relevance of their knowledge of the skill, but they started doing so as they moved to the next stage. The context was analyzed analytically to begin and developed into a more holistic assessment at higher stages. They contend that there was an observable shift from analytical approaches to intuition-based approaches while making decisions. Decision-making was rational for all the learners except for the experts who made decisions intuitively. The degree of immersion increased from a detached commitment to highly involved, along with the understanding of the task, deciding and the outcomes (Dreyfus & Dreyfus 1986, 2004, 2005).

Based on these shifts, they developed the characteristics of five stages a learner passed through towards higher proficiency. A general description of the five stages based on the collective characteristics suggested not only by Dreyfus & Dreyfus (1986) but also by later researchers who applied this model in various professions, e.g., clinical (Peña (2010), healthcare (Khan & Ramachandran 2012); correctional services (Scobey 2006); education (Bedi 2003); and nursing (Ramsburg (2010) are as follows:

Novice: A novice is someone who does not know much about the new topic or domain. The only mechanism usually they have is some form of training. A novice is typically placed in training where s/he learns some facts about the skills and the rules to apply the skills. While applying these skills, the novice sees everything context-free. For every new thing, they need rules and maxims to solve it. Usually, they are trained to follow these rules without exceptions. At this stage, they do not have a contextual understanding of how to evaluate a situation and how to decide whether a given rule will be applicable in that situation. Therefore, the novice cannot discriminate between situations (Dreyfus & Dreyfus 1986, 2004, 2005).

PROFICIENT PERFORMANCE

Advanced beginner: The novice moves up as an advanced beginner as s/he starts gaining some experience in real situations. The advanced beginner starts grasping the concepts underlying the situations and starts comprehending the facts about situations. As they gain more experience, they start comparing and discriminating the situations. They can apply the rules in a structured setting, but they do not yet have the experience to tackle real-world situations. As the new situation is encountered, they tend to identify the unrecognized aspects of the situation, tend to apply the previously learned rules and try to relate to the situation. They develop some situational perception, but it is still very limited. Task involvement is increased. At this point, the performance is improved marginally (Dreyfus & Dreyfus 1986, 2004, 2005).

Competent: As the advanced beginner starts gaining more experience, s/he handles more situations. The performer starts developing an understanding of context-free elements and situational elements. They can now recognize various aspects of the problem, and they can set goals. They may not apply rules all the time depending on the situation, but they try to tackle situations in novel ways. At this point, they have a better contextual understanding of whether a rule should be applied in a given situation. However, decision-making is still analytical. A competent performer is highly involved with the task, as well as the outcome of the task (Dreyfus & Dreyfus 1986, 2004, 2005). The term competent has seen the appeal in training and instruction design for a long time as an indication of someone's qualification. However, Eraut (1994, p. 126) clarified that 'the Dreyfus definition of competence is based on how people approach their work, not on whether they should be judged as qualified to do it'.

Proficient: At this stage, the involvement of the performer with the task, as well as its outcome, is very high. The context is considered holistically, and among those, the proficient performer is able to make situational discriminations and pay attention to what is important and what is not. Pattern recognition is strengthened whereby s/he can recognize new unrecognized elements of a novel situation. S/he has very little dependence on the rules of familiar situations, but s/he may use maxims in novel situations. At this stage, the decision-making is very quick. Performance is improved drastically. In clinical practice, Khan & Ramachandran (2012, p. 5) observed a proficient person as one who was able to handle complex routine work unsupervised but may need supervision for non-routine complex tasks, and performance was usually based on experience. Benner (2004, p. 198) observed that there was a change in perception used by proficient performers regarding a situation. At this stage, they were deliberate about changing the strategies based on an understanding of the new situation.

Expert: This last stage in skill progression was seen to be acquired with concrete experience. Deep involvement with the understanding of the situation, task, and its outcome resulted in highly contextual experiences. The learner developed deep tacit knowledge; a learner developed the intuitive grasp on situations. Thus, the decision-making became intuitive rather than analytical at this stage. At this stage, they also developed highly developed skills to make subtle discriminations between situation and knowledge used in different situations. Based on experience, they could even work out the solution for novel and never-seen-before problems (DiBello & Missildine 2011). Based on prior experience, they can even come up with a solution for new or never experienced before situations. Experts adopt a contextual approach to problem-solving and understand the relative, non-absolute nature of knowledge. Reflection comes naturally, and experts solve problems almost unconsciously. At this point, an expert's skills became automatic to the point that they were not even aware of it (Dreyfus & Dreyfus 1986, 2004, 2005).

Earlier researchers like (Eraut 1994) recognized the strength of this model was in 'the case it makes for tacit knowledge and intuition as critical features of professional expertise in 'unstructured problem areas''. Further, this model emphasized the process view which positioned progression towards the expertise as 'the way in which experts solve problems, rather than simply by the amount of knowledge that experts possess' (Ge & Hardré 2010, p. 24).

It has proven to be an extremely useful model for depicting levels of expertise in any profession. Most significant of this research has been the work of Benner (2004, p. 194) who tested the applicability of the Dreyfus and Dreyfus model in nine studies spanning over 21 years and found that it was 'predictive and descriptive of distinct stages of skill acquisition in nursing practice'. The author described the nature of expertise at each stage that added richer perspectives to the Dreyfus and Dreyfus model. Lately, researchers have expanded and characterized each stage.

Despite widespread simplicity and appeal of the Dreyfus and Dreyfus model, another school of thought questioned the validity of the same. For example, Day (2002) noted that it is difficult to apply five stages in professional settings because practitioners perform a range of tasks in their jobs and they will not fit into one stage for all the tasks they do. Thus, the most common objection raised was a representation that proficiency acquisition is a linear process independent of the influence of external factors and domain expertise (Grenier & Kehrhahn 2008).

Another objection to this model was 'its failure to explain how someone becomes an expert and its stress on the importance of experience and not of its impact' (Farrington-Darby & Wilson 2006, p. 29). Other concerns included the absence of social structure in knowledge and skill acquisition, lack of objective quantification in regards to how to measure attainment of each stage or where a particular stage ends, and lack of operational definitions of intuition (See Peña 2010). Even though these staged skill acquisition models conceptually explains how an individual learns, 'one cannot accurately predict where people are in the skill-acquisition process' (Langan-Fox et al. 2002, p. 106).

Though studies have either detected or forced-fit the characteristics of individual proficiency to the description of stages found in such models, it is not clear from those studies if there was any business benefit to the organization or any development benefit to the individual (Benner 2004; Beta & Lidaka 2015; Ramsburg 2010; Scobey 2006). Dall'Alba & Sandberg (2006) observed that experience and the understanding of practice were the major determinants of any professional skill development, and it may not have level-like stages. Attri (2018) raised the question on the usefulness of the meaning or representation of stages of skill/proficiency acquisition for the workplace and whether or not proficiency tracking in the workplace should rely on staged-transition models.

The major implication of the Dreyfus and Dreyfus model was an evolution of the concept of scaling the proficiency in the form of stages so that suitable instructional design could be implemented for learning at different stages. Researchers have translated the stages into appropriate instructional methods to be used at each stage to move a novice through to higher stages of proficiency (Benner 2001; Clavarelli, Platte & Powers 2009). Despite its limitations, the Dreyfus and Dreyfus model appears to be a starting point in identifying the methods and strategies to develop the proficiency of a learner.

3.3 PROFICIENCY SCALING

While the Dreyfus and Dreyfus model explained the novice-to-expert transition in terms of stages, it was based on how people approach work. The second foundational view towards novice-to-expert transition was to quantify the level of proficiency at each stage somehow. Hoffman et al. (2014) assumed proficiency scaling as a fundamental action that needs to happen in any accelerated proficiency studies 'to forge a domain – and organisationally appropriate scale for distinguishing levels of proficiency'.

3.3.1 Hoffman's proficiency scaling

Hoffman (1998) recognized the challenges in defining expertise and posit that the differentiation between novices and experts itself suggested the presence of some qualitative shifts of knowledge and performance between the two extremes of development continuum. He commented 'If one acknowledges that expertise develops, and that qualitative changes occur over the developmental period, then one must make some attempt at stage-like categorization, if only to motivate research' (Hoffman 1998, p. 84). If one can define novice and experts in terms of characteristics, knowledge, and performance, remaining stages in this continuum of development can be retrieved from the literature. Hoffman, Feltovich, et al. (2010) further stated, 'The analysis of proficiency and proficiency scaling can usefully commence by distinguishing experts (high and very high proficiency) from novices (very low proficiency)' (p. 32). In that view, experts were believed to possess a large body of knowledge. Novices, on the other hand, were believed to have not reached as high a proficiency level as an expert, even though they could be highly experienced individuals in their domains. Hoffman, Feltovich, et al. (2010) proposed the continuum view of progression in terms of proficiency: 'We are considering a concept of expertise referred to as "high proficiency."' (p. 28). They viewed proficiency as an indicator of one's level of experience or expertise in the skills, and thus there was a need for some sort of mechanism to scale proficiency. That also meant that the notion of high proficiency, as suggested by Hoffman, Feltovich, et al. (2010), was akin to the stage of expertise in the Dreyfus and Dreyfus (1986, 2004, 2005) model.

Chi (2006, p. 22) supported a similar position of using the term *proficiency* to mean mastery in skills as 'expertise is a level of proficiency that novices can achieve'. Researchers also viewed proficiency as a qualitative indication of expertise or mastery (Scobey 2006).

Hoffman et al. (2014, p. 26) contended that it was important to develop 'a scale that is both domain and organisationally appropriate, and that considers the full range of proficiency'. They believed that it was possible to scale proficiency by using various inputs such as interviews, age, seniority, experience, education, training, professional certifications, performance measures, and social standing.

Hoffman et al. (2014) concept of proficiency is expressed as a continuum of mastery in a skill or function or job in which a novice is someone who has low or very low proficiency, while an expert is someone with very high proficiency in that particular aspect (skill, task, function or job). On this continuum, one progresses towards higher proficiency through stages like naïve, novice, initiate, apprentice, journeyman, expert and master (Hoffman 1998). Based on the Middle Ages craft guilds in Europe, Hoffman (1998) proposed that novice-to-expert transition could be represented through seven stages, similar to gaining mastery in a craft (*Table 2*).

Table 2: Proficiency scaling proposed by Hoffman (1998)

Stage	Characteristics
Naïve	Completely ignorant about the domain.

Novice	A member in the domain who has minimal exposure to the domain.
Initiate	A novice who has started on the profession.
Apprentice	Someone who is taking up instructions beyond introductory level. S/he is working with and assisting an experienced person.
Journeyman	One who is executing orders and performs a day's work and duties unsupervised. S/he has achieved some level of competence, has become experienced and is a reliable worker.
Expert	A distinguished journeyman regarded for his/her accurate judgements, is efficient and delivers reliable performance. Special skills attained due to extensive experience and can deal effectively with rare or "tough" cases.
Master	A journeyman or expert who is also qualified to teach those at a lower level. Highly experienced experts whose judgments establish regulations, standards, or ideals. Equally regarded by other experts as the "real" expert in certain subdomains.

Source: adapted from Hoffman (1998)

Instead of differentiating between confusing constructs of competence, proficiency, and expertise, Hoffman, Feltovich, et al. (2010, p. 28) viewed all such levels in terms of proficiency in which expertise is referred to as 'high proficiency'. From that standpoint, they appeared to suggest proficiency in knowledge and skills as a continuum along which novices, journeymen, and experts can be placed. Hoffman's (1998) progression was based on changing knowledge and skills that are associated with the experience. Macmillan (2015, p. 36) explained this approach as:

> Hoffman's Scheme, on the other hand, presumes a progression of knowledge and capabilities associated with different amounts of instruction and domain-specific experience. It describes relative levels of expertise or proficiency within a single knowledge domain. In doing so, it fulfils its traditional function as a means of describing the progression of increasing knowledge and skills as one

moves, over many years, from the status of novice to a master in a specific field.

3.3.2 Jacobs' taxonomy of human competence

On similar lines, (Jacobs 1997) proposed a 'taxonomy of human competence' which suggested that human competence could be scaled with designations such as novice, specialists, experienced specialist, expert, and master. The distinction was based on someone's ability to produce outcomes. At the same time, it was recognized that '*master*, *expert*, a *specialist*, or a *novice* are usually relative notions' (Jacobs 2003, p. 7). While, on the one hand, novices are the ones whose 'outcomes are less valuable or who produce no outcomes can have lower of competence' (Jacobs 2003, p.5), on the other hand, experts are those who 'achieve the most valuable outcomes in organisations'. Masters were considered the 'experts of the highest order' (Jacobs 2003, p. 5). The taxonomy of human competence (Jacobs 2001, 1997, 2003; Jacobs & Washington 2003) specified the definitions of novice, expert and master, which are almost similar to Hoffman (1998), while the definitions of *specialist* level and *experienced specialist* are closely aligned with the *apprentice* and *journeyman* levels of Hoffman (1998).

3.3.3 Implications of proficiency scaling

The major implication of this scaling was that it envisioned a full spectrum of proficiency and suggested that individuals at different stages of their career may possess a different level of proficiency (Hoffman 1998) or competence (Jacobs 2001, 1997, 2003; Jacobs & Washington 2003). Thus, these scaling taxonomies did not propose proficiency as a specific stage in the Dreyfus and Dreyfus (1986, 2005, 2006) model. Rather it views that even a competent person has a certain level of proficiency in skills, tasks or job functions, though qualitatively and quantitatively (if it can be measured) less than a proficient performer. Moreover, the stage of journeyman (Hoffman 1998) or experienced specialist (Jacobs 1997, 2001, 2003) corresponds to the competent or proficient stages of Dreyfus and Dreyfus (1986, 2004, 2005). In subsequent research, Hoffman et al. (2014, p. 3) clarified about journeyman that 'they have practiced to the point where they can perform their duties unsupervised (literally, they can go on a journey)'. They further point out that:

> While there may be some requirements for more senior experts in select areas, there is more profound and continuing need for journeyman and senior journeymen to carry out the complex cognitive work effectively to ensure current and future success. (Hoffman et al. (2014, p. 3)

Some researchers criticized the lack of scientific rigor of Hoffman (1998) framework. For example, Farrington-Darby & Wilson (2006, p. 29) commented '[w]hat this classification does not provide is the process that has to occur to move between the classifications'. Hoffman (1998) suggested this model to advance the research thinking in the absence of any scientifically validated model. It should be noted that the implication of these stages is not really to create another staged view of proficiency; rather it is to introduce the concept of scaling of the proficiency at each stage of the progression, whether using the progression suggested by Dreyfus and Dreyfus (1986, 2004, 2005) or any other measurements.

However, there is no easy answer on how to map any proficiency scale to the performance measures used in the workplace. While proficiency scaling in terms of stages is generally accepted in the literature, no literature was found that included evidence of methods to quantify the proficiency to distinguish one stage from another objectively or in measurable terms. Even among researchers, there is less agreement on performance measures in regards to whether to measure job performance in terms of tasks or behaviors or outcomes (Koopmans et al. 2011). The literature does not provide much guidance on the nature of proficiency at each stage on any of the staged models.

While most of the classic studies focused either on novice-to-expert differences or purely on the construct of expertise, the mid-range proficiency levels have been ignored (Hoffman et al. 2014). Mid-range proficiency levels refer to journeyman (Hoffman 1998) or an experienced specialist that is proficient (Dreyfus & Dreyfus 1986, 2004, 2005; Jacobs 1997). The literature is so focused on novice-expert differences that it lacks development focus on the intermediate phases completely (Alexander 2003b). The mid-range of proficiency levels became important as researchers noticed that organizations started paying attention to the proficiency of employees: 'Proficiency ... is the primary objective of both formal and informal learning undertakings in organisations' (Enos, Kehrhahn & Bell 2003, p. 371).

3.4 PROFICIENT PERFORMANCE

3.4.1 Role of proficiency in performance

Performance measurement deals with how well someone meets the standards set for tasks, actions, behaviors, results or accomplishments to meet organizational goals. If performance is defined in terms of actions and behaviors, managers need to know how proficiently an individual is demonstrating those actions or behaviors. Performance could be a task performance, outcome performance or job performance depending upon what is being measured for proficiency. The prevalent view of proficiency is that it represents mastery of skills, tasks, knowledge or job function what someone acquires as a result of experience (Enos, Kehrhahn & Bell 2003, p. 371). Thus, the concept of performance has an important dimension of proficiency (Griffin, Neal & Parker 2007; Koopmans et al. 2011). In general, proficiency is an indicator of a level of mastery in a given task, skill, or function, i.e., how good someone is in that domain. In most studies, the performance was considered as the final outcome as a result of the level of proficiency one exhibited. The higher the proficiency, the higher is the performance. Campbell & Wiernik (2015, p. 48) highlighted the importance of proficiency: 'For those [actions and behaviours] that are relevant, the level of proficiency with which the individual performs them must be scaled'. Most commonly, an individual's proficiency indicates a level of performance.

Several performance-related studies use the term *proficiency* in the context of the task performance in a job (Borman & Motowidlo 1993, 1997; Campbell & Wiernik 2015; Koopmans et al. 2011;

Motowidlo, Borman & Schmit 1997; Motowidlo & Van Scotter 1994; Viswesvaran & Ones 2000; Viswesvaran 1993). Campbell (1990, 1999) was among the first to use proficiency as a measure of performance, though it was in the context of the performance of specific tasks. He proposed *job-specific task proficiency* as a key determinant of an individual's performance, which communicated the sense of the ability of someone to do the task well. In the context of job performance, Kanfer & Kantrowitz (2002, p. 30) observed that 'job proficiency is generally more narrowly defined as a task-relevant outcome'. They indicated that in some studies performance was measured with a cognitive ability that in turn was measured in terms of task proficiency. However, these instances limited the reference to proficiency in the context of job-specific tasks.

One may be less proficient or highly proficient in a specific set of tasks (or skills). This calls upon the concept of proficiency scaling. If the proficiency level of an individual can be quantified, it may be possible to plot it on the proficiency scale to see where an individual is in the progression towards high proficiency.

3.4.2 Development of proficient performers

From a development standpoint, Alexander (2003b) explained strategies demonstrated by proficient performers. She described a three-stage model of learning based on studies conducted in educational settings. She characterized proficiency as the interplay of knowledge, strategies, and motivations. She observed that at the proficiency/expertise stage, performers demonstrated the use of a broad and deep knowledge-base on the topic or domain knowledge-base, and at the same time, were seen using deeper processing strategies. It was also seen that they have high individual interest and engagement, as similar to the observation made by (Dreyfus & Dreyfus 1986, 2004, 2005) regarding involvement with the task.

The researchers suggested the role of reasoning skills as a differentiator as: 'Proficiency is defined not just in terms of knowledge but also in terms of reasoning strategies and skills' (Hoffman, Feltovich, et al. 2010).

3.4.3 Characteristics of proficient performers

As indicated before, another view suggested viewing proficiency as a specific stage characterized by behaviors demonstrated by the individual, as indicated by the Dreyfus and Dreyfus model. Dreyfus (2004) stated that a proficient performer is deeply involved with the task. A proficient performer can identify the important part of tasks and pay requisite attention. A proficient person sees situations holistically in terms of various elements: 'With holistic understanding, decision-making is less labored since the professional has a perspective on which of the many attributes and aspects present are the important ones' (Benner 1984, pp. 13–34). As the situation changes, his/her deliberation, plan and assessment may change. With changing situations, s/he is able to see new patterns which deviate from normal. Decision-making is very quick and fluid because of his/her experience in a similar situation in the past. 'Action becomes easier and less stressful as the learner simply sees what needs to be done rather than using a calculative procedure to select one of several possible alternatives' (Dreyfus & Dreyfus 2005, p. 786). The proficient performer considers fewer options and will focus on the correct aspect of the problem (Benner 1984).

PROFICIENT PERFORMANCE

Subsequently, Benner (2004) noted that nurses at the proficiency stage exhibited a situated understanding of their patients' responses: 'The nurse feels increasingly at home in the situation and can now recognise when she or he has a good sense of the situation' (id. 195). Dreyfus & Dreyfus (2005, p. 787) further clarified that 'the *proficient performer*, immersed in the world of skillful activity, *sees* what needs to be done, but *decides* how to do it'.

The mainstream literature continues to emphasize the composition of proficiency in terms of knowledge, skills, behaviors, and competencies to perform the desired function (Dixon 2015). However, notable business leaders have shown a different trend in their writings in the organizational context. For a given job, a pre-defined level of performance is expected from the individuals which can be expressed in terms of customer satisfaction scores, revenue generated, the number of transactions conducted or defect rates (Rosenbaum & Williams 2004, p. 14). *Business Dictionary* defines proficiency: 'Mastery of a specific behavior or skill demonstrated by consistently superior performance, measured against established or popular standards' [http://www.businessdictionary.com/definition/proficiency.html].
To do a job to satisfaction, one needs to be operating at this level set for the job. A performer is said to be proficient when s/he meets these standards. Leading thought leaders on *Learning Paths* defined proficiency as: 'Being able to perform a given task or function up to a predetermined standard. Proficiency and independently productive are often used as synonyms' (Rosenbaum & Williams 2004, p. 5). They further iterated: 'This is the point in time when you are left totally on your own and that *[sic]* you can do your job without

asking questions or making mistakes' (Rosenbaum & Williams 2004, p. 13). On the same lines, a white paper from Alorica (2017, p. 7) defines: 'To be truly proficient, an agent must master not only the required skills for the position, but be able to work independently while meeting all KPIs.' The consistency is specified as one of the key components of proficiency, that is, achieving performance thresholds once is not proficiency: 'Proficiency is when a new employee achieves a predetermined level of performance on a consistent basis' (Rosenbaum & Williams 2004, p. 14).

Though there are not many studies in which the role of consistency is studied, consistency is seen as an expected attribute of proficiency in high-risk or life-threatening jobs. For instance, in a study involving 200 patients who underwent thoroscopic lobectomy surgery by two different surgeons, Li, Wang & Ferguson (2014, p. 1154) noticed that efficiency and consistency defined the proficiency of surgeons. They found that while the personal experience of more than 100 cases developed efficiency, 'attaining consistency requires 200 or more cases' (id. 1154). Consistency in the sports arena is valued in terms of pay-for-consistency in performance (Deutscher et al. (2017). The idea of consistency implied that proficiency is a level or a state that is described as a non-negotiable state. This minimal level of proficiency referred to as *desired or target proficiency,* varies from organization to organization and from job to job. Depending on how desired or target proficiency measures are defined, an individual may or may not have reached the desired or target proficiency in a given job.

The business leaders set proficiency as a business metrics, that is, proficiency needs to be measured in business key performance indicators (KPIs), and metrics associated with a job role. A highly regarded business leader, Fred Charles, considered to be the first one to coin and define 'proficiency' as:

> Proficiency is the use of knowledge in action for the purpose of producing value for a customer. The proficiency threshold, therefore, is the exact moment when a worker can convert knowledge through action into the promised value for the customer. (Fred 2002, p. 43)

He further qualified it by saying:

> The proficiency threshold is reached when sales and marketing team can sell and advertise value to customers with confidence, when orders are filled on time, when services meet customer expectations, and when management team is leading as envisioned. (Fred 2002, p. 44)

As we can see, he specified proficiency in terms of business metrics about which an organization would care. Beta & Lidaka (2015, p. 1961) indicated that state of proficiency has 'no clear-cut explanation of the word, which allows the use of different interpretations according to the application'. Supporting that, Kim (2015, p. 2) stated that 'missing accounts of the middle stages [of proficiency] leave the developmental process somewhat unclear'. In a recent study, Attri (2018) found that most of the business leaders thought proficiency in terms of how well someone performs a job or function as opposed to skills/knowledge, which of course are ingredients that form the proficiency but do not reflect the whole. The business leaders emphasized the business metrics as a way to define proficiency. The research analysis identified it as 'job-role proficiency' to differentiate it from definitions of proficiency used in task and skill domains:

> Job-role proficiency is *[sic]* state of performance at which performers produce business outcomes or deliverables consistently to the set performance thresholds expected from a given job role. It refers to achieving and maintaining one pre-established performance level and does not imply progression through different stages or levels of performance. It refers to the business performance of the job role and does not convey an individual's performance demonstrated on a task or skill' (Attri 2018, p. 236).

Thus, proficiency in the workplace is a much larger construct which signifies overall work performance (Griffin, Neal & Parker 2007). Studies in HRD acknowledge that such overall job or work proficiency include aspects of behavioral performance, task performance, contextual performance, team, and organizational performance and also recognized the challenge to develop individuals to such levels (Campbell & Wiernik 2015; Dumas & Hanchane 2010; Houger 2006; Kanfer & Kantrowitz 2002; Khan, Khan & Khan 2011; Quartey 2012; Wallace 2006). The job-role proficiency is qualitatively different from the constructs of job-specific task proficiency (Campbell et al. 1993), task performance (Borman & Motowidlo 1993), technical proficiency (Griffin, Neal & Parker 2007), human competence (Jacobs 1997, 2001, 2003), stage of proficiency (Dreyfus & Dreyfus 2005) and proficiency as a continuum (Hoffman 1998). This distinction set the premise that proficiency for a job role is much more than an individual's performance. Theoretically, the basis of the construct suggested in this study is similar to the one suggested by concept of work role performance employing role theory: 'It is possible to assess proficiency when the requirements of a work role are formalised because there is a clear standard against which these judgments can be made' (Griffin, Neal & Parker 2007, p. 329).

3.4.4 Measuring proficient performance

Recently, there is more management focus on job role-based performance tracking. From the management consulting firm Deloitte, Bersin (2013) indicated on his blog that 'in today's high performing companies, people now take on "roles" not "jobs"'. It is also contended by some that 'job roles better encapsulated the totality of performance' (Baker 2016). Every job role in an organization is designed for a purpose, and thus, has defined and specific expectations in terms of outcomes, results, and deliverables measured with some metrics. A performer justifies being in a job role because s/he produces outputs to those established standards.

On the same lines, using an outcome-based view, leading practitioners stated that 'Proficiency can be defined in numbers of transactions, dollars sold, defect rates, customer satisfaction scores, or anything else that is measurable and related to results' (Rosenbaum & Williams 2004, p. 14). Supporting this view, Jacobs (2003) indicated that '[p]eople whose outcomes are less valuable or who produce no outcomes can have lower levels of competence'. However, there are instances when it is not possible to measure the end business results or outcomes (e.g., strategy related jobs). In those situations, proficiency was measured in terms of observable actions (i.e., quality and quantity of activities, comparison with experienced peers, the number of repetitions, verifiable and observable behaviors, and evidence from authentic work). For example, evidence of authentic work is producing a business report. Such observable behaviors can be translated to the outcomes. Pollock, Wick & Jefferson (2015) emphasized the value of actions that directly lead to the outcome as '"good performance', in the business sense, and deemed to be activity that produces high value outcomes at relatively low input cost'.

In a study conducted by Attri (2018), 85 project leaders who were interviewed emphasized that proficiency is a state or level of performance of achieving business outcomes to pre-established standards consistently. They differentiated it from being good in some skills, knowledge or attitude or ability to perform some activities, steps or tasks. Thus, proficiency is about results rather than about demonstrating a skill, task or activity. Certainly, without knowledge, skills, and behaviors and without the ability to perform required tasks, procedures or activities, it is not feasible to produce the desired outcomes. Fred (2002, p. 43) perhaps suggested the closest relationship of knowledge and the outcome, and valued the outcomes that come out of learning knowledge: 'The proficiency threshold, therefore, is the exact moment when a worker can convert knowledge through action into the promised value for the customer.' However, being able to produce the designated results independently ultimately determines whether or not someone is proficient, and if not there yet, how soon s/he could be in that state.

3.4.5 Importance of proficient performance

Enos, Kehrhahn & Bell (2003, p. 371) position proficiency as 'the primary objective of both formal and informal learning undertakings in organisations'. Nevertheless, workforce proficiency appears to be an important determinant of how successfully organizations handle business challenges on a daily basis (Hoffman, Feltovich, et al. 2010). Having employees with high proficiency level is crucial to organizations:

Domain practitioners who achieve high levels of proficiency provide technical judgment to speed decision-making in time-critical events. They provide resilience to operations by resolving tough problems, anticipating future demands and re-planning, and acting prudently by judgment rather than by rule. (Hoffman et al. 2014, p. 2)

3.5 EXPERT PERFORMANCE

In the novice-expert continuum, stage of expertise has invited the most attention among researchers in the field of cognitive psychology, training, learning, performance and business practices, leading to volumes of academic research by leading expertise researchers such as *The nature of expertise* (Chi, Glaser & Farr 1988), *Exploring expertise* (Williams, Faulkner & Fleck 1998), *Cambridge handbook of expertise and expert performance* (Ericsson et al. 2006), *Development of professional expertise* (Ericsson 2009a), and *Expertise out of context* (Hoffman 2012). Most of the expertise discussion in these publications are based on classic and seminal works dating back to the 1960s. The expertise researchers regard extensive classic and seminal works by leading researchers such as De Groot (1965; 1966), Chase & Simon (1973), Chi, Glaser & Rees (1982), Glaser & Chi (1988), Dreyfus & Dreyfus (1986) and Ericsson et al. (1993) as the foundation to most expertise theories which continue to be used in modern research.

3.5.1 Attributes of expertise

According to Hoffman (1998), three dimensions can define expertise: (1) development of expertise; (2) the knowledge structures possessed by experts; and (3) the reasoning processes used by experts. On the other hand, Novak (2011) suggested that expertise could be viewed from four perspectives: (1) attributes; (2) cognition; (3) stages; and (4) community. The attribute perspective defines expertise based on years of studies in several fields, which revealed certain characteristics about how experts operate. The cognition perspective is based on cognitive studies of experts in fields like chess, music, and sports. Such studies reveal how experts think and organize knowledge. The stage perspective represents expertise as a sort of progression of knowledge and skills. Lastly, the community perspective represents expertise as a quality that emerges from the interactions individuals have with people and their environment.

One stream of literature is almost entirely devoted to novice-expert differences. The pioneering research by De Groot (1965; 1966) on the differences in performance of novices and experts in the game of chess has motivated other studies (e.g. Chi, Glaser & Farr 1988). Subsequently, several studies revealed how experts were different from novices, and others have attempted to explain the general nature of expertise (Chi, Glaser & Rees 1981; Farrington-Darby & Wilson 2006; Schraagen 1993). Expertise is best understood by understanding what an expert does. In the proficiency scale, Hoffman (1998, p. 85) considered expert as a person who has special skills, extensive experience and ability to crack tough problems. From that perspective, expertise has been defined as 'the possession of a large body of knowledge and procedural skills' (Chi, Glaser & Rees 1982, p. 8). In their seminal work, Glaser & Chi (1988) made a point that knowledge structures, processing capability and problem solving are the collective ingredients to develop expertise. An argument for expertise being acquired and hence an outcome or goal of skill acquisition was posited by Chi (2006, p. 23) as 'presumably the more skilled person became expert-like from having acquired knowledge about a domain, that is, from learning and studying' and 'from deliberate practice'. Moreover, experts within their domains are considered to be skilled, competent and think in qualitatively different ways from novices (Anderson 2000; Chi, Glaser & Farr 1988).

In a study conducted by Klein (1998), he interviewed several first responding emergency workers such as firefighters, military officers, nurses and air traffic controllers who made decisions under stress. He noted that expertise or expert performance has the key attribute of pattern recognition which is an ability possessed by an expert to recognize aspects of a new situation based on the exhaustive repertoire of previous experience. Experts recognize patterns, select a course of action and then assess the course of action through mental simulation before executing it. Klein (1998) strongly emphasized that experts have well-developed intuitive capabilities. Thus, exclusivity was one feature of expertise that set it apart from any other construct in skill acquisition. This means expertise typically has been viewed as knowledge, skills, abilities and performance characteristics being possessed by only some people and usually are not common enough to be possessed by all (Dror 2011). These abilities may contain a range of skills such as superior well-organized knowledge, specific mental representations, cognitive skills, the ability to process a large amount of information, ability to identify patterns, ability to filter signal from noise and highly automatic skills (Dror 2011).

A continuum view of the novice-to-expert transition has usually been used to explain the actions and characteristics of experts. On that continuum, Dreyfus & Dreyfus (2005) contended that an expert operates and behaves differently from a novice, advanced beginner, competent performer or proficient performer. An expert exhibits experience-based deep understanding. 'An immense library of distinguishable situations is built upon the basis of experience' (Dreyfus & Dreyfus 1986, p. 32). Thus, experts treat knowledge in context, and they can recognize the relevance. Similar to the observation made by Klein (1998), Dreyfus & Dreyfus (2005) also made the observation that actions by an expert are driven by intuition and from tacit knowledge and usually are unconscious. They suggested that at the expert level, an individual relies on intuition and the analytical approach is only used in new situations or unrecognized problems not previously experienced. They appear to grasp the conceptual understanding and principles governing the situations intuitively. Thus, they have the ability to recognize the relevant features of new situations. Selectivity also eventuates because of experience, whereby an expert performer can selectively know quickly what needs to be achieved and how to achieve it. The experts can see alternative approaches in a given situation. An expert 'focuses on the accurate region of the problem without wasteful consideration of a larger range of unfruitful possibilities' (Benner (1984, p. 34). Therefore, an expert is able to make unobvious discriminations in situations that a proficient performer may not be able to make. Thus, the expert performer can adapt his/her approach based on the situation. Based on prior experience, the expert can even devise and implement a solution for situations they have never experienced before (DiBello & Missildine 2011).

At this stage, skill attains the automaticity, as indicated by Fitts (1964; 1967), Anderson (1981, 1982) and Ackerman (1988). The skill becomes so automatic sometimes that even an expert may not be aware of it. The performance of an expert at automaticity is fluid. Therefore, it is believed that the expert could move effortlessly between intuitive and analytical approaches and they have the ability to see the overall picture. Furthermore, reflection also characterizes the expertise: 'Experts not only possess extensive domain knowledge through experience and proceduralization, but also utilise self-regulatory knowledge in monitoring progress' (Ge & Hardré 2010, p. 25). However, experts are most critical reflections of their own assumptions, while considering a different course of actions, especially in time-critical situations (Klein 1998).

3.5.2 A holistic view of expertise

In almost all the expertise development models, expertise progression has been considered quite one-dimensional, especially in stage models. Such approaches viewed proficiency as a trait possessed by an individual. However, contemporary researchers appeared to recognize that expertise development depends on 'becoming socially embedded in the appropriate groups of experts so that one can acquire 'specialist tacit knowledge'' (Collins 2011, p. 255). Recognizing the social aspect of expertise, Collins et al. (2006) and Collins (2011) proposed the construct of interactional expertise. They propose that there are two extra dimensions to expertise. One deals with the degree of exposure to tacit knowledge and the other deals with esotericity (specialized knowledge). They argued that those dimensions create 3-D *expertise space* in which expertise can be explored in a number of ways. The postulation by Collins (2011, p. 255) was based on the fundamental premise that '[t]acit knowledge can be acquired only by immersion in the society of those who already possess it'.

Furthermore, expertise in an organizational context appears to be more encompassing for the whole job itself rather than on representative tasks, as suggested in the expert performance model. On those lines, Cornford & Athanasou (1995, p. 15) suggested a concept of occupational expertise: 'People build up highly specialised knowledge about an operation, about a company, about equipment or solving particular problems'. Subsequently, professional expertise in the occupational space and practice oriented-professions (e.g., legal, consulting) have been studied (Billett 2010; Boshuizen 2003; Evers et al. 2011; van der Heijden 2002; Holt, Mackay & Smith 2004; Lajoie 2009; Mieg 2009; Mott 2000)

3.5.3 Construct of expert performance

Among classic theories, the Fitts & Posner (1967) model asserted the value of practice in developing automaticity during skill acquisition. However, Ericsson (2009b) believed that practice, as described by Fitts and Posner's (1967) model, was helpful in achieving automaticity only in everyday skills and was no way a mechanism to attain superior expert performance. While classic expertise studies characterized experts and expertise, (Ericsson et al. 1993) suggested a mechanism of achieving *expert performance* based on several studies in domains like music, chess, and sports. They maintained that the construct of expert performance was special. Ericsson & Charness (1994, p. 731) described expert-level performance (or expert performance) as 'if someone is performing at least two standard deviations above the mean level in the population, that individual can be said to be performing at an expert level'. Such superior performance is achieved with a combination of high-level skills and domain-specific knowledge and skilled memory (Charness & Tuffiash 2008).

3.5.4 Deliberate practice mechanism

In studies in the domain of music and chess, the findings indicated that individuals normally used extensive training, deliberately and carefully designed professional practice and extended domain-related activities that improved their performance incrementally (Ericsson et al. 1993). The deliberate efforts included constant engagement in similar domain activities, exposure to new issues in his/her domain, and subject to the certain special type of practice called *deliberate practice*. Deliberate practice is not just practice or any other domain-related activity such as work or on-the-job training event (Ericsson & Charness 1994). Rather, deliberate practice is a highly individualized training on tasks selected by a qualified teacher to build expertise in an individual. The deliberate practice is based on the premise that 'expert performance requires the opportunity to find suitable training tasks that the performer can master sequentially.... typically monitored by a teacher or coach' (Ericsson 2006, p. 692). The feedback from a designated coach is considered an important factor in deliberate practice. With such efforts, the individual may be able to increase expertise.

ACCELERATED PROFICIENCY FOR ACCELERATED TIMES

In several studies, Ericsson emphasized and characterized the nature of deliberate practice (Ericsson, Prietula & Cokely 2007; Ericsson 2000, 2002, 2003, 2004, 2006, 2007, 2008, 2009c). In their studies, they identified four components in the deliberate practice model: focused goals which are determined by a teacher in order to improve a specific aspect of performance, concentration and effort, feedback from a teacher comparing actual to desired performance, and further opportunities for practice (Ericsson 2007, 2008, 2009c). Deliberate practice activities are designed to allow repeated experience to allow learners to observe various critical aspects of tasks. Constant stretching and correcting of mistakes were central to the expert performance model because 'attempts for mastery require that the performer always try, by stretching performance beyond its current capabilities, to correct some specific weakness while preserving other successful aspects of function' (Ericsson 2006, p. 700). Such stretching of skills leads to gradual changes in cognitive mechanisms leading to long-term skill retention. Ericsson (2014, p. 81) suggested that 'new cognitive mechanisms are gradually acquired during the extended period, and they mediate the superior performance, thus leading to qualitative differences in structure compared to untrained performance'. Ericsson (2000, 2002, 2003, 2004, 2006a, 2007, 2008, 2009c) further hypothesized that dramatic differences in performance between experts and non-experts could be attributed to the amount of deliberate practice. Thus, the acquired performance of an individual is a direct function of the amount of time engaged in deliberate practice activities.

3.5.5 Time to expertise

In their earlier studies, Ericsson et al. (1993) confirmed that it takes 10,000 hours or ten years of intense training and deliberate practice to become an expert in almost anything. Since then, researchers have applied the concept of deliberate practice in other domains such as science, weather forecasting, engineering, military command and control, surgery and sports and have seen that the framework reasonably explained or supported the development of expertise (Ericsson & Ward 2007; Kirkman 2013; Roth 2009; Ward et al. 2007; van de Wiel & Van den Bossche 2013). Ericsson et al. (1993) hypothesized that true measurement of expert performance could happen only in laboratory settings by studying the reproducibility of superior performance on representative tasks. The expert performance, as suggested by the deliberate practice mechanism, is defined and measured on the representative and specific set of tasks on which reproducibility and superiority of the performance could be verified in the laboratory (Ericsson 2014).

3.5.6 Relevance of expert performance

Studies on expert performance have also faced criticism. Recent studies have reasoned that deliberate practice as the only method to achieve expertise is probably not realistic and cited some deficiencies of the approach. For instance, some of the deficiencies were that it discounted the effect of innate talent; it did not explain the performance in novel situations; it possibly ignored the effect of task complexity and task characteristics; and it exhibited a large variance of performance among individuals (Ackerman 2014; Gobet 2013; Hambrick, Altmann, et al. 2014; Hambrick, Oswald, et al.

2014; Kulasegaram, Grierson & Norman 2013; Lombardo & Deaner 2014). Most of the objections appear to stem from the issue that the deliberate practice approach was based on the repetition of familiar or routine tasks in relatively closed and repetitive domains such as sports and music, in which standards of measurements are defined and finite. In a domain in which problems were novel or non-repetitive in nature, the applicability of this model is not well established.

On the contrary to the claims that deliberate practice was the only mechanism explaining expert performance, some studies indicated that more factors were contributing to expert performance (Kulasegaram, Grierson & Norman 2013; van de Wiel & Van den Bossche 2013). For example, experience stood out as a key differentiator in both Dreyfus and Dreyfus's (1986, 2004, 2005), as well as Hoffman's (1998) account of expertise. However, there has been conflicting evidence in regards to the contribution of experience towards expert performance. Contrary to a common belief that experience leads to expertise, Ward et al. (2007) negated the sole effect of experience in gaining expert or superior performance in a study involving 203 male soccer players between 8 and 18 years of age. The participants consisted of experienced elite players from professional clubs, while sub-elite players were recruited from local schools. The study found that accumulated weekly hours in practice most consistently discriminated between skill levels, rather than the experience of the players. Ericsson (2006, p. 685) supported this observation by saying that '[e]xtensive experience in a domain does not, however, invariably lead to expert levels of achievement ... further improvement depend [sic] on deliberate efforts to change particular aspects of performance'. However, van de Wiel & Van den Bossche (2013) study involving 17 residents undergoing an internal medicine program and 28 experienced physicians in internal medicine appeared to contradict these claims. In this study, the researcher tried to examine the effect of work-related deliberate practice on performance. They found that deliberate engagement in work-related activities was not related to case test performance of the experienced physicians. However, work experience showed a clear positive relationship with the performance of the resident students.

These impracticalities and the long period of ten years have been viewed as a daunting obstacle in the organization (Fadde & Klein 2010, 2012; Kirkman 2013). Ericsson maintained that there was probably no shorter or faster way to expert performance stating that 'researchers have not uncovered some simple strategies that would allow non-experts to rapidly acquire expert performance' (Ericsson & Charness 1994, p. 737). Despite the criticism of the ten-year rule, there is only limited evidence to the contrary showing the possibility to reduce the ten-year period (Lombardo & Deaner 2014). Nevertheless, deliberate practice and expert-performance characteristics have guided scaled versions of the training approaches for specific skills (Fadde 2013, 2016; Ward et al. 2007). A major implication of this expert performance approach and deliberate practice framework was to identify the representative tasks and then design training activities with focused, deliberate practice in a certain sequence to develop expertise. The deliberate practice framework placed value on the sequence of exercises, the amount of deliberate practice, feedback and coaching mechanisms.

Another implication was the role of deliberate personal efforts by an individual in terms of disciplined, deliberate practice, as well as training efforts on achieving expert performance.

3.6 EXPERT VS PROFICIENT

Organizations are continuously striving to develop peoples' skills to the next level of proficiency due to new business challenges and competition. To develop employees to desired proficiency is not the same as developing expertise. Expertise is considered to be an elite status bestowed on few domain specialists, and not everyone may need to be developed to that level. For example, for some critical functions or roles in organizations such as CEO's position, there may be a need to develop individuals to a very high level of proficiency as determined by the nature of the challenges faced. Such brilliant individuals may be experts in their domains. However, not everyone needs to be or could be an expert of that order. Hoffman, Andrews & Feltovich (2012, p. 8) supported that:

> We do not assume that every organisation needs to have every employee be expert at every task. Instead, we are recognizing that for the majority of employees achieving a degree of competence to become journeymen is just fine. Hence our general reference is to accelerated proficiency.

Most of the methods in the literature for the development of proficiency and expertise (*high proficiency,* as Hoffman et al. called it) were informed by expertise studies (Fadde 2016). However, the limitation of those methods is noted as being mostly focused on developing the expertise of individuals on specific representative tasks and often time within laboratory settings (Hambrick, Oswald, et al. 2014). The notion of expertise specifies deliberate practice in a specific set of non-changing tasks. However, in the workplace, professionals hardly ever get to work on the same set of tasks that long. For those reasons, Fadde & Klein (2010) contended that deliberate practice, and hence, the achievement of expert performance, is not an even realizable goal in any job for any organization. At ground level, proficiency and expertise are not the same things.

An increasing trend in the literature revealed that several researchers thought that employees should be prepared to proficient level or journeyman level as a minimum in organizations (Hoffman et al. 2014; Jung, Kim & Reigeluth 2016; Moon, Kim & You 2013). For instance, (Hoffman et al. 2014) believed that skills of most employees needed to be developed at least at the journeyman level, that is, one who can do his/her job productively and independently. Lately, the organizations expect a minimum journeyman level of proficiency from their employees while they would still develop a few selected employees as experts.

3.7 SUMMARY

This chapter presented a review of studies on how novice progresses into an expert. The stages of proficiency and proficiency scaling along that progression was discussed. The nature and dimensions of proficient performance were explored. Finally, the chapter explored the concepts of expertise and expert performance.

The organizations typically require most of their employees being while they still need few experts. While there is extensive literature on performance and proficiency, it does not fully explain the nature of proficiency as required by the organizations in a given job function. Several interrelated but unanswered questions arise from this review, such as: What proficiency means to organizations? How do organizations measure proficiency? How do the stages of proficiency play a role in performance assessment at work? Such questions should be addressed in future research studies.

4

ACCELERATED PROFICIENCY: MEANING AND DRIVERS

Over the past few decades, the research focus has been on skill acquisition, development of workplace proficiency and higher level expertise. From a practical standpoint, the business challenge is to bring people to a certain level of proficiency so that they can do their job to desired standards. However, changing organizational challenges and attempts to apply principles derived from expertise studies appears to have raised concerns about the time it takes to acquire proficiency. Recent research studies have shown that the business world has reacted to increased competition and pace of business. Thus, there is increasing use of new business metrics to track the speed with which workforce attains proficiency and demonstrates the required performance. In the last decade, accelerating the rate of acquisition of proficiency has become an important topic. Newly evolved business metrics tied to 'time' and 'speed' are *time to proficiency, time to competence, time to full productivity* and *speed to proficiency*. This chapter introduces the terms and also set the ground for the importance of accelerating proficiency of employees at the workplace.

4.1 ACCELERATING PROFICIENCY

Organizations have witnessed tremendous turmoil and growth between 2000 and 2016, which has led executives to be concerned about the success of their business in the new world (Deloitte 2017). The foremost organizational concern is increased competition. With globalization, most organizations now have access to the same markets, similar technologies and similar capabilities (Kraiger, Passmore & Rebelo 2014; Kraiger 2014). The relative success of organizations may ultimately depend upon time-to-market of their products, services or solutions they develop or offer. Capabilities, competencies, and skills of the workforce are the most critical determinants of time-to-market and hence the competitive distinction among organizations (Wright & McMahan 2011). Changing business landscapes and market dynamics bring different expectations on workforce competencies. A decade ago, the *Implications for 21st Century Work* report forecasted:

> One expected consequence of the technological advances is a continued growth in the demand for a high-skilled workforce capable of undertaking the basic R&D to develop new technologies, developing the applications and

> production processes that exploit the technological advances, and bringing the resulting products to the commercial marketplace. (Karoly 2007, p. 3).

The ability and readiness of the workforce to meet new business needs is a topic of constant concern to modern business managers (Salas et al. 2012). Thus, providing employees with the required skills and developing them to the desired proficiency level is a key goal of organizations for their sustainability. Once the desired level of proficiency is defined, the next challenge is to reach to that proficiency in a shorter time. The corporations worldwide have started shifting their focus (or started including the focus) on the expectations for acceleration and speed to develop their workforce at a faster rate, increase the rate of skill acquisition and reduce times with which workforce becomes ready to do their jobs.

Most commonly, scholarly research calls this concept of accelerating employee skills or performance as '*accelerated proficiency*.' Hoffman, Feltovich, et al. (2010) defined *accelerated proficiency* as the 'phenomenon of achieving higher levels of proficiency in less time' (p. 9) and dealt with 'how to train and train quickly to higher levels of proficiency' (p. 8). The level of proficiency is the desired level decided by organizations for the job. Hoffman, Andrews & Feltovich (2012, p. 8) considered that accelerated proficiency deals with 'achievement of knowledge and skill across the proficiency spectrum, all the way from apprentice to expert levels' in a shortest possible time. Hoffman et al. (2014, p. 13) further qualified accelerated proficiency as 'getting individuals to achieve high levels of proficiency at a rate faster than ordinary.' They expressed accelerated proficiency in terms of time to proficiency measurement (id. 169). Acceleration of proficiency is measured in terms of reduction in the time someone takes to reach the desired proficiency. In business language, measurement of acceleration is expressed as *time to proficiency* or *speed to proficiency* or similar variations of these terms such as time to competence, or time to full productivity among others which essentially mean the same thing (Bruck 2015; Fadde & Klein 2010; Fred 2002; Hoffman et al. 2014; Rosenbaum & Williams 2004). Accelerated proficiency, thus, is the deliberate and conscious effort of shortening time to proficiency. In the latest time to proficiency study, Attri (2018) interviewed 85 business leaders and experts with proven experience of shortening time to proficiency. The study led to identifying core characteristics of the concept of accelerated proficiency:

> *Accelerating proficiency* means shortening the time someone takes in a given job role to reach to a state of consistent performance that meets the set thresholds. This is measured in time-to-proficiency. (Attri 2018, p. 236).

This is the most comprehensive definition of accelerated proficiency, supporting the views of previous studies.

The intent behind these terms is conceptually portrayed in Figure 1. Proficiency levels are plotted on the vertical axis and time is plotted on the horizontal axis. Proficiency paths are shown as a straight line for simplicity. The dotted horizontal line indicates desired or target proficiency. Assuming an employee starts a job role at time T_0, s/he reaches target proficiency following a *normal proficiency path* at time T_1. Conceptually, if some strategies or mechanisms exist which could accelerate the rate of proficiency acquisition to follow the *accelerated proficiency path*; it could have allowed the individuals serving the same job role at time T_2. The difference, T_2-T_1, is a net reduction in time to proficiency. The result of shorter time to proficiency leads to substantial financial and operational benefits to the organization and higher value to customers (Fred 2002).

Figure 1: Simplified concept of accelerated proficiency

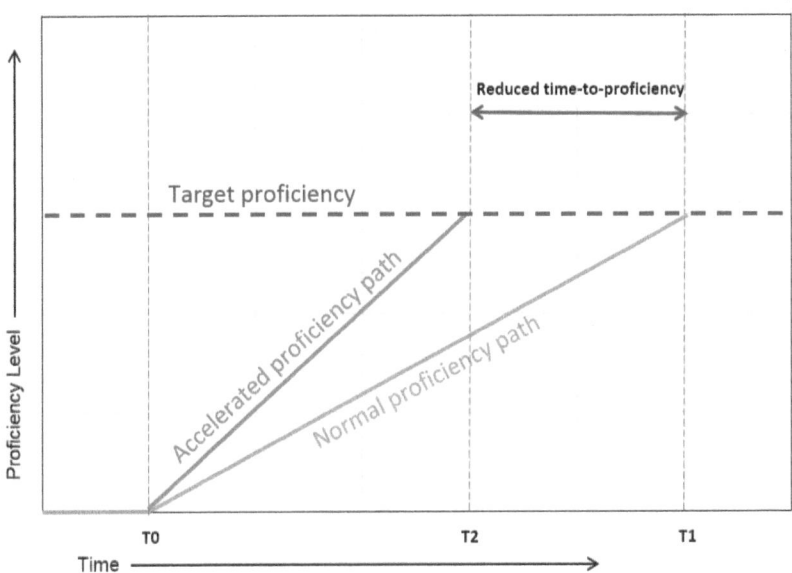

Source: *modified from Rosenbaum and Williams (2004) and Hoffman et al. (2014)*

4.1.1 Time to Proficiency Metrics

Business leaders consider that it is very important to identify the point when an individual demonstrates performance that signifies his/her being operating at or above desired or target proficiency

(Fred 2002). Every job role requires a certain amount of time to develop performance to the desired proficiency level. This time is referred to as *time to proficiency* (TTP). Bachlechner et al. (2010, p. 378) defined time to proficiency as 'the amount of time an individual spends in a new job environment before it [*sic*] is able to fulfil most tasks without help from colleagues or supervisors.' For instance, *Training Industry*'s glossary pitches it as: 'Time to proficiency refers to the time needed or taken by an individual to acquire the skills and knowledge necessary to reach an acceptable level of performance' [https://trainingindustry.com/glossary/time-to-proficiency/]. Time to proficiency is usually measured from the date of hiring or when someone takes up a new role or the first day of the training s/he attends. However, measurement of the starting point and end state may vary significantly based on the context and definition of desired proficiency. Time to proficiency is not measurement of one activity, rather it involves time required for several activities such as onboarding, formal as well as informal training required to understand the basics of the job, on-the-job training and on-the-job learning to understand specifics of job tasks, and other activities to gain experience on specific tasks or skills required to do the job (Attri & Wu 2015).

Some leaders like to refer to other terms like time to full productivity, time to competence or speed to proficiency. Nevertheless, these terms mean essentially the same thing (or similar things) as the time to proficiency.

Cornerstone (company) places 'Time to productivity is a metric that measures how long it takes a new hire to contribute to an organization' [https://www.cornerstoneondemand.com/glossary/time-productivity]. Millington (2018) states:

> Time-to-full productivity can mean one of two things. It can refer to the time it takes a new recruit to ably complete every aspect of their job role as measured by their manager. Alternatively, it can refer to the time it takes a recruit to reach an equivalent level of performance as their closest colleagues. Essentially, it means how long it takes a newcomer to be proficient in their job.

In a survey conducted by i4cp (2011) [https://www.i4cp.com/productivity-blog/2011/09/14/why-you-should-measure-time-to-full-productivity], it was observed that 16% of the organizations used time to full productivity metrics while the other 64% acknowledged that they should be using it to manage the talent more effectively.

KPS (company) coined the term *time to competence* as 'the time to achieve the target performance level' [https://www.kpsol.com/speed-to-competency-service-agents-measurement-action/].

The term 'speed to proficiency' is most commonly used in the business arena. The earliest usage of the term "speed to proficiency" came from book *Breakaway: Deliver value to your customer – Fast!!!* in which Fred (2002, p. 16) defined:

> Proficient workers speed things up: organizational change, operational improvement, problem solving, and delivery of service all happen faster. When you shorten the time it takes for workers to become proficient, the capital and resources required to introduce a new product, maintain operations and infrastructure, and perform a service are also proportionally reduced. I call this *speed to proficiency*.

The last decade has seen this term becoming a common buzzword in business discussions. Cedar Interactive (company) positioned it as: '"Speed to Proficiency" refers to the time required to bring a person up to a proficient level of performance at a job or task' [http://cedarinteractive.com/serv-speedtopro.htm]. Bruck (2007) identified its value as: 'In any business arena where the demonstrated mastery of new knowledge and skills is critical to the success of the business speed to proficiency is the name of the game' [http://www.q2learning.com/docs/WP-S2P.pdf]. Recently, in a white paper, Alorica (2017, p. 7) defines:

> To be truly proficient, an agent must master not only the required skills for the position, but be able to work independently while meeting all KPIs. How long an individual or team takes to reach this level of competence is the speed to proficiency.

Lately, the term *speed to proficiency* has taken its own little life in the business world. In a recent study, over 85 business leaders expressed how poorly the term "speed to proficiency" and for that sake "accelerating time to proficiency" is understood by their frontline managers (Attri 2018). At the same time, they also indicated the concerns of how academic community and scholarly literature view these terms differently.

4.1.2 Studies on time to proficiency

Studies on time to proficiency have been conducted since the late 1980s. Carpenter et al. (1989) and Faneuff et al. (1990) were among the first to develop a time to proficiency model in a military context for recording aviator proficiency. In their study involving avionics communication specialists, Carpenter et al. (1989) measured time to proficiency in terms of performance in a selected set of tasks. They defined time to proficiency as 'the length of time it takes to bring people with different attributes (especially mental aptitude) to targeted levels of task performance' (Carpenter et al. (1989, p. 1). They correlated productivity, attrition, cost, and aptitude in their model with the time to proficiency. Based on the model, they found that time to proficiency metrics were viable performance measurement methods in the job which 'provides sufficient information for the modeling of productivity' (Carpenter et al. 1989, p. i).

In a different application of the same concept, Pinder & Schroeder (1987) conducted time to proficiency study which involved 354 managers from eight companies in Canada, who were surveyed regarding their time to proficiency after job transfers. They conceived time to proficiency as 'the length of time that elapses between the individual's movement into a new job and ascendancy of that individual to a level of performance at which a balance between inducements and contributions exists' (Pinder & Schroeder 1987, p. 337). Inducements were the investments made in the person when s/he started a new job, while contributions were his/her productivity on the new job. This definition reveals the key implication that while someone is working toward desired proficiency and trying to be productive in a new job, his or her performance has a financial impact on the business, thus making it a compelling reason to monitor time to proficiency in a given job.

Figure 2: Accelerated proficiency growth curve and time to proficiency

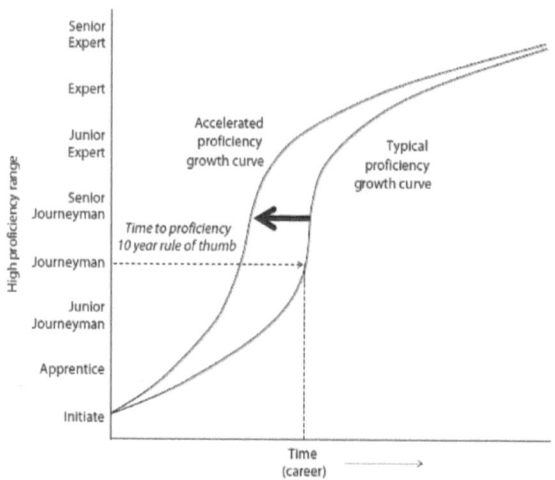

Source: adapted from Hoffman et al. (2014)

Renowned academic researchers on *accelerated proficiency,* Hoffman et al. (2014, p. 169) referred to time to proficiency in terms of career stages as the time taken by an individual to reach a desired level of proficiency. The career stages they most frequently referred to were journeyman and senior journeyman. The journeyman career stage exhibited characteristics like being reliable, experienced, able to work unsupervised, and having achieved a certain level of competence. These characteristics, in general, though not entirely, lined up well with the proficiency stage of Dreyfus & Dreyfus (2005) model. Hoffman et al. (2014, p. 169) explained reducing time to proficiency in terms of an S-curve of proficiency acquisition, as shown in Figure 2.

The proficiency scales show the stages of initiator, apprentice, journeyman, and expert. They further broke the journeyman and expert stages into three different levels to indicate seniority, given that time is plotted in terms of career. The basic inference drawn from this graph is that there could be some methods or mechanisms that can accelerate the time to proficiency, at least at the journeyman level.

4.1.3 How long is time to proficiency

The overall time to proficiency could be in months or years, depending on the jobs. Ericsson et al. (1993) estimated that at least ten years of deliberate practice was required to acquire expertise (time to expertise). Though developing every employee as an expert may not be a feasible goal for organizations, there is a general consensus that time to proficiency could also be long.

Few studies have focused on how much time it takes for someone to reach high proficiency (expertise), and they were mostly situated within classic studies on expertise or expert performance. Ericsson & Charness (1994) proposed, '[t]o measure the duration of the acquisition process, we analyze the length of time it takes for best individuals to attain the highest levels of performance within a domain'. Measurement of time taken to acquire high proficiency has long intrigued researchers. Chase & Simon (1973) found that several other domains exhibit the patterns of achieving high proficiency in ten years, similar to the observations made in the domain of chess. Since then, the ten-year rule to achieve expertise has been empirically tested by researchers (Hayes 1989; Simonton 1997).

The most extensive work on this has been carried out by Ericsson et al. (1993), who analyzed the effect of deliberate practice by comparing three groups of 30 under-training violinists and two groups of 24 expert and amateur pianists. Through extensive modeling and measurements, they concluded that it required about ten thousand hours or ten years of intense training and deliberate practice activities to attain expertise in almost anything. However, this estimate of ten years was for attaining an elite performance on a specific set of tasks or skills, mainly in a closed domain where standards of performance are well established.

In a study involving 215 modern writers, their best works since the time they wrote their first publication were evaluated (Kaufman & Kaufman 2007). They found that the several famous writers required ten years to reach a point of writing to achieve a well-regarded publication, which required, in addition, an even longer preparation time. Nevertheless, they also stated that 'it takes 10 years to become not just an "expert" but a "world-class" expert' (id. 115).

While all of these studies refer to the ten-year period as time to expertise at world-class status, there are only a few studies which report measurements of time to proficiency (Carpenter et al. 1989; Faneuff et al. 1990). An air force communication specialist's time to proficiency was noted in the range of 18 months to 36 months depending upon their aptitude scores (Carpenter et al. 1989). According to an estimate, a pilot takes a minimum of 1500 hours (the equivalent of two years flying two hours every day) to be certified to fly a commercial plane (Government Publishing Office 2013).

In another study involving 300 call center agents, Borton (2007) noted that time to proficiency of the agents was more than six months. More recently, a survey conducted with chief sales officers of 1,200 companies worldwide by Accenture (2013) indicated that time to proficiency of 73% of the new sales representative workforce was approximately one year or more. The time to proficiency of new bankers in a study was estimated to be between eleven and fourteen months (Thompson 2017, p. 173).

Thus, time to proficiency is usually very long—much longer than any training program one attends to get initial operating readiness.

4.2 ACCELERATING LEARNING VS PROFICIENCY

One concept that is interrelated with accelerated proficiency is that of accelerated learning. In the literature *accelerated learning* is often used synonymously with the intent of accelerating proficiency and accelerating expertise. Two schools of thoughts have emerged.

In more traditional terms, Adams, Karthaus & Rehak (2011, p. 1) described it as: 'Accelerated learning allows a shortened timeframe for learning with a comparative amount of material learned and retained'. Historically, accelerated learning has been considered as a set of techniques to enable students to think fast and learn more (Rose 2000). Over the years, accelerated learning has become a buzzword. The literature review indicated a range of claims and methods towards accelerating learning. For instance: brain-based learning (Smith & Call 1999); blended online learning (Patchan et al. 2015); accelerated fast-track training programs

(Trekles & Sims 2013); social learning and involvement (Meier 2000); experiential learning (Abston & Rhodes 2013); intelligent computer-based tutoring (Sottilare & Goldberg 2012); electrocardiograph feedback to accelerate learning (Berka et al. 2010); and as extreme as direct current stimulation to the brain (McKinley et al. 2013). However, none of the accelerated learning viewpoints appear to match.

Some studies have attempted to accelerate learning of employees and teams in the workplace (Lynn, Akgün & Keskin 2003; Seow et al. 2005). In an organizational context, accelerated learning means to learn some task in a shorter time and be able to produce results. Andrews & Fitzgerald (2010, p. 5) expressed accelerated learning in terms of its goal to 'speed up knowledge acquisition in ways that are not detrimental to learning'. Hoffman, Feltovich, et al. (2010) asserted that accelerated learning means several things including the idea of training people to the minimal level of proficiency in a shorter time; getting individuals to achieve higher levels of proficiency at a faster rate; and making learning less prone to decay. In a subsequent development, Hoffman, Andrews & Feltovich (2012) considered accelerated learning as an umbrella concept, of which accelerated proficiency is a sub-set:

> "Accelerated learning" refers not only to the idea of hastening the achievement of basic-level proficiency; it reaches across the proficiency scale to the question of how to accelerate the achievement of expertise, and whether that is even possible. (Hoffman, Andrews & Feltovich 2012, p. 8)

The traditional view of accelerated learning and the one submitted by Hoffman et al. ((Hoffman, Andrews & Feltovich 2012;

Hoffman, Feltovich, et al. 2010) do not seem to intersect with each other. The goal of the traditional meaning of accelerated learning is more geared towards speeding up the learning curve of a specific individual, that is, learning a given content in a shorter time or learning more content in the same time (e.g. Imel 2002; Patchan et al. 2015; Radler & Bocianu 2017; Trekles & Sims 2013).

However, a study by Attri (2018) with 85 industry experts revealed that learning something quickly did not necessarily mean an individual would start producing consistent business results quickly too. For example, if a sales engineer's monthly quota were $1M, learning the details of the product features, sales processes and sales technique would not mean s/he could surely produce $1M consistently month after month. S/he would have to develop relationships, connections, and leads, and gain experience in all aspects of the job role to be able to produce that many sales every month. Such outcomes require more than just learning content, knowledge or skills. Thus, the effect of accelerating learning or learning more content in a short time may or may not always contribute toward a shorter time to proficiency.

The reality at the workplace is that people (even in the same job) learn at different rates and with different styles. Controlling every individual's learning curve is not feasible, and that is not the intent of any project involving accelerating proficiency. As outlined in earlier chapters, accelerated proficiency refers to the performance of a job role as a whole and a group of people serving that role as a whole. Thus, it is not about the learning of one person, unless it is achieved collectively for the entire group in a job (Bologa & Lupu 2007).

Further, it was noted that accelerated proficiency projects are generally not started with the intent of shortening training duration or rapidized training, that is, 'the idea of training individuals to achieve some minimal level of proficiency at a rate faster than usual' (Hoffman et al. 2014, p. 13). On the contrary, attaining such initial operating readiness to put someone on-the-job to do basic duties does not serve the goal of accelerated proficiency toward reducing time to proficiency (Attri 2018). Attri (2018) noted that accelerated proficiency (or efforts to reduce time to proficiency) is entirely different from similarly worded topics such as *accelerated learning* and *accelerated training*:

> Accelerated proficiency is not about learning a body of content faster or shortening the training duration because the solution to a shorter time-to-proficiency lies beyond training interventions (Attri 2018, p. 236).

In that sense, observations by Attri (2018) sets grounds for better qualification of terms accelerated learning, accelerated training and accelerated proficiency and extends the ones given by Hoffman et al ((Hoffman, Andrews & Feltovich 2012; Hoffman, Feltovich, et al. 2010) into the organizational context. Nevertheless, accelerated learning methods continue to be part of any accelerated proficiency discussions for the lack of any clear-cut distinction or characterization.

4.3 BUSINESS DRIVERS FOR SPEED

Irrespective of the actual length, there is a general consensus that time to achieve a high level of proficiency to do any job consistently and reliably with a high degree of repeatability is generally very long. Organizations do not have that much time (Fadde & Klein 2010). Market pressure, particularly over the last decade, has warranted accelerating the expertise cycle as a necessity (Clark & Mayer 2013). Several market forces collectively drive the need for shorter time to proficiency in the workplace, such as time-to-market competitiveness (Lynn, Akgün & Keskin 2003); constant obsolescence of skills (Korotov 2007); increasing complexity of jobs and skills (Hoffman, Feltovich, et al. 2010); attrition of senior or ageing workforce constantly getting replaced (Hoffman et al. 2014).

The need for acceleration of proficiency has been explained in the literature for sectors such as the military, sports, utility, research, biotech and information technology sectors (See examples in Hoffman et al. 2014). Some researchers have speculated that in some professions such as military and air force time to proficiency was very long. Hence a need to accelerate proficiency was recognized as: '[In the US Air Force] it still ordinarily takes many years to achieve proficiency. Therefore, there would be great advantages if the USAF could establish regimens of training that could accelerate the achievement of that proficiency' (Hoffman, Andrews & Feltovich (2012, p. 1). However, proponents of 10-year of deliberate practice, Ericsson & Charness (1994, p. 737) pointed out that there are no proven ways to develop expertise faster:

> Although these studies [on expertise] have revealed how beginners acquire complex cognitive structures and skills that circumvent the basic limits confronting them, researchers have not uncovered some simple strategies that would allow nonexperts to rapidly acquire expert performance.

On the contrary, Hoffman, Feltovich, et al. (2010, p. 61) criticized the ten years of deliberate practice as a rule to gain high level of proficiency: 'Our reason for calling out the ostensive limitations of the "approach" is that if expertise is achieved only after deliberate practice (the 10-year rule of thumb), then acceleration would not be possible'. Hoffman, Andrews & Feltovich (2012, p. 9) pointed out that the fact that it takes a long time to achieve proficiency, is the basis of accelerating the same. Very recently, Hoffman, Andrews & Feltovich (2012, p. 9) raised the issue that 'empirical fact about expertise (i.e., that it takes a long time) sets the stage for an effort at demonstrating the acceleration of the achievement of proficiency.'

The general literature showed several case studies indicating financial and business benefits of training (Bartel 2000; Kirkpatrick & Kirkpatrick 2009; Phillips 2012). The result of a shorter time to proficiency leads to substantial financial and operational benefits to the organization and higher value to customers (Fred 2002). Some researchers pointed out financial reasons of accelerating proficiency: 'If any time could be shaved off the "10000 clock', there would be potentially significant saving of money and time, an increase in overall organisational capability...' (Hoffman et al. 2014, p. 169). Several studies indicated substantial financial or cost benefits of shorter training duration and faster readiness of the workforce (Jacobs 2014b; Liu & Batt 2007; Sullivan, Brechin & Lacoste 1999) and from the reduction of time to proficiency (Borton 2007, p. 32; Pollock, Wick & Jefferson 2015, p. 285; Thompson 2017, p. 169). More recently, Attri (2018) showed quantified benefits of a shorter time to proficiency in over 60 projects in different industries. These benefits were categorized in four groups as business gains, improvement in operational metrics, improvement in productivity and cost savings.

However, several non-financial reasons such as the impact of non-proficiency in critical professions have also led researchers to investigate the concept of accelerating proficiency. For example, in a study involving firefighting commanders, lack of events to gain experience and become proficient was perceived to endanger life and property when those events occur which require proficient people to handle them (Kuchenbrod 2016).

Therefore, the business has a pressing need to accelerate speed to proficiency of their employees in almost every job. Fred (2002, p. 16) makes a compelling argument:

> Speed to proficiency is more than a theoretical advantage: It is the most devastating competitive weapon in the world where the competitive forces of scale, automation, and capital are subordinate to the power of proficient workforce.

The efforts to accelerate time to proficiency, thus lead to the faster readiness of workforce, cost savings and increased competitiveness in the market. Therefore, researchers appealed to hasten the process of acquiring expertise or at least acquiring a certain level of mastery in the skills (Fadde & Klein 2010, 2012; Fadde 2007, 2009a, 2009b, 2009c, 2012, 2013, 2016; Hoffman et al. 2008, 2009, 2014; Hoffman, Andrews & Feltovich 2012; Hoffman & Andrews 2012; Hoffman, Andrews, et al. 2010; Hoffman, Feltovich, et al. 2010).

Also, corporations and business leaders have emphasized the need for speed to proficiency and made recurring appeals to tackle this new business metric in several white papers, blogs, business case studies, commercial conferences and business books (Bruck 2007, 2015; Cross 2013; Harward 2017; Rosenbaum & Pollock 2015; Rosenbaum & Williams 2004). Several notable business leaders have contributed to raising awareness about this business challenge and need for speed through their works - *Learning paths: increase profits by reducing the time it takes employees to get up-to speed* (Rosenbaum & Williams 2004); *Breakaway: deliver value to your customers—fast!* (Fred 2002); and *Speed to proficiency: creating a sustainable competitive advantage* (Bruck 2015); and *Up to Speed: Secrets of Reducing Time to Proficiency* (Rosenbaum 2018). While all of these books were based on practitioner experiences and not grounded in research-based evidence, the author's recent scholarly work highlights the need to reduce time to proficiency - *Speed to Proficiency in Organizations: A Research Report on Model, Practices and Strategies to Shorten Time to Proficiency (Attri 2019)*, *Designing Training to Shorten Time to Proficiency (Attri 2019)* and *Modelling accelerated proficiency in organisations* (Attri 2018). Collectively, these works recognized that shortening time to proficiency was a crucial business challenge that needs to be solved.

Leading workplace learning expert, Jay Cross stated that 'the faster a worker becomes proficient, the more profitable the firm' (Cross 2013). Similarly, leading business consultants, Rosenbaum & Williams (2004) stressed the importance of identifying the point at which desired performance is delivered: 'You need to know the *level of performance* required to do the job and *how long* it takes to get there.... when you can get employees up-to speed in far less time, productivity rises at far less expense'.

As a result of these appeals by business leaders, organizations now realize that the faster employees learn the skills required to do the job up to set performance standards, the faster they are able to handle new customer needs, meet new market needs, perform to new expectations, and deliver new technologies or adopt new changes (Attri & Wu 2015; Attri 2014). These appeals have indicated that time to proficiency is becoming one of the most important business metrics for fast-paced technological organizations. Accordingly, organizations worldwide are striving to figure out interventions, systems, and strategies to shorten time to proficiency of employees (Fred 2002).

While the magnitude and scale of the problem are the triggers for organizations to think of shortening time to proficiency, Attri (2018) showed that one or several of three drivers drove organizations to institute accelerated proficiency initiatives: time-related pressures, speed-related competitiveness, and skill-related deficiency while cost or financial gains were not so much of the main trigger. This study confirmed that speculations made in the literature regarding the retiring workforce, complexity, changing nature of work, time-to-market pressures, competitiveness and business pressures, as the drivers for accelerating time to proficiency (Bruck 2015; Fred 2002; Hoffman et al. 2014; Langerak, Hultink & Griffin 2008; Lynn, Akgün & Keskin 2003).

4.4 THEORY OF ACCELERATED PROFICIENCY

The general theories underlying the concept of accelerated proficiency are grounded in seminal and classic works conducted between the 1960s and 2000s by leading theorists such as Murphy (1989), Campbell (Campbell 1990; Campbell, McHenry & Wise 1990; Campbell et al. 1993), Borman and Motowidlo (Borman & Motowidlo 1993; Motowidlo, Borman & Schmit 1997; Motowidlo & Van Scotter 1994), Dreyfus and Dreyfus (Dreyfus & Dreyfus 1986, 2004, 2005), Fitts (Fitts 1964; Fitts & Posner 1967), Anderson (1981, 1982, 2000), Ackerman (1988, 1992), Chi (Chi 1982; Chi 2006; Chi, Glaser & Rees 1982; Chi, Glaser & Farr 1988; Chi, Glaser & Rees 1981; Glaser & Chi 1988), Ericsson (Ericsson 2000, 2002, 2003, 2004, 2006a, 2007, 2008, 2009a, 2009b, 2009c; Ericsson et al. 1993; Ericsson & Charness 1994; Ericsson, Prietula & Cokely 2007; Ericsson & Towne 2010; Ericsson & Ward 2007), Spiro (Spiro & Jehng 1990; Spiro et al. 1987; Spiro et al. 1990; Spiro et al. 2003) and Klein (Klein 1993, 1997, 1998, 2003; Klein & Baxter 2009; Klien & Borders 2016; Klien, Hintze & Saab 2013; Klein et al. 1997), among others. Despite that, a limited research has been carried out directly on this concept.

4.4.1 Theoretical aspects

The literature on the topic of accelerated proficiency is in nascent phases. Hoffman & Andrews (2012) raised the point that understanding of the concept of accelerated proficiency remains to be crystallized. While their comprehensive synthesis on expertise and accelerated expertise advanced the understanding of the nature of accelerated proficiency, a unified theory remains elusive, more so in natural settings of organizations (Hoffman et al. 2014). Extending it to the theoretical underpinning of the concept and process of accelerated proficiency, Hoffman et al. (2014, p. 132) contended that there was no unified theory yet that could explain the nature of accelerated proficiency phenomenon (more so in the natural settings of organizations):

> A considerable number of theories or approaches are manifestly pertinent to the topic of accelerated proficiency. But on close examination, not all of them fit well with what we know about expertise, and not all of them fit well with the complex and ever changing tasks that characterize the "real world".

They observed that two theories — *cognitive transformation theory* (CTT) and *cognitive flexibility theory* (CFT) — appeared to explain certain aspects of acquiring and accelerating proficiency: 'Both try to achieve proficiency, but in different ways' (Hoffman, Feltovich, et al. 2010).

4.4.2 CTT as Basis of Accelerated Proficiency

Spiro et al. (1992, p. 9) believed the unlearning was a key component of learning: 'We now know that the path from novicehood to expertise is not one of monotonic progress, but rather requires a stage of *undoing* the results of earlier learning before further progress can be made'. Researchers noticed that as individuals go through cognitive development, they keep getting fixated on the mental model (Feltovich, Spiro & Coulson 1997). Extending further, Klein & Baxter (2009) developed cognitive transformation theory (CTT) and noted that cognitive skills, unlike behavior skills, depend heavily on the mental model. Mental models (or knowledge structures or schemata) are models to organize one's knowledge. Klein & Baxter (2009) believed that cognitive skills were not about adding anything more to the existing mental models, but it was about *sense making* to see and think about things differently. To learn a cognitive skill, one needed to reorganize his/her knowledge structure, which did not happen with the usual components of learning – diagnosis, learning objectives, practice, feedback, etc. They believed that for cognitive skills it is difficult to diagnose the subtle aspects of cognitive skills. Instead, they proposed that to help people reorganize existing mental models, learners have to first unlearn some of their existing flawed models. Therefore, to develop and accelerate proficiency, it is necessary to figure out ways to unlearn and reject flawed mental models. To build and accelerate proficiency, Klein & Baxter (2009, p. 7) stated that training instructions need to 'diagnose limitations in mental models, design interventions to help students appreciate the flaws in their mental models, and provide experiences to enable trainees to discover more useful and accurate mental models'. CTT emphasized that it is important to design systems which allow learners to recognize their flaws in their current mental models and then discard flawed models in favor of less flawed models.

CTT is one of the theories with several implications for developing and accelerating expertise. In a review, Hoffman et al. (2008) concluded that CTT explained the mechanisms to accelerate the proficiency and beyond. 'Cognitive transformation theory describes the changes to knowledge and reasoning that proficient workers need to undergo in order to make the jump from mere proficiency to superior levels of expertise' (Hoffman et al. (2008, pp. 5–2). Using a similar concept, in multiple operational simulation experiments conducted by DiBello et al. (DiBello, Missildine & Struttman (2009; 2008, 2011; 2019), it was shown that when performers were exposed to multiple cycles of failures, their flawed mental models were revealed. The rapid failure cycles helped them reorganize their mental models. The fundamental premise of their approach was to develop 'cognitive agility' (DiBello & Missildine 2011, p. 17) based on a concept of 'disequilibration', which involved showing learners their flawed mental model, whereby they get to unlearn their previous model, reorganize the new mental model and develop a sustainable change in their behavior in shorter time (DiBello, Missildine & Struttman 2009, pp. 27–28). The mechanism observed in these studies is explained as: 'Only when something traumatic occurred, such as a failure, would the experts reexamine their mental models and replace questionable aspects' (Klein & Borders 2016, p. 269). Therefore 'unlearning the flawed mental model' appears to be a key strategy to develop and accelerate adaptive expertise. Some of the methods to accelerate proficiency that share theoretical underpinning of CTT are simulation-based training, tough cases, desirable difficulties, scenario-based training, and time compression.

4.4.3 CFT as Basis of Accelerated Proficiency

In their original studies, Spiro et al. (1988, 1987) noticed that knowledge acquisition was accelerated in ill-structured domains when instructions supported learners to develop flexible mental models. Based on their empirical results, Spiro et al. (1988, 1987,

1992; 1990) viewed expertise in ill-structured domains as the ability to develop flexible mental models, and spontaneously change one's mental model adaptively to respond to changing situational demands. This changed mental model enabled them to apply knowledge from multiple perspectives depending on the situation. Based on this premise, cognitive flexibility theory (CFT) was developed focusing on the nature of learning in complex and ill-structured domains and concerned about the transfer of knowledge and skills beyond initial learning situations (Spiro & Jehng 1990). The fundamental mechanism suggested by CFT was to build "cognitive flexibility" in learners so that they understand deeply and then apply flexibly. Cognitive flexibility was emphasized as one of the most basic requirements to accelerate proficiency. As Spiro et al. (1992, p. 7) put it: 'A learner who has developed "cognitive flexibility" will be able to utilize conceptual knowledge in an adaptive fashion'. CFT advocated presenting content to learners from several different perspectives and themes. This allowed learners to present their knowledge in multiple dimensions rather than in a single conceptual dimension. The core of CFT was to use multiple mental and pedagogical representations, promote multiple alternative systems of linkage among knowledge elements, and promote abstraction of functional and conceptual understanding and the need for participatory learning. It also emphasized not to over-simplify the content, rather support context-dependent knowledge. CFT advocated a constructivist view and specified using case-based learning for knowledge construction from highly interconnected knowledge sources in which all ranges of complexity may exist (Hoffman et al. 2014). Studies conducted by Spiro et al. (1987), Coulson, Feltovich & Spiro (1997), Jonassen (1992) and Jonassen et al. (1997) suggested that learners studying the material designed using cognitive flexibility theory were better able to transfer the principles to the novel, unrelated cases. Spiro et al. (2003) contended that by suitably designing instructions using hypermedia based on CFT principles, they could accelerate the experience of learners in complex learning. CFT as the theoretical framework has also shown up in case-based learning scenario-based simulations and games.

4.4.4 Unified Theory to Explain Accelerated Proficiency

Both CTT and CFT appeared to explain certain aspects of accelerated proficiency. Hoffman et al. (2008, p. 5.2) stated that:

> Core ideas of cognitive flexibility theory (what makes problems difficult for learners and the simplistic understandings that result for those learners) and cognitive transformation theory (the need for unlearning experiences) are certainly pertinent to shaping any program of accelerated learning.

Hoffman, Feltovich, et al. (2010, p. 139) suggested that both theories could be merged to form a new theory for accelerated proficiency because they are complementary to each other. However, none of them appears to describe the phenomenon of accelerated proficiency completely. They implied that potentially two theories—cognitive flexibility theory (Spiro & Jehng 1990) and cognitive transformation theory (Klein & Baxter 2009), could be merged to form a new theory for accelerated proficiency: 'Both tap into same general empirical base about the phenomenon of proficiency, expertise, and high-end learning' (Hoffman et al. 2014,

p. 136). The absence of a unified theory or model makes it even more important to understand this phenomenon, more specifically in organizations.

From the scarce literature on this topic, it appears that researchers are yet to develop a better understanding of the process of accelerated proficiency because there is no comprehensive theory yet. Hoffman & Andrews (2012, p. 5) raised the importance of crystallizing understanding of the concept of accelerated proficiency:

> There are theoretical and practical issues with regard to what we mean by accelerated learning and whether the training and scientific communities are conceptualizing this problem as a topic demanding programmatic research. As such, concepts of accelerated learning and accelerated proficiency bring in a host of interesting questions, issues, and challenges in the area of instructional design, training, transfer, retention, the role of feedback, mentoring, and others. (Hoffman & Andrews 2012, p. 5)

4.5 SUMMARY

In this chapter, the meaning, nature, and process of accelerated proficiency were discussed. This chapter also established grounds for business drivers that necessitate to accelerate proficiency of employees. The chapter explored various studies on theoretical aspects of accelerated proficiency and highlighted that the phenomenon and process of accelerated proficiency remained inadequately explained. Despite the recognition of its importance, the body of knowledge appears to be lacking in the business domain. The literature provides speculations and assumptions, as opposed to concrete cases, to understand the business dynamics and challenges that drive the need for accelerated proficiency. Hoffman, Andrews & Feltovich (2012, p. 9) specified a set of research questions for future time to proficiency research that they believed were the gaps and problems for which there were no direct answers in the literature:

> What is it within the work itself that takes time to master? What is it about the nature of the cognition within the work that requires time to achieve high levels of proficiency?... What might be the payoff if this problem were solved, say, by reducing the time to achieve journeyman level skill by some significant amount (e.g., from 4 years to 2)? (Hoffman, Andrews & Feltovich 2012, p. 9)

These apparent gaps in the literature, therefore, require further investigation.

5

METHODS TO ACCELERATE PROFICIENCY

Noticing the need to accelerate the achievement of proficiency and a lack of proven methods to do so, Hoffman, Andrews & Feltovich (2012, p. 9) appealed to training professionals:

> Our vision is that methods for accelerating the achievement of proficiency, and even extraordinary expertise, might be taken to new levels such that one can accelerate the achievement of proficiency across the journeyman-to-expert span post-hiring (Hoffman, Andrews & Feltovich 2012, p. 9).

In this chapter, the literature is reviewed for methods and

techniques that appear to provide some empirical evidence or support to accelerate proficiency. Both classic and recent studies have been reviewed for methods of acceleration.

5.1 THEMATIC CATEGORIES OF METHODS

From a detailed literature review of a range of studies in the last four decades, thematic analysis led to the emergence of six categories of potential methods which either generated evidence of accelerating proficiency or have shown good promise in that direction. The methods which provided evidence towards accelerating proficiency appear to have some form of synergy or similar theoretical basis. The six categories that emerged in this process are:

- Cognitive task analysis (CTA) based training methods
- Simulation-based training methods
- Scenario-based training methods
- Part-task based methods
- Workplace activity-based methods
- Technology-based methods

Several early classic studies advocated variations of a method that involved modeling the experts in terms of capturing their thinking, strategies, and behaviors through cognitive task analysis (CTA). Most studies advocated developing a curriculum based on elements revealed by CTA methods to train novices or transfer that knowledge quickly.

Another set of studies, categorized under 'Simulation-based training methods' showed methods that suggested using simulations-based and games-based methods to provide exposure and practice to novices in a highly time-compressed fashion.

A massive number of studies converged into the category 'Scenario-based training methods'. This included methods that suggest the use of scenarios, cases and problems which have shown evidence in accelerating proficiency by subjecting the performer towards multidimensional understanding, developing adaptive expertise, developing flexibility and challenging their mental models, and showing them ways to unlearn or reorganize their mental models. Key techniques to accelerate proficiency include using desirable difficulties, tough cases, difficult problems and failures presented in time-compressed fashion.

A completely different approach suggested for accelerating the acquisition of complex skills came from studies categorized under 'Part-task based methods'. These methods focus on isolating representative part-task, providing practice and accelerated expertise on those part-tasks and then integrate those part-tasks inside the whole-task context.

The large percentage of studies across several disciplines like HRD, training, learning, and psychology led to the formation of category 'Workplace activities-based methods'. Several methods have been specified by HRD studies that advocated using the workplace itself while developing employees to prepare them with the skills/competencies required to perform their job. The major methods that emerge in this category included both informal and structured methods such as informal and social learning; experiential and action learning; structured workplace activities;

cognitive apprenticeship, structured on-the-job training; deliberate practice; deliberate performance and learning organizations. The studies on structured on-the-job training (S-OJT) and CTA provided encouraging evidence of accelerating employee proficiency.

One of the latest trends is that of 'technology-based methods' which requires much more in-depth analysis than the one presented in this book. The rapid evolution of technology is seeing several unimaginable methods with an excellent promise to accelerate time to proficiency. For this book, classic studies suggested using technology to capture knowledge and transfer it to new employees and personalized learning through technology-driven efficient learning sequences.

5.2 COGNITIVE TASK ANALYSIS (CTA) METHODS

Researchers have indicated that the key to expertise development is first to elicit this knowledge structure or mental models and then teach that to novices to develop expertise (Lajoie 2003). Lajoie (2003) suggested observing explicit exemplars or models of expertise from experts and then mapping them to create a trajectory that can help novices to develop similar competencies. She maintained that '[t]he transition from student to expert professional can be accelerated when a trajectory for change is plotted and made visible to learners' (Lajoie 2003, p. 24). She also proposed that cognitive task analysis (CTA) can help reveal that trajectory to the expertise. However, it depends on how well expertise can be modeled by an expert. Past studies have confirmed that experts developed automaticity, which was usually 'implicit or unconscious' (Clark & Estes 1996, p. 407) as a result of repeated use of declarative knowledge which developed into production knowledge (Anderson 2000). At the stage of automaticity, experts were believed to be so intuitive or unconscious about the decisions they made that they sometimes cannot fully articulate why they do what they do (Logan 1988). Early researchers developed CTA to capture these unconscious processes of how experts operate, think, behave and process a task. These methods revealed the cognitive structures and processes involved in performing a task (Clark & Estes 1996). Expert knowledge often takes different forms that enable different performances at different stages of expertise. Therefore, different CTA methods were introduced which varied in process and intent. In an earlier study, Merkelbach & Schraagen (1994) presented three frameworks, namely task modeling, knowledge modeling and cognitive modeling to develop an integrated view of how experts perform tasks, think and approach problems, handle challenging situations and decide their plan of action.

Over the years, studies have introduced over 100 different methods to conduct CTA (Clark, Feldon, et al. 2008; Clark 2014). Major methods include hierarchical task analysis; goals, operators, methods and selections; knowledge analysis and documentation system; precursor or reason for action, result and interpretation of result; integrated task analysis model; critical decision method; work domain analysis; concept mapping; and think-aloud protocols among others (Clark, Feldon, et al. 2008; Clark, Feldon & Yates 2011; Hoffman & Lintern 2006).

5.2.1 Using CTA to design training

The most popular study that combined CTA-based training design and simulation-based training together is the one using the Sherlock (1 & 2) intelligent tutoring system. This classic study conducted jointly by researchers at the University of Pittsburgh and US Airforce, has been noted in several publications such as Katz, Hall & Lesgold (1997); Lajoie & Lesgold (1992); Gott, Lesgold & Kane (1996); (Gott, Lesgold & Kane 1996; Lajoie & Lesgold 1992; Lesgold et al. 1988; Lesgold 1991). Though conducted in the late 1980s and 1990s, these studies have continued to be influential towards specifying the cognitive principles used in modern-day time-compressed simulations. This intelligent computer-based coach provided experience to the learners on 'the most difficult aspects of cognitively-intense jobs in a simulated work environment' (Gott, Lesgold & Kane 1996, p. 2). This system packed meaningful problem-solving cases within a brief period of time. The cases were developed from the actual real-world problem-solving process, and decisions flow captured using CTA methods from the experts troubleshooting F-15 aircraft electronic problems. The model of the system, the knowledge representations used by experts to solve the problem and cues/decisions they used to solve the problem were programmed. The cases progressed based on actions inputs by the novice learners while they were solving the apparent problems. The system incorporated not only on-demand coaching and feedback (critique of the student's activity) but also during task reflection and post-performance reflection, when necessary. In the end, the system also presented the experts' solutions to the same problems so that learners could learn from the experts (Lesgold 2001). To demonstrate this system's potential in accelerating proficiency, they tested three control groups of 54 F-15 avionics repair technicians. One group comprised master technicians with proven experience, while the second group was a control group which was comprised of untutored technicians and the third group was the experimental group who were tutored with the Sherlock system. The technicians were presented novel problems after they had practiced a sequence of cases. They found that new learners using the Sherlock system were far more successful in troubleshooting novel problems than the experienced technicians. They suggested that those learners used their newly developed mental models and troubleshooting task schemata as 'interpretive structures' and 'flexible blueprints to guide their performance' to solve novel problems (Gott, Lesgold & Kane 1996, p. 5). They showed that novice technicians could score comparable troubleshooting proficiency scores to that of master technicians with over four years of job experience in just 20 hours of CTA-driven coaching over the three weeks. Gott & Lesgold (2000) reasoned that on-the-job experience takes years to attain and the job mostly provides routine opportunities, whereas the Sherlock system compressed that time by providing meaningful cases within a compressed timeframe.

Traditional studies have employed CTA methods to elicit the knowledge and information from experts and then designing training for the novices. While the primary goal of such studies was to investigate the effectiveness of training, it was seen that in some cases it also accelerated proficiency. For example, Schaafstal et al. (2000) conducted a study of 21 navy technicians responsible for repairing electronic equipment. The technicians formed two groups: one went through a regular traditional training course, while other group attended a course of troubleshooting designed using CTA methods. Both groups were given the same set of faults to troubleshoot. They were evaluated for the quality of the solution, systematicity of reasoning and functional understanding. It was observed that the technicians attending CTA-based course solved twice as many problems compared to the group who took the standard course. The findings of that study implied that learners took less time to reach to required performance thresholds, while their effectiveness was higher.

One study involving 26 new interns with similar backgrounds at the department of surgery were divided into two groups: one attending a standard "see-do-teach" course and the other group attending a CTA-based course. At the end of the respective courses, both groups appeared in the same practical and knowledge tests. It was noticed that the group with the CTA-based training required fewer attempts to find the vein (which means fewer needle punctures to locate the vein) and also showed a trend towards less time to complete the procedure (Velmahos et al. 2004). This study showed that time-to-training could be reduced, while at the same time accuracy and efficiency of the learners could be improved using CTA. The study also demonstrated that two and half months later the group of students who attended the CTA-based course retained their competence, even in a clinical stress environment. Retaining competence in the workplace and the ability to perform to the same standards also implies that CTA may have the potential to accelerate proficiency.

On similar lines, Kirschenbaum, McInnis & Correll (2009) reported using the CTA method for training submarine sonar technicians. They reported that new sonar technicians exhibited faster acquisition of skills during training, as well as a higher level of proficiency on the job. Training times were reduced by up to six months, and the technicians were able to start their on-the-job training sooner and carry out their work more effectively.

Incidentally, it is seen that CTA could be applied in critical and life-saving professions, which demand high accuracy and efficiency, especially medicine and surgery. The success of the CTA method in these fields is attributed to its ability to capture an accurate account of an expert's thinking process over the traditional self-reported techniques. This was demonstrated by several studies conducted by Clark. Clark, Pugh, et al. (2008) conducted a study with 11 trauma surgeons responsible for administrating emergency treatment in urban settings and war settings. The authors selected a task of insertion of a femoral artery shunt. Nine of the urban trauma surgeons unaided described the procedure. One Iraq-returned surgeon was interviewed using CTA methods. The eleventh surgeon, with experience in both settings, was used as the gold standard for comparative purposes. It was found that the account of surgeons matched 68% when using the CTA-based interview versus 31% without CTA support. This study demonstrated that CTA was far more successful in obtaining an accurate account of knowledge from experts. Subsequent papers by Clark supported evidence that experts not using CTA methods for interviews omitted nearly 70% of the necessary decision steps (Clark, Feldon, et al. 2008; Clark et al. 2011).

Other studies using different surgical procedures found similar results in that experts omitted over 70% of the decision steps (Sullivan et al. 2014; Yates, Sullivan & Clark 2012). This evidence suggested that experts' cognitive processes can be accurately adapted in training materials which allow more effective expertise development. A significant acceleration to better performance was observed with training courses designed with CTA (Campbell et al. 2011; Clark et al. 2010).

5.2.2 Complimenting CTA with other methods

CTA methods were found to be complementary to other methods of curriculum development. Clark, Feldon, et al. (2008) asserted that CTA and 4C/ID models leveraged each other's strengths towards the development of expertise. As a note, 4C/ID (four components instructional design) model purports breaking a complex work into smaller recurrent part-tasks which can be practiced independently, identifying just-in-time information that is required before and during part-task practice, integrating part-tasks into a concrete whole-tasks, and providing supportive information for non-recurrent portion of tasks (van Merriënboer, Clark & de Croock 2002). A study by Tjiam et al. (2012) supported the claim that CTA and 4C/ID models can be complementary to each other. In this study, 12 urologists who were experts at performing nephrostomy procedures were interviewed using CTA-based interviews to create a blueprint of the procedures. This information was then used to design simulation-based training using the 4C/ID approach, which allowed integrating the part-task practice into the whole-task of performing the surgery. The more prevailing trend seen in the literature is that of using CTA methods to design simulation-based training or scenario-based training (Cannon-Bowers et al. 2013; Geissler et al. 2012; Munro & Clark 2013).

In the context of the systems engineers' jobs, Squires et al. (2011) used a combination of CTA methods to develop competency maps or taxonomies of expertise in complex system engineering jobs. These competencies were then used to design an 'experience accelerator' simulator to shorten time to competence of systems engineers. In a recent study, Patterson et al. (2013) recruited fourteen pediatricians at a children's hospital. They were interviewed using critical decision methods (CDM) and were asked to describe a challenging incident they handled which involved the diagnosis of sepsis. Scenarios were designed based on the cues expert physicians described that they used to recognize sepsis. These cues were then integrated into rich scenarios, and novice physicians were trained through scenario-based simulation. This method claimed to accelerate the expertise curve of novices.

The literature appears to place CTA-based methods as one of the forefront methods to accelerate the trajectory towards proficiency and expertise. It is apparent that CTA has become a standard method to identify 'the opportunities to improve performance through new forms of training, user interfaces, or decision aids' (Roth & O'Hara 2014, p. 320). The studies mentioned above have clearly shown innovative use of CTA, providing evidence that when used appropriately with other expertise development techniques, CTA has the most potential in accelerating proficiency.

5.2.3 Challenges and benefits

It appears that apart from high-risk professions such as medical, fire control and military, the applications of CTA methods in business settings is lacking, more so towards accelerating time to proficiency in the workplace. One possible explanation could be that CTA methods are very effort intensive endeavors. For instance, Clark & Estes (1996) indicated that efforts to design a one-day CTA-based course from a standard two days long course were roughly 30 times.

However, the financial benefits appear to outweigh such time-intensive efforts. For example, in the same study, Clark & Estes (1996) indicated that using the CTA-based design, the 'new course resulted in a 50% savings in training time on the part of the trainee managers'.

In a meta-analysis of training literature, R Lee (2004) and Tofel-Grehl & Feldon (2013) reported an average of 53% to 87% post-training performance gain if the training was designed using CTA. In addition, there have been some advances in using tools and software to rapidly conduct CTA (Zachary et al. 2012). CTA-based methods have been used in some studies for job roles such as top executive positions (e.g. Baxter 2015), life-saving jobs (Klein & Borders 2016) or disaster response personnel (Crichton & Flin 2004).

5.2.4 Cogntive work analysis

The key issue with the CTA-based method is its focus on tasks only. However, work in organizations is performed amidst several other variables, such as the environment and other influencing factors, which CTA-based methods do not address. In acknowledgment of this issue, a more encompassing approach called *cognitive work analysis* (CWA) was proposed by Rasmussen, Pejtersen & Goodstein (1994). The multi-stage framework was evolved to analyze how work is accomplished in complicated socio-technical systems. Socio-technical systems are the ones that rely heavily on the social process of communication and cooperation. This method involved conducting a range of analyses including work domain analysis (general characteristics and functional purposes of the system), control task analysis (tasks relevant to functional purposes of the system), analysis of possible strategies (to address the factors that may prevent a task from happening), team analysis, social and organizational analysis (interactions among people and with constraints), and analysis of workers' competencies (knowledge, training, skills and experience) to understand all possible interactions between work, worker and work elements (Ashoori & Burns 2013; Naikar, Lintern & Sanderson 2002; Naikar 2011; Roth & O'Hara 2014). Unlike CTA, there is no evidence of application of CWA towards accelerating performance despite several reviews and experimental studies being carried out (Demir, Abou-Jaoude & Kumral 2017; Naikar 2017).

5.3 SIMULATIONS-BASED TRAINING METHODS

5.3.1 Time compression

On similar lines of the Sherlock training system, Fletcher (2010) demonstrated that using an automated troubleshooting expert system developed by DARPA, novice technicians solved 97% of the problems with 90% rated excellent compared to experienced technicians who produced 85% of the problem solved with 60% of the solutions rated excellent (See Hoffman et al. 2014). Studies on such intelligent systems have hypothesized that adaptive learning experience leads to accelerated performance. Implications of the studies on these coached-practice environments (e.g., Sherlock) in terms of strategies to accelerate expertise primarily included using authentic scenarios and difficult problems, making use of situated learning in a work context, employing models of expertise using CTA and coached cognitive apprenticeship principles, incorporating on-demand feedback, and making learners learn by doing and by reflection (Lesgold & Nahemow 2001; Lesgold 2001). These findings also indicated that simulation and feedback played an important role in accelerating proficiency. In a recent synthesis, Hoffman et al. (2014, p. 102) concluded that '[f]rom the Sherlock project, we know that it is possible to time-compress the experience-feedback cycle for acceleration from apprentice to journeyman proficiency levels'. The literature further suggested that time compression was the most basic method to accelerate proficiency:

> All of the methods used in training for rapidization and for accelerated proficiency depend on one or another form of time (or experience) compression. One form is that of packing more varieties of experience into the training and not merely shortening the training.... A second sense of time compression is to truncate events that transpire within a scenario... (Hoffman et al. 2014, p. 118)

In other words, time compression is achieved by developing a library of real and 'tough cases' and presenting them to learners within an accelerated time frame. 'Tough cases' are the challenging and difficult cases encountered in work. The literature also suggested various other ways such as simulation-based training, scenario-based training, game-based learning, scenario-based simulation and such variations to achieve time compression.

5.3.2 Expert-based simulation

The convergence of scenario-based learning with simulation-based learning has seen computer-based simulations replaced with expert-system based simulations. Recently, Arnold & Collier (2013) proposed simulating the experience through a web-based expert system which was designed based on a corpus of cases to accelerate expertise of financial knowledge workers. In that system, they developed a library of cases by interviewing the experts, understanding how they made the decisions in those cases and then tied those rationales to known financial principles. The new employees were trained through a web-based system which presented them the cases in a piece-meal fashion and asked learners to make decisions at different points in a case. Learners were able to compare their rationale with that of the experts, which acted as a feedback loop. Arnold & Collier (2013, p. 19) claimed that their research 'demonstrates the feasibility of one such methodology for using technology to accelerate experiential knowledge acquisition'. Further, recent studies have shown computer-based, expert-systems based and web-based intelligent tutoring systems using simulation-based training (Darzi et al. 2011; Sottilare & Goldberg 2012).

5.3.3 Above Real-time Training

In complex domains, such as engineering, some researchers have proposed complex simulations shown to accelerate proficiency. In the 1980s, in the context of high-risk jobs such as air combat maneuvering and air traffic controllers, time compression was demonstrated by a technique called *above-real-time training* (ART). This method was based on the concept that learners are required to perform tasks to the same performance criteria as the real environment but the events or the sensory cues were presented to them in high-fidelity simulation at a faster rate than the actual real-time speed. (Guckenberger, Uliano & Lane 1993) demonstrated a 50% time saving while training the high-performance skills like gunnery tasks in a tank and emergency procedures of F-16 aircraft using ART versus traditional real-time methods. They cited another study by Vidulich, Yeh & Schneider (1983) in which the technique had seen the application in training air traffic controllers. The controllers were found to be better at identifying the aircraft turn point in actual practice after they were trained with a simulator, which used an airplane approaching a speed 20 times faster than the actual speed. Guckenberger, Uliano & Lane (1993, p. 7) maintained that 'a new task that is practiced and learned in accelerated time (i.e., a difficult task) would require the learner to expend more than normal attention and effort, and hence accelerate the development of automaticity patterns'. Similar to the concept of 'tough cases', this method encompassed making training environment slightly more difficult than the real-world (like sports or athletics).

Similar results were repeated in a study by Donderi et al. (2012) in which a PC-based simulation of fighter plane chase scenarios was used with 54 participants. The screen resolution was varied, and the speed of stimulation was increased in the second session. They found that post-test scores were significantly higher by using high-speed simulation. The studies on 'contextual interference' suggested that using more difficult tasks than actual difficulty levels, led to better long-term retention of skills (Paas & van Gog 2009).

5.3.4   Gamification

Gamification has also emerged as a form of simulation which employs games or game-type concepts to replicate reality and provide close-to-reality experiences to the learners 'to accelerate the dialogue between knowledge and practice for efficient learning without risk of failure in real life' (Smeds 2003, p. 107). Learning by trial-and-error is a risky endeavor, especially for life-critical jobs. The idea of games, gamification, serious games through simulation or scenario-based games, is to create an immersive experience that engages learners and allows experiments by learners and trial-and-error among a range of variables to allow learners exposure to different situations. 'Well-constructed game-based scenarios can effectively compress several years of experience into a much smaller amount of learning time' (Higgins (2015, p. 8).

A form of gamification and scenario-based training in the workplace is *decision-making exercises* (DMXs), as indicated by Klein (2003), and is used to accelerate complex decision-making in the workplace without taking professionals out of their job. In a study conducted by Harris-Thompson, Malek & Wiggins (2010) among board operators in oil and gas process control, they involved 17 CTA-based interviews to gather expert stories on critical, non-routine incidents. They analyzed those scenarios and developed piece-meal scenarios called DMXs out of it. Appropriate additional data, as well as fabricated noise (irrelevant data similar to actual situation), were embedded into the piece-meal scenarios. The exercises were designed as paper-and-pen exercises feeding piece-meal information of a scenario to the new board operators as it would unfold in the real situation, but in time-compressed fashion. The learners were required to make decisions within specified time-frames based on the information available at a given moment. The study asserted that it was possible to accelerate cognitive skills and natural decision-making of professionals in natural settings.

As a corollary, in some studies, CTA method was used in gamification while extending methods like tactical decision games (Schmitt 1996) or decision-making exercises (Klein 1993, 1998, 2003) by seeking expert view or rationale for their decisions. Demonstrating such forms of gamification, Hintze (2008) evolved a technique called *ShadowBox*, which allows novices to follow the thinking of experts. He conducted an experimental study among 43 fire department officers. They were divided into three groups: control, expert and experimental. Experts had more than 15 years' experience, while the control and experimental group represented new employees. The method employed interpretation of pre-design scenarios and comparing the interpretations with that of the experts. The method employed the expert modeling as a way to allow trainees to discover what experts believed was important in a situation and how they focused their attention (Borders et al. 2015; Klein & Borders 2016; Klein, Hintze & Saab 2013). This method used the CTA method for knowledge elicitation and to capture how experts viewed and solved a given situation. However, during the facilitation, an expert presence was not required. This method appeared to accelerate the decision-making of novice fire control officers.

In other studies, Klein & Borders (2016, p. 270) applied the technique of *ShadowBox* in a study in the defense setting on 59 commissioned and non-commissioned officers of the army. They were divided into two groups: one had access to the expert to seek feedback, while the other group did not have any such option. Both groups were exposed to four challenging scenarios, and their responses to the actions they would take were recorded. The findings showed that for groups who received feedback from experts, their choices and ranking of course of actions matched those of the experts. The researchers concluded that 'it is possible to train cognitive skills in a reasonably short amount of time and in a way that can scale up' (Klein & Borders 2016, p. 276). They claimed: 'ShadowBox training can be seen as a platform for achieving rapidized training, higher levels of proficiency (accelerated proficiency), better transfer (rapidised transposition), and facilitated retention' (Klein & Borders (2016, p. 270).

As an alternative, Vandergriff (2012) proposed a model called *adaptive course model* (ACM) which employed scenario-based tactical decision games presented to learners under time constraints and uncertainty. Learners were required to solve the problem and justify the solution. ACM tended to add on to the experience of the learner. The focus was on the ability to quickly review the problem, prepare a solution and suggest a course of action. The model involved group discussions as an additional technique. The games were presented to the learners in progressively increasing difficulty. Employing experiential learning and a recognition-primed decision-making (RPD) process, this model was believed to accelerate decision-making skills.

5.3.5 Virtual or synthetic environments

The organization may assign an individual to available on-the-job assignments or may decide to design and provide training interventions in a compressed timeframe deliberately. This observation supports the *synthetic learning environment* method proposed by Cannon-Bowers & Bowers (2008). A similar assertion was made in a study with battlefield officers in which Shadrick & Lussier (2009) identified the recurring themes of cognitive behaviors among officers and then designed deliberate training methods on the line of the *Think Like a Commander* (TLAC) program to impart complex expertise and adaptive thinking. Fundamentally, they noticed that manufacturing 'crucible experiences' (id. 302) through 'deliberate focused training approach and research-based scenario development' (id. 303) in a compressed timeframe could 'accelerate the development of adaptable thinking that would otherwise require long time' (id. 302).

5.3.6 Immersive strategies

While computer-based simulations were grounded in expertise, development principles were used for problem-solving, troubleshooting, diagnostic type of problem domains. However, for business problem solving, a different approach is needed. The literature indicated that immersive strategies showed promise in accelerating proficiency in the workplace for skills like naturalistic decision-making or leadership because it can deliver valuable experiences sooner than they may be experienced on the job. Such immersive strategies included simulation, game-based learning, tabletop exercises, interactive stories, board games, and alternate reality games. Some researchers used immersive simulated games to accelerate leadership skills which incorporate storytelling and real-time feedback from leaders (Backus et al. 2010). These games involved a 'series of turns to allow players to try different game strategies and learn from them' (id. 147). Extending gamification further, Grossman et al. (2013) specified that decision-making expertise could be accelerated using simulation-based games in the workplace, among other strategies.

5.3.7 Operational simulation

Operational simulation has been shown to be a promising method to compress the experience in a shorter timeframe (DiBello, Missildine & Struttman 2009; DiBello & Missildine 2008, 2011; Hoffman et al. 2014). In an earlier study conducted by DiBello (1996), they demonstrated a time-compressed full-scale business scenario called OpSim (operational simulation) as a technique to accelerate higher-order skills in actual business settings. The shop floor workers acquired mastery in a computer-based material management system within two months, as opposed to the usual 18 to 24 months. In a subsequent study at a biotech firm, DiBello, Missildine & Struttman (2009) simulated time-compressed replica of business operations. They simulated business activities to be carried out in the normal course of six months into a few "game months" with the same target as actual business activities. The researchers reported that they could provide transferable expertise to the workplace, and the organization realized the benefits of accelerated expertise that were gained over a few days rather than several years. DiBello & Missildine (2008) reported similar results in another study. DiBello & Missildine (2011) extended the operational simulation methodology into the virtual world using immersive computer technology. They maintained that a technology-enhanced immersive virtual world provided a 'number of opportunities for enhanced accelerated learning, and the rehearsal and planning of complex strategies and tactical plans' (DiBello & Missildine 2011, p. 19). Their simulation was based on the theory of showing learners their flawed mental model and helping them to unlearn it and then reorganizing the new mental model that allowed them to acquire a sustainable change in their behavior in a shorter time (DiBello & Missildine 2011, p. 17). Another premise of their approach was that expertise development required repeated encounters with highly challenging problems, active problem-solving and immediate performance feedback (DiBello & Missildine 2011, p. 17). To accelerate expertise, they proposed that providing multiple failures on 'tough cases' within a compressed timeframe allowed learners to recognize their flawed mental model quickly.

The *Production and Control Journal* dedicated one full issue to studies on simulation for accelerated learning in production settings which spanned the food supply chain, electrical engineering, production planning, project management and corporate management, problem-solving and change management (See Smeds 2003). In other complex jobs, such as engineering, serious simulations have also been introduced. Slootmaker et al. (2014, p. 563) called this as '*scenario-based serious games* are games where learners are placed in complex problem spaces, which mimic real world situations'.

Robinson & Pennotti (2013, p. 2) designed multiple simulations exposing engineers responsible for designing complex systems to different challenges of complexity, confusion, decision-making, and leadership. They observed that '[e]ngineers at different levels of experience, who have been immersed in these simulations, have demonstrated insights usually associated with time on the job. This raises the possibility that useful experience might be acquired at the dramatically reduced time, cost and risk' (Robinson & Pennotti 2013, p. 2).

5.3.8 Benefits

The results of most of the simulation studies conducted have shown improved performance, and in several cases, accelerated performance. Researchers have reported that learners need fewer real-world hours by using simulators and overall experience was accelerated (Brudnicki, Ethier & Chastain 2007; Butler 2012; Clavarelli, Platte & Powers 2009; Robinson & Pennotti 2013). That also meant that learners spent more time in the simulator than traditional course learners did. For those reasons, Ward, Williams & Hancock (2006) commented that simulation-based training may not necessarily be a time-efficient method of training. However, when the goal is accelerating proficiency, training duration may be less of a consideration. The simulation also played a role in manufacturing events which were known to be rare.

5.4 SCENARIO-BASED TRAINING METHODS

Researchers have maintained that learning around scenarios, cases or problems provided the contextual experience of real-world, or as close to the real-world, is key to gaining a higher level of expertise (Clark & Mayer 2013).

Popularly known as scenario-based learning (SBL), the variations of these methods are known as problem-based learning, project-based learning, and case-based learning. These methods situate knowledge in a real-world context. 'After all, expertise is based on experience. With a well-designed program of SBL you can compress experience spanning years in the work environment, into a few hours of training time' (Clark 2009, p. 84). These techniques have attempted to provide a real-world experience or equivalent to novices to begin the process of getting them to think like experts.

5.4.1 Scenario-based training

Scenario-based training has been demonstrated as a successful strategy to accelerate the experience of the performer and increase the transfer of learning to the workplace (Clark 2009; Kreutzer et al. 2016; Salas et al. 2009; Sottilare & Goldberg 2012; Thomsen et al. 2010). The learning started with a real-life or close to real-life problem or scenario and participants learned how to analyze a problem, identify relevant facts and generate hypotheses, identify necessary information/knowledge for solving the problem and make reasonable judgments about solving the problem (Buch & Wolff 2000). These interventions, due to their real-world context and appropriate guidance to solve problems, held significant potential to accelerate expertise (Jonassen & Hung 2008). Fundamentally, all of these approaches have created learning interventions around well-constructed problems from the real-world which learners were required to solve (Clark & Mayer 2013; Jonassen & Hernandez-Serrano 2002; Thomsen et al. 2010). This approach was seen to be the only feasible method in which risks of the actual job were not permissible. In some cases, it would be unreasonable and undesirable to wish for a high occurrence rate of certain events (e.g., fire, flood, plane crash, etc.) in order to experience the event in the real-world (Kuchenbrod 2016).

The literature provided an abundance of evidence on accelerating proficiency using realistic simulation strategies (Brundage et al. 2014; Brydges et al. 2012; Butler 2012; Clavarelli, Platte & Powers 2009; Fiorella, Vogel-Walcutt & Fiore 2012; Lee 2011; Macdonald 2014; Patterson et al. 2013; Robinson & Pennotti 2013; Seto & Kern 2016).

5.4.2 Desirable difficulties

However, the key idea to accelerate proficiency is time compression of scenarios. While scenario-based methods hold the potential to accelerate proficiency, if the cases chosen are not representative of reality, the training becomes disconnected from the workplace when learning is complex in nature (Vaughan 2008). Selecting the right problems was identified as a key determinant of the effectiveness of these methods (Jonassen & Hung 2008). Two kinds of problems have been suggested in the literature. Bjork (2013) suggested adding 'desirable difficulties' into training as a problem. Desirable difficulties were useful failures, bugs or mistakes intentionally introduced into the learning that makes a learner struggle. The desirable difficulties, though they impeded the initial rate of skill acquisition, were seen to accelerate the transfer of abilities to solve tougher problems. Studies using the desirable difficulties approach have been conducted for many years. Doane et al. (1996) performed an experiment in which they gave difficult problems of discrimination to one group of participants and simpler problems to another group. At a later stage when both groups were given a block of difficult problems to discriminate, they found that learners who started with difficult problems first, outperformed compared to the control group learners who start with simpler problems first.

On those lines, Pandy et al. (2004) demonstrated the *How People Learn* (HPL) framework (Bransford et al. 2004) could accelerate the learning of engineering students. They advocated challenge-based instruction accelerate expertise development. 'These findings indicate that challenge-based instruction, when combined with an intellectually engaging curriculum and principled instructional design, can accelerate the trajectory of novice-to-expert development in bioengineering education' (Pandy et al. 2004, p. 220).

5.4.3 Tough case time compression

On the other hand, for developing higher level proficiency, a concept of 'tough case time compression' is suggested which involved creating a library of tough cases and then exposing the learners to the tough cases within a short time (Hoffman et al. 2010, p. 14). The fundamental premise was that people become proficient faster on rare problems by exposure to difficult real-world cases from the past or designing something that is likely to happen in the future. Hoffman et al. (2014, p. 105) stated 'one could do a form of time compression in which one taps into a corpus of cases that present opportunities for perceptual learning, and thereby "hasten expertise"'. This involved exposing learners to tough or difficult cases which allowed them to recognize their flawed mental models. 'Accelerated proficiency can be achieved through the use of case-based instruction and realistic tough cases with focus on errors and "desirable difficulties"' (Hoffman, Feltovich, et al. 2010). In a recent research study, Soule (2016) tested the hypothesis that difficult cases could accelerate the expertise of the learner. He concluded that expertise in complex decision-making was accelerated because tough cases triggered both experiential and social cognitive learning in a single process. He also asserted that learning involved in tough cases was 'substantial experiential, social, emotional, and practical features' (Soule 2016, p. 172).

Collectively, the literature review indicates that desirable difficulties appeared to accelerate post-training transfer of beginners, the tough cases, on the other hand, appeared to accelerate proficiency on the higher end of the scale. The tough cases suggest developing adaptive expertise in handling non-routine, novel and unfamiliar situations (Hesketh & Ivancic 2002). To represent expertise to handle unfamiliar novel problems, early researchers developed a construct of adaptive expertise and differentiated it from routine expertise (Hatano & Inagaki 1986). 'Adaptive experts not only have knowledge that is well organised, but also display the ability to transfer their knowledge, skills, beliefs, and attitudes to new situations' (Pandy et al. 2004, p. 211). Adaptive experts developed some form of conceptual skills with which they were more effective in novel situations than non-routine experts (VanLehn & Chi 2012). The adaptive experts built extra knowledge about the task domain (such as the mental model of structure and function of a system) that helped them solve novel problems in the new domain. Important components of adaptive expertise were conceptual abstraction, knowledge structures, and representation and pattern recognition (Feldon 2006).

Adaptive expertise becomes important from the point of accelerating proficiency as: 'Transfer, or the ability to use knowledge flexibly and effectively across application areas, is an important component of proficiency' (Hoffman et al. 2014, p. 4). Based on the assumption that adaptive expertise would take longer to achieve, researchers maintained that '[t]raining must promote flexibility and adaptability' to address complexity (Hoffman et al. 2008, pp. 5–3). Adaptive expertise methods have been suggested as key methods to accelerate proficiency. Schwartz, Bransford & Sears (2005) established that knowledge representation accelerated the rate at which an expert solved novel problems. That is why it was believed that the key aspect of developing adaptability and flexibility was to prepare learners for significant complexity. That was the fundamental premise of CFT (Spiro et al. 1992) and CTT (Klein & Baxter 2009).

One example of accelerating expertise in a complex situation was using tough cases to develop adaptive performance is demonstrated in a program called *think like a commander* (TLAC). For example, Shadrick, Lussier & Fultz (2007) reported an experiment in which they subjected 143 army officers to three challenging and dynamic tactical problems. Officers were exposed to several scenarios in a compressed timeframe; they were coached on how an expert would think in the same scenario, and learners were allowed to correct their mental model and decision-making. A key focus of this program was to provide officers with the ability to evaluate rapidly changing situations through deliberate practice on several scenarios and develop an understanding of an expert tactician's thinking pattern. Shadrick, Lussier & Fultz (2007, p. v) found that officers trained through TLAC performed better in adaptive thinking skills than the officers having lived the real-world experience. They concluded that 'deliberately training complex cognitive skills may be substantially more effective and efficient than the experiential learning methods that take place in live and virtual environments' (id. 5). That method was believed to accelerate officers' proficiency in making tactical decisions, as reported in a number of studies by Shadrick et al. (Shadrick & Lussier 2009). The approach suggested that practice activities allowed the subjects to ingrain the task and to perform the task under a variety of conditions that led to developing the ability to perform the task with little or no conscious attention, as opposed to the trial-and-error method of the real-world (id. 18).

A similar approach was taken by van den Bosch, Helsdingen & de Beer (2004) in a study in which they developed a number of scenarios about air defense and trainees who were provided a range of information to make decisions, defend their positions and explain their plans in a given situation. In three different studies, adaptive flexibility was found to be a predictor of performance, as well as acceleration. The first study involved 140 expert and novice businesspeople solving complex problems in a business simulation of a chocolate factory (Güss et al. 2017). The second study involved 14 US SWAT officers who were monitored for their in-event real-time decision-making under real situations (Harris et al. 2017). The third study involved 23 expert and novice authorized firearms officers during armed confrontations (Boulton & Cole 2016). These three studies proposed exposing performers to a range of varied real scenarios that would lead to developing adaptive flexibility, which in turn accelerates expertise.

5.4.4 Conceptual skills

Bransford & Schwartz (2009, p. 765) contended that a learner's preparation to absorb new information and develop performance to new standards also was a determining factor for adaptive expertise development and helping them "work smarter". In the context of adaptive expertise, developing conceptual skills and principles of domains to prepare learners for future roles and demands was another area which had implications on accelerating proficiency. In a case study involving 44 college students with an algebra background but no background in statistics, VanLehn & Chi (2012) conducted an experiment. The participants were divided into two groups. The first group were given domain principles of probability with the help of an intelligent tutoring system and asked to solve some problems. They were not allowed to go to the next domain principle until they solved a given problem. The other group was asked to solve problems whichever way they wanted. Then, both groups were taught physics principles. Researchers found that the group which was taught explicit problem-solving strategy in probability showed improved performance in the physics task domain over the other group of students who were not provided such principle-based knowledge. They concluded that when students were taught using principle-based learning, and students were taught to focus on conceptual skills rather than the procedures of a domain, it tended to accelerate the rate at which they learned a new task domain. They stated that *acceleration of future learning* (AFL) occurred when prior knowledge increased the rate at which some students learn, relative to others (id. 31). Future learning was also believed to be accelerated by teaching students the metacognitive skills and learning-to-learn skills, note taking, and explanations, as VanLehn & Chi (2012, p. 32) contended: 'These are domain-independent skills (e.g., selfmonitoring, note taking, self-explanation), in that they can in principle accelerate the learning of almost any content'.

Clark & Feldon (2008) suggested some training strategies to build adaptive expertise: application environment, motivation, increasing novelty, variable practice, and targeted feedback. Clark (2006) supported that by providing varied practice and declarative knowledge that allowed the learners to adopt a procedure to handle a novel situation. Some researchers have recommended using training design strategies as advance organizers, analogies, guided discovery, error-based training, metacognitive instruction, learner control, and mastery-oriented learning (Smith et al. 1997). In a review of the training literature, Lazzara et al. (2010) recommended eight training strategies which worked well for adaptive expertise, including cue-recognition training, sense-making training, planning and forecasting, metacognition skills training, error-based training, and guided self or team correction.

The research on adaptive expertise suggested that such methods might accelerate proficiency. Furthermore, it also suggested the applicability of the concepts from CTT and CFT to develop adaptive expertise.

5.5 PART-TASK BASED METHODS

Most of the methods available in the literature are whole-task methods, in which a particular task is taught as a whole (van Merriënboer, Clark & de Croock 2002). However, a new method of representative part-task approach was evolved by van Merriënboer & Kester (2008; 2019), which extended their previous work on whole-task. The key idea of the part-task technique is to isolate a specific sub-skill and teach within a whole-task to build skills on the part-task. In a study conducted by Klein et al. (1997) among 30 US Marin corps squad leaders, they interviewed several fire ground commanders and workers in a number of other high-risk professions in dynamic situations to understand how professionals make decisions and how they evaluate options. He found that experts typically made decisions by recognizing the aspects of a new situation by comparing it to the previous situation. He called this as *recognition primed decision making* (RPD) (Klein 1993). In later studies, Klein isolated the pattern recognition sub-skill as a representative part-task and then used that to accelerate the decision-making of a novice (Klein et al. 1997; Klein 1997, 1998).

Fadde (2007) extended this recognition technique using principles of expertise studies such as Ericsson & Charness (1994) and developed an approach called *expertise-based training* (XBT). He maintained that any complex skills like intuitive decision-making can be broken into sub-skills or sub-tasks such as detection, categorization, and prediction, situational awareness and pattern recognition. Once decoupled, one can then develop targeted instructional design activities in workplace settings to accelerate those sub-skills (Fadde 2009a). Fadde (2007) applied this approach to baseball and called the method *temporal occlusion* in which part-task practice of pitch recognition skills was taught using video-based or computer-based simulation. Once the sub-skill of pitch recognition was mastered in video-based or computer-based training, the skill was integrated into real drill practice by having a player to shout out aloud the incoming pitch. The XBT approach involved designing instructional interventions on repurposing those tasks which have been identified as differentiators between experts and novices (Fadde 2009c). In these interventions, the sub-skills that led to expertise were systematically targeted using a part-task approach which could accelerate the performers towards a higher level of proficiency in whole-tasks.

In several studies, mainly in baseball and similar sports, evidence of using this approach was shown (Fadde 2007, 2009b, 2009c, 2010, 2012, 2013). A similar approach has been reported in soccer (Belling, Suss & Ward 2014a); baseball (Belling, Sada & Ward 2015); tennis (Williams et al. (2002); and cricket (Müller & Abernethy 2014). Particularly, the XBT approach has seen applications in high-performance sports (Fadde (2016), classroom teaching (Fadde & Sullivan 2013), online masters programs (Tokmak, Baturay & Fadde 2013) and nursing education (Razer, Blair & Fadde 2015).

In an early study, Starkes & Lindley (1994, p. 218) demonstrated that decision-making time of baseball players was reduced by approximately 540 milliseconds just in six video sessions. This time is enough for them to anticipate an opponent's move or making their own decisions. Subsequently, several of the studies showed that representative tasks can be trained using video simulations or computer-based programs which can be run in workplace settings (Belling, Sada & Ward 2015; Belling, Suss & Ward 2014a, 2014b; Fadde 2007, 2009a, 2012, 2013). A computer or video-based training on representative tasks was believed to be accelerating situational awareness of novices. Recently, the literature has reported the application of the XBT approach using video for accelerating proficiency of science teachers (Sancar-Tokmak 2013). Another variation of this strategy was to integrate model-based feedback via video-simulation. In a university education setting, a study conducted by Fadde (2012) on 55 university students reported that the participants in a group which received video-based training annotated with expert feedback aligned more with the content expert than did participants in the control group who did not receive such training.

The key implication of representative part-task methods is to isolate representative sub-skills and then put focused, deliberate activities in the workplace or in training settings to conduct practice on those sub-skills to allow the learners to use it in a whole-task manner as part of the larger work.

5.6 WORKPLACE ACTIVITIES-BASED METHODS

HRD literature approaches workplace training/learning methods from theoretical orientation put forward by noted philosophers: behaviorism (Thorndike, Watson, Hull, Tolman, Skinner), cognitivism (Kohler, Piaget, Bruner, Gagne), humanism (Buhler, Maslow, Rogers), social learning (Bandura, Rotter) and constructivism (Dewy, Lave, Piaget, Vygotsky). Workplace learning and training methods in HRD mostly fall under two schools of thought. Some researchers agree to informal work-based approach (Piskurich 1993) while some prefer a more structured approach to on-the-job learning (Jacobs & Jones 1995; Rothwell & Kazanas 2004).

On-the-job training has been a way to impart the necessary experience and practice to a new employee to meet job expectations. Hoffman et al. (2008, pp. 7–4) observed that '[o]n-the-job training is the first, and often only, strategy corporations rely on for learning—indeed, as much as 60% of all training is on-the-job training'.

5.6.1 Informal and social learning

In the first school of thoughts, some leading studies by Cseh, Watkins & Marsick (1999), Watkins & Marsick (1992) and Marsick & Watkins (1997, 2015, 2001) proposed informal learning and incidental learning as the core mechanism of workplace learning. Informal learning is something that happens uncontrolled in the workplace. Incidental learning is a by-product of other interventions. Cseh, Watkins & Marsick (1999) described workplace learning through a model of informal and incidental learning. In a study conducted with 84 managers at a Fortune 500 company, Enos, Kehrhahn & Bell (2003) found that primary mechanism that developed proficiency of managers was informal learning that allowed them to transfer learning quickly to real-world situations. Some researchers pointed out the value of the social aspect of learning from each other as an important component of informal learning (Eraut 2004, 2007a; Marsick et al. 2017). Lately, studies proposed situated learning at the workplace and learning through communities of practices as key workplace learning methods that emphasize the informal learning through social interactions at the workplace and learning from each other (Carter & Adkins 2017; Farnsworth, Kleanthous & Wenger-Trayner 2016; Mills 2011; Wenger 2000).

5.6.2 Experiential and action learning

HR practitioners valued experiential learning (Kolb 1984) and action learning (Pedler 2011; Revans 1982) as a means to develop expertise and improve performance. Experiential learning included different things such as learning from experience, context, non-routine conditions, the tacit dimension of knowledge, reflection and critical reflection, informal and incidental learning (Garrick 1998). Andresen, Boud & Cohen (2000, p. 208) define 'the ultimate goal of experiential learning involves the learner's own appropriation of something that is to them personally significant and meaningful (sometimes spoken in terms of the learning being "true to the lived experience of learners")'. Garrick (1998, p. 4) viewed informal learning also as experiential learning itself because 'experience of the learner occupies the central place in all considerations of teaching and learning'. Studies on the transfer of learning also contended the value of experiential learning (Bates, Holton III & Seyler 1997; Holton, Bates & Ruona 2000). While experiential learning methods appealed for the involvement of learners during learning, action learning, on the other hand, appeal for the participation of learners in the real scenarios. Participation, sharing with each other, learning from each other and group learning are some key elements of action learning methods. Miller (2003) conducted a study at a 400 people hospital which demonstrated the use of action learning as a primary mechanism for workplace learning for 35 managers. Fadde & Klein (2010, 2012) suggested that action learning activities could accelerate the performance in natural settings.

5.6.3 Structured workplace activities

However, several studies maintained that workplace was not a place conducive to learning and posed several barriers that hampered learning at the workplace (Hager 1998; Kooken, Ley & De Hoog 2007; Schulz & Roßnagel 2010). Brooker & Butler (1997) conducted a study at six industrial sites to explore perceptions of trainees and trainers towards the workplace as a learning context. It was found that both trainers and trainees considered workplace more as production place than learning place and at the time the learning was more disruptive.

Extending training into the workplace is challenging because workplaces are considered as unstructured entities. Rosenbaum & Williams (2004) noted that 70% to 80% of learning happens on the job through unstructured activities that hamper speed to proficiency. Contrary to this, Billett (2004) and Billett (1996) negated the common arguments of viewing workplace learning as an unstructured or informal entity. Rather, he believed that 'workplace activities and interactions are highly structured and regulated' (Billett 2004, p. 314). He contended that workplace activities are highly goal-oriented, structured, organized and measured which in fact should accelerate the learning and hence performance at the workplace. He further stressed that workplace participatory activities engaged professionals in developing competence leading to making workplaces as a legitimate learning environment.

In another study, Billett (2006) concluded that workplace activities could be organized and sequenced as a curriculum or a learning pathway, in such a way that overall trajectory to performance could be made more systematic. Though the study did not lead to evidence of acceleration, it emphasizes an important aspect of structured workplace learning, the use of experiential learning, and learning through work.

The second school of thought in HRD emphasized a more structured approach to workplace learning. In a study conducted at a large food manufacturing plant with 17 learners, Billett (2002) proposed guided participation in work activities, guided learning at work and guided learning transfer. His method advocated learning through undertaking everyday work activities, organising and sequencing of workplace experiences, access to routine and non-routine practice, monitoring learners' progress on pathway of activities, providing goals with work practice, modeling the tasks to be performed, demonstrating procedures, coaching with an activity, providing opportunities to participate observe and listen and opportunities to reflect and abstract situation. In such studies, mentoring or coaching has been seen as a central mechanism of workplace learning which has provided some weak empirical evidence towards improving career outcomes for employees (Allen & Eby 2007; Allen et al. 2004; Billett 2003; Ramaswami & Dreher 2007). Based on the core principle of mentoring in the context of complex tasks or jobs, cognitive apprenticeship method, originated from cognitive science research, has shown evidence of accelerating expertise (Boling & Beatty 2010; Cash et al. 1996; Collins, Brown & Newman 1988; Collins 1990; Dennen & Burner 2008; Dennen 2004; Jin & Corbett 2011; Kuo et al. 2012; Woolley & Jarvis 2007).

5.6.4 Cognitive apprenticeship

While the previous methods discussed were implanted through some training intervention (mostly in a classroom or controlled setting), accelerating proficiency in the workplace is a key challenge for organizations. In their seminal work, Collins, Brown & Newman (1989) developed a method of direct modeling of experts in performing complex cognitive tasks. They called the approach *cognitive apprenticeship* and defined it as 'learning through guided experience on cognitive and metacognitive, rather than physical, skills and processes' (Collins, Brown & Newman 1989, p. 456). Fundamentally, the cognitive apprenticeship challenged the traditional apprenticeship model's ability in delivering cognitive skills in situated settings. When using cognitive skills such as decision-making or performing other complex tasks, most of the thinking is internal to the performer. While in traditional apprenticeship, the learner builds his skills under a mentor by direct observation, and it becomes challenging when cognitive skills are involved. The main premise of the cognitive apprenticeship model was to make thinking visible through actions or other means: 'Applying apprenticeship methods to largely cognitive skills require [*sic*] the externalization of processes that are usually carried out internally' (Collins, Brown & Newman 1987, p. 4). From a process standpoint, the methodology involved breaking larger or more complex tasks into smaller tasks which were within the *zone of proximal development* (Vygotsky 1978) or within the reach of the learner, and then support and offer guidance in situated settings on authentic and representative tasks, rather than classroom-type tasks.

The cognitive apprenticeship process consisted of six key components: modeling, coaching, scaffolding (and fading), articulation, reflection, and exploration. Modeling involved revealing knowledge structures used by an expert and having him/her to externalize the process, actions or thinking. This included factual or conceptual knowledge, heuristics, and strategies. Coaching involved observing learners and offering them prompts, feedback and questions. Scaffolding involved support, suggestions or cues provided during the task execution to the learner. Reflection involved bringing moments when learners could compare their processes with that of an expert. Articulation involved learners to explain, summarize and clarify or ask questions. Lastly, exploration involved making learners explore new goals and formulate new tests for their hypotheses (Druckman & Bjork 1991) (Woolley & Jarvis 2007, p. 75). The cognitive apprenticeship model also incorporates several approaches including a model of expertise, collaborative learning, communities of practice and mentoring (Dennen & Burner 2008; Lajoie 2009).

Cash et al. (1996) studied the effect of cognitive apprenticeship in 28 college students taking up automotive air-conditioning training courses. Students were divided into two groups. They were measured at three time periods. The group receiving experimental treatment of cognitive apprenticeship scored significantly higher than the other group. They found that compared to the classroom-based methodology, cognitive apprenticeship resulted in a more effective acquisition of technical concepts and troubleshooting skills. Stalmeijer et al. (2013) in a study of 17 clinical teachers also confirmed that clinical teaching practice followed cognitive apprenticeship.

Though applied in several educational settings, the main implication of the cognitive apprenticeship model is its application during everyday practice in the workplace. In business studies, Backus et al. (2010) suggested two methods to accelerate leadership development: (1) immersive learning such as simulations; and (2) cognitive apprenticeship. They contended that cognitive apprenticeship offered an immersive solution considering the dynamics of the workplace. In a review of research studies on six components of cognitive apprenticeship, Dennen & Burner (2008, p. 436) affirmed that cognitive apprenticeship matches with how learning happens in the workplace:

> Empirical studies have confirmed much of what theories have suggested: (1) that the cognitive apprenticeship model is an accurate description of how learning occurs naturally as part of everyday life and social interactions, and (2) that the instructional strategies that have been extracted from

these observations of everyday life can be designed into more formal learning contexts with positive effect.

Recently, Kuchenbrod (2016) used CTA and the DACUM (design a curriculum) process to accelerate the expertise of live-burn instructors in the firefighting domain. Their method involved using CTA-type analysis with subject matter experts to capture the necessary skills required for the occupation, identifying a required proficiency level for each skill and then designing a curriculum for proficiency. Using the learner's self-assessment and demonstration of the skills to the desired proficiency quickly moved the learner to the next skills, thus, leading to shorter time to proficiency for the job. The key implication of cognitive apprenticeship and guided mentoring was its ability to provide authentic and highly job-specific learning and experience to the performer. Such authentic learning appears to accelerate learning. Trekles & Sims (2013) stated:

> When learners engage in authentic learning situations, they have the opportunity to synthesize all of the skills and concepts that they have learned thus far, allowing them to develop practice that in turn leads to the development of more extensive and complex schemata and expertise regarding the topic of study. (Trekles & Sims 2013, sec. method, para 1)

Evidence suggests that technology can be used to design all of the six components of cognitive apprenticeship (modeling, coaching, scaffolding (and fading), articulation, reflection, and exploration) as described in previous paragraphs. The demonstration on the coached-practice environment and computer-based intelligent tutoring systems such as the Sherlock system were examples of the technology-assisted cognitive apprenticeship model

(Collins 1990; Gott 1988; Katz, Hall & Lesgold 1997; Lesgold et al. 1988; Lesgold 1991).

Graesser, McNamara & VanLehn (2005) designed a computer-based learning environment which supported self-explanation and coaching students in metacognitive strategies. The study demonstrated that a deeper level of metacognitive skills could be developed using computer-based systems. In the last two decades, several researchers demonstrated the use of cognitive apprenticeship through computer-based, technology-based or web-based solution to provide expert guidance to the performers (Boling & Beatty 2010; Hausmann, van de Sande & VanLehn 2008; Hong et al. 2007; Jin & Corbett 2011; Kuo et al. 2012; Lesgold & Nahemow 2001; Mitrovic, Ohlsson & Barrow 2013; Ong & Ramachandran 2003; Sottilare & Goldberg 2012). Thus, the literature suggests that cognitive apprenticeship methods, either as they are or through technology, are a powerful accelerator of proficiency.

5.6.5 Structured on-the-job training

A variation of the cognitive apprenticeship is seen as an approach popularly known as *structured on-the-job training* (S-OJT (Jacobs 2014b). Among all the HRD methods, S-OJT has emerged as the most promising methods in organizations for experiential learning (Jacobs & Jones 1995). This method develops the expertise of new employees with the help of mentoring/coaching from experienced employees (Jacobs 2014b). This is a structured process of defining, tracking, monitoring and managing OJT. S-OJT approach incorporated analysis of work activities, checklists and mentor sign-off. In an early study in clinical practice, the positive effect on S-

METHODS TO ACCELERATE PROFICIENCY

OJT at the workplace was shown which included improved customer satisfaction without having to take people away from work (Sullivan, Brechin & Lacoste 1999). The key result of this approach appears to be a reduction in time to proficiency. In a study conducted by Jacobs & Bu-Rahmah (2012) at a petroleum company in the Middle East, they applied S-OJT to train new engineers. The new engineers were put under a pool of pre-qualified mentors for various tasks. They noted that 53 months of time normally required to advance an engineer to the desired performance, was reduced to 36 months using S-OJT. Among other benefits, the S-OJT approach has reported a reduction in training times as suggested by 'the results related to training efficiency suggest that S-OJT usually takes less time to conduct and it achieves the training objectives when compared to unstructured OJT, classroom training, and blended versions of the training' (Jacobs 2014b, p. 281).

Further, Jacobs (2014b) reported nine case studies which showed that S-OJT can accelerate proficiency in the skills which were of low to medium complexity, have predictable or pre-defined outcomes and for which well-documented procedures were available. However, evidence was lacking on if and how S-OJT could be applied to highly complex cognitive tasks as well. Although there are several studies to manage and track S-OJT systematically, no literature was found that offered an explanation of techniques to shorten the S-OJT cycle, which may still extend to several months in complex jobs (Jacobs & Bu-Rahmah 2012).

HRD literature has long inclined towards training and development as the core activity towards developing the expertise of employees at the workplace (Jacobs & Jones 1995). However, recently Billett (2014) contended another viewpoint that most of the learning at the workplace occurs outside the boundaries of intentional mentoring and other structured HRD interventions. He argued that the process of observation and imitation play a key role in workplace learning. Thus, the nature of workplace activities determines the pace at which learning happens.

5.6.6 Deliberate practice at work

The deliberate practice mechanism, as proposed by Ericsson et al. (1993), has been investigated for its applicability to the workplace also. In a study involving 100 sales agents working for 10 German insurance companies, Sonnentag & Kleine (2000) found that workplace activities such as extensive preparation of task accomplishment, gathering information from domain experts, or seeking feedback can be used to develop performance through deliberate practice. They noted that performance was directly associated with the amount of time spent on the deliberate practice of those work-related activities. They implied that the deliberate practice mechanism can also be used in work settings which include a range of usual job activities and tasks. However, they also cautioned about the complexity of work performance as 'a number of factors in addition to deliberate practice that might impact an individual's work performance.... these factors override the effects of deliberate practice' (Sonnentag & Kleine 2000, p. 90).

5.6.7 Deliberate performance through action learning

On the contrary to this attempt to apply deliberate practice mechanism in business settings, Fadde & Klein (2010, 2012) argued that professionals and business personnel do not have the time and luxury to engage in a narrow set of skills and years to engage in the focused, deliberate practice besides their regular roles. Another aspect is that job rotation — reassignments to different roles and other job duties — precludes the conscientious deliberate practice on specific skill sets at workplace settings (Hoffman et al. 2014). Therefore, deliberate practice mechanisms may not work for organizations and in particular in the job involving knowledge work. Hoffman, Feltovich, et al. (2010, p. 402) quoted Gary Klein's perspective: 'Deliberate practice usually involves motor or perceptual-motor skills, whereas most of the skills needed in business and industry involve cognitive work'.

To address this challenge, Fadde & Klein (2010, 2012) proposed a framework called *deliberate performance*, also called *action learning activities*, based on routine day-to-day workplace events as the opportunities for professional and business people to accelerate expertise in domain-specific tacit knowledge and intuitive expertise. They intended to incorporate tacit knowledge to develop expertise-based intuition and to base activities on everyday situations that were authentic to the particular workplace and job performance and were mostly self-guided. They suggested doing so by engaging the individuals in routine work activities using on-the-job or just-in-time training opportunities. They proposed it as 'an instructional method designed to accelerate the process by making it more systematic, that is, more drill-like (in the fashion of deliberate practice)' (Fadde & Klein 2012, p. 12). This expertise in natural settings could be accelerated using four types of deliberate performance exercises: estimation, experimentation, extrapolation, and explanation (Fadde & Klein 2010). Estimation of time and resources needed to complete a task or project was an important skill that increased awareness of the individual. Experimentation was trying new ways to do the things allowing professions to apply induction, deduction, and abduction processes. Extrapolation referred to deliberate exercises that allowed professions to reuse their previously learned information or experiences. The last exercise they recommended was an explanation, which includes a group analysis of a recent event or project. Fadde & Klein (2010) positioned this feedback and coaching were deemed essential components of deliberate performance.

Recently, Jung, Kim & Reigeluth (2016) developed instructional guidelines based on the deliberate performance model and proposed four phases – development plan, action, reflection on action and remedies to accelerate the proficiency of journeymen. However, there are no studies confirming this framework to-date.

5.6.8 Learning organizations

From an HRD perspective, managers are supposed to play a big role in enabling their employees with workplace learning (Beattie 2006; Gratton 2016; McLaughlin 2016; Yen, Trede & Patterson 2016). Despite the advances in work-based learning (Morris & Blaney 2010) or learning through work (Billett & Choy 2013; Billett 2010, 2014; Chan 2013), it seems that managers do not know how to support such learning. In a study, Woodall (2000) found that despite recognition of the importance of the workplace as an important place for learning, managers typically did not know much about work-based learning interventions and systematic approach to workplace learning was lacking. Similarly, in a study, Hughes (2004) noted that while workplace learning is expected to be influenced by supervisors, there was no noticeable attempt by supervisors to enable their staff to learn. Marsick & Volpe (1999) acknowledged that business practitioners know a little about how informal learning can be best supported, encouraged and developed.

Further, the work environment plays an important role in accelerating proficiency. From the literature review, it is evident that accelerating proficiency in the workplace could be a complex phenomenon. However, existing literature on proficiency lacks an explanation of influencing conditions on proficiency development, as well as acceleration (van der Heijden 2002). In a meta-analysis to investigate instructional interventions to accelerate the novice-expert transition, Welch (2008, p. 208) concluded that one needs to examine if the work environment indeed supports shortening the novice-to-expert transition. Most expertise and proficiency theories have discounted the influence of a range of contextual factors such as job environment, nature of the job, and dynamism of the business environment. For instance, in a study aimed at understanding the expertise development process of 11 instructional design students, Ge & Hardré (2010, p. 24) identified several factors that influenced the development of expertise. They found that despite a large body of research on expertise 'little research has focused on the interactions of internal and external factors influencing novices' expertise development'. Therefore, the methods and solutions for accelerating proficiency have to consider the workplace dynamics, environment and other influencing factors (Moon, Kim & You 2013).

Therefore, at a holistic level, HRD studies indicated that to develop performance at the workplace, organizations must become learning organizations (Marquardt 1996; Matthews 1999; Watkins & Marsick 1993). The originators of the concept of *learning organizations*, Senge (1994a, 1994b) and Senge et al. (1994) proposed personal mastery, mental models, shared vision, team learning and system thinking as key ingredients of making an organization a learning organization. Kaiser & Holton III (1998) proposed learning organizational performance model which emphasized that learning outcomes at individual, team and organization level lead to performance outcomes.

HRD literature explored several workplace learning theories and methods and several of those looked promising as well. Ironically HRD research typically does not seem to make the acceleration of proficiency, performance or expertise as a primary goal or a strategic initiative. The literature review suggests that most of the methods of workplace learning and training have been used with the goal of *building* proficiency rather than the goal of *accelerating* it. There are limited direct evidence of accelerating performance, proficiency or expertise. Though researchers have appealed, there are insufficient studies regarding how the work environment supports or hampers accelerating proficiency in the workplace in business settings.

5.7 TECHNOLOGY-BASED METHODS

Most modern-day simulation methods use some form of technology. Some technologies are used in the workplace and in training to improve performance. Performance support systems and automation are also argued as a means of accelerating proficiency (Hoffman et al. 2014).

5.7.1 Expert-based systems

A multitude of modern technologies has been used to accelerate expertise in controlled environments in a handful of studies. For example, Raphael et al. (2009) presented an 'adaptive performance trainer' system that involves modeling an expert in terms of 'psychophysiological profile' of expertise in the form of an EEG signature and other physiological metrics that change during the stages of learning. The system provides continuous psychophysical monitoring and feedback to the trainee and customizing the training based on that feedback. This approach has been demonstrated to accelerate skill acquisition in marksmen training (Behneman et al. 2012).

5.7.2 Tutoring systems

Technology offers distinct advantages in accelerating learning and allows learners to learn more content in a short time. Sottilare & Goldberg (2012) proposed that a technology-based tutoring system could minimize the intrinsic cognitive load by appropriately selecting the problems of appropriate difficulty while presenting information that increases the germane load (domain-specific activities) as per cognitive load theory (CLT). Such a system could use multiple representations of information or content to apply to flexible mental models, as per CFT. Lastly, such a system can be designed which would allow learners to recognize their flaws in their current mental models and then discard flawed models in favor or less flawed models, as per CTT. More contemporary techniques, such as blended learning and a blend of online and face-to-face training, are believed to accelerate learning. For example, in a controlled group study, Patchan et al. (2015) found that students learned basic and additional content at a considerably higher rate when blended learning was used via online technologies. While the literature indicates that technology supports learning flexibly and accelerates learning, Jipp (2016, p. 92) argued the opposite view that automation of information hinders expertise development because such automation does not put any load on working memory.

5.7.3 Performance support systems

One key area of technology-based methods is performance support systems (PSS). PSS entails providing performers with on-demand content, information, job aids, JIT knowledge and learning resources close to the point of need and during the workflow (Gottfredson & Mosher 2011). Information and support at the time of need in the context of the job or task appeared to support acceleration, while keeping the focus of the performers on producing outcomes rather than learning the content (Cagiltay 2006; Gal et al. 2017; Gannan 2002; Nguyen 2006; van Schaik, Pearson & Barker 2002). In a study, Nguyen, Klein & Sullivan (2005) reported significant differences in performance by using PSS. Some studies established that time on task was significantly reduced when PSSs were used in combination with training, as compared when using only PSS (Mitchell 2014). Some studies viewed PSS as performance interventions, and in certain cases they were the only interventions required for a given performance issue (Villachica, Stone & Endicott 2006).

5.7.4 Knowledge capture systems

Accelerating knowledge acquisition is one key goal identified by researchers. Hoffman, Feltovich, et al. (2010, p. 28) reasoned that '[t]o accelerate proficiency, one must accelerate the acquisition of knowledge that is extensive and highly organized'. Alongside training interventions, knowledge capture and sharing in organizations helped new professionals to make quick decisions and accelerate their own expertise. In a study conducted among 100 top-level executives and next-in-line executives in Fortune 500 companies, Baxter (2013) demonstrated that proficiency or expertise in complex workplace skills like strategic thinking, situational awareness, and decision-making, could be accelerated by capturing and using tacit knowledge. She demonstrated that tacit knowledge could be captured through knowledge elicitation methods such as in-depth interviews of senior professionals on how they made a decision in a case. This study demonstrated another use of CTA to capture knowledge and quickly transfer to junior practitioners, as opposed to the traditional approach of designing training programs. The captured knowledge was then transformed into scenarios and presented to professionals to practice decision-making and receive feedback from senior professionals.

In two separate studies, one using a case study on 19 employees at a call center (McQueen & Chen 2010) and the other using in-depth interviews with 15 client-facing consultants at a levy-fund company (McQueen & Janson 2016), it was found that scripting the tacit knowledge led to accelerating the speed to proficiency in handling clients. Hoffman et al. (2008) supported knowledge capture and sharing as a method to accelerate proficiency. However, they also cautioned that 'knowledge management by knowledge capture and knowledge repositories is only a part of the solution to workforce problems' (p. 3.6).

5.7.5 Personalised learning systems

Traditional literature has suggested some approaches involving designing a personalized or non-personalized learning sequence (of things to learn or preferred order of topics) (Hong et al. 2007; Hsieh & Wang 2010; Janssen, Berlanga & Koper 2010; Zhao & Wan 2006). Some studies have advocated designing and optimizing the learning path based on learner profiling and dynamic assessment using automated systems or technologies (like learning management systems) to speed up content learning and providing multiple pathways (Mostafavi & Barnes 2016; Mostafavi, Liu & Barnes 2015; Muhammad et al. 2016; Tam, Lam & Fung 2014, 2014; Yang, Li & Lau 2014).

Another variation is seen in professional practice studies in which professional competencies are sequenced with appropriate proficiency checks in the form of multi-tier certification (ten Cate 2013). These approaches have claimed to increase the learning speed of learners or making a curriculum shorter (e.g. accelerated curriculum advocated by some universities). The core goal suggested by these studies leans towards sequencing the learning objectives in the instructional interventions through a topic-based or task-based curriculum.

However, professional and academic literature has seen a similar but characteristically different approach that involves mapping and sequencing the learning journey of a learner from day one of taking up a role and then work it up towards desired proficiency with the goal to reduce the time taken to reach the desired proficiency. The idea for this type of method to accelerate proficiency is that by focusing on most essential and important tasks and by breaking the skills into smaller skills, one can plot an efficient learning journey which potentially can take the time away from the journey. Thus, a correctly designed sequence forces learners to perform a set of tasks, acquire skills or attend curriculums in a specific order, which eventually leads to faster acquisition of desired proficiency.

Among early advocates, Lajoie (2003, 2009) in concept emphasized that to accelerate the journey from novice to expert, the 'trajectory' to expertise must be established and made clear. Billett (2006, p. 38) proposed a concept of workplace learning pathway claiming that 'an ideal intended workplace curriculum comprises the identification and sequencing of work activities that represent the "course to be run"—that lead to full participation in the particular work-practice'. Sports studies have shown the impact of development speed by an appropriate sequence of skills (Taghizadeh & Daneshfar 2014).

The approach of breaking the larger task into smaller parts and then sequencing based on complexity and recurrence was the fundamental premise of the 4C/1D model presented by van Merriënboer, Clark & de Croock (2002). Within the whole-task, clusters of part-tasks are sequenced appropriately based on complexity, as well as recurrence (frequency) to build performance as a whole (Paas & van Gog 2009). This model supported building the whole-task sequence from a training perspective so that performers could integrate the part-tasks efficiently (van Merriënboer, Clark & de Croock 2002; van Merriënboer & Kester 2008).

The sequence of learning can be developed based on several factors. Several studies suggested a range of criteria to sequence the learning journey which involved sequence by content/tasks by practice sessions (Healy 2007); sequence by content type (Koubek, Clarkston & Calvez 1994); sequence by experience level of learners (Kalyuga et al. 2003); sequence by type of skills (Dodd 2009); and sequence by increasing complexity (Bunderson 2011). Sequencing the tasks/activities appropriately was one of the key principles of cognitive apprenticeship advocating sequencing the tasks in an order of increasing complexity and from global to local skills (Boling & Beatty 2010; Collins 2002; Dennen & Burner 2008; Jin & Corbett 2011; Kuo et al. 2012; Lajoie 2009; Vihavainen, Paksula & Luukkainen 2011; Woolley & Jarvis 2007). Similarly, appropriate sequencing of workplace activities, mentoring sessions, and job shadow sessions is also a core idea of structured OJT approach (Jacobs 2014b).

METHODS TO ACCELERATE PROFICIENCY

The concept of sequencing a complete learning path has been referred to as with many names in the literature – learning path (Rosenbaum & Williams 2004); learning pathway (Alchemy 2000), among others. In the business world, the *Learning Paths* methodology has seen quite a traction that involves making the learning sequence more efficient was by eliminating waste, overlap, redundancies, repetitive content and non-value-added activities that do not lead to desired proficiency goals (Rosenbaum & Williams (2004) Rosenbaum (2014). While there are no academic studies on this, Rosenbaum (2018) claimed that by using their methodology of creating efficient learning sequence, organizations have attained up to 30% shorter time to proficiency. Some studies provided limited evidence of using process improvement tools like Lean Six Sigma, a methodology to remove wasteful activities from any process (See Furterer 2009), to improve the efficacy of curriculum, which is a relatively new area with a limited number of studies (Thomas et al. 2017).

The study conducted by Attri (2018) positioned that if one focus on the most important things that matter to deliver a business outcome to attain required proficiency, several things would not be required to be master upfront. Thus, he suggested three-step approach - first segmenting the tasks and activities based on characteristics using data analytics, secondly creating a logical sequence of experience as a complete *proficiency path,* and thirdly to optimize the proficiency path for efficiency and time saving using several different techniques. A large number of project leaders affirmed the direct effect of such an approach to accelerate proficiency. In this study, the experiences were sequenced by several criteria such as by tasks characteristics (e.g., frequency, complexity, importance, and impact); by some organizing principle or central themes (e.g., process flow and product manufacturing sequence); or by methods that ensure proficiency development (e.g., interleaved job shadow with training sessions and spiral practice sessions).

In some studies, it was seen that by breaking a block of knowledge into shorter segments made it efficient to deliver information through technology-based platforms for quick access and immediate application. Such a method emphasizes that applying learning close to the point of need in the context of the work, improves retention and transfer of skills, cuts the need for multiple repetition cycles and improves the speed of learning (Hug, Lindner & Bruck 2006; Hug 2015; Souza et al. 2015; Zhamanov & Zhamapor 2013). Such shorter chunks sequenced appropriately invariably used spaced practice and interleaving and delivered through technology that led to a slow-down of forgetting, improved learning, increase rate of skill acquisition and resulted in long-term retention (Birnbaum et al. 2013; Karpicke & Bauernschmidt 2011; Sobel, Cepeda & Kapler 2011; Spruit, Band & Hamming 2015; Wang, Zhou & Shah 2014).

5.8 SUMMARY

Several approaches in past research studies has given some leverage points for acceleration of learning and proficiency. That includes but not limited to studying how mentors do it; blocked practice sequenced; problem-based learning with reduced scaffolding;

mentoring; appropriately timed meaningful corrective feedback; simulation and immersion; scenario-based training; presenting case-based instructions with desirable difficulties; compressing a library of tough cases in a short time; presenting decision-making exercises; virtual reality or operational simulation; building knowledge structures; and cognitive tutoring systems (Andrews & Fitzgerald 2010; Hoffman et al. 2008, 2009, 2014; Hoffman, Andrews & Feltovich 2012; Hoffman & Andrews 2012; Hoffman, Feltovich, et al. 2010).

6

CHALLENGE TO ACCELERATE PROFICIENCY

Most of the methods discussed in the previous chapters are grounded into the training of the employees, either traditional or at the workplace. However, these methods present its own challenges. This chapter outlines some of the foreseeable difficulties that one may face while following the training and workplace methods reviewed earlier. In addition, briefly some guidelines to apply lessons from this book are presented.

6.1 CHALLENGES TO ACCELERATE PROFICIENCY

The review in the preceding sections recognized the fact that time to proficiency was generally very long, and hence it called for methods to shorten it. For instance, the leading authority on accelerated proficiency, Hoffman, Andrews & Feltovich (2012, p. 9) recognized this need:

> This empirical fact about expertise (i.e., that it takes a long time) sets the stage for an effort at demonstrating the acceleration of the achievement of proficiency – an effort that sets out to address a number of inter-related questions concerning the path to expertise.

From the literature review, two challenges have become evident in regards to accelerating proficiency. First, the literature has suggested a lack of understanding of the actual mechanisms of how someone gains proficiency, despite a large amount of research on the higher end of expertise. Second, the literature has suggested challenges in regards to methods and solutions to accelerate the acquisition of proficiency.

The first challenge is expressed as: 'One also needs to understand how expertise is acquired, how it can be taught, and how new employees can be presented with appropriate experience and management activities' (van der Heijden 2002, p. 55). Among other things, understanding the mechanisms of learning and how they interact to develop a novice into an expert is extremely crucial to develop suitable instructional design and training interventions to ensure acceleration of novice-to-expert development (Welch 2008). The actual process of how one becomes proficient using training or other methods remains under-explored in the literature, as pointed out by Lajoie (2003). The gap identified by researchers two decades ago still persists today. For instance, some researchers noted: 'Most studies can't explain how the expertise reaches to a specific level or stage by multiple mechanisms. Accordingly we have to develop specific and realistic model for how expertise develops' (Moon, Kim & You 2013, p. 226).

There is another aspect to this gap. The classic studies focused either on a range of issues related to novice-expert differences (e.g. Chi, Glaser & Farr 1988) or on the development of higher-end expertise (Ericsson et al. 1993). However, developing and accelerating proficiency to the stages of journeyman and senior journeyman, in between extreme ends of novice and expert, have not received much attention (Alexander 2003b; Hoffman et al. 2014). These mid-range proficiency stages have been positioned as the most important stages 'considering the significant impact of the journeyman stage and the need for hastening performance in that stage' in organizations (Jung, Kim & Reigeluth 2016, p. 58). However, there are scarce empirical studies on how to accelerate proficiency, particularly at the mid-range of the journeyman and senior journeyman proficiency levels.

The basic question about the possibility of acceleration, as well as methods of acceleration, appears to be under-researched, particularly in workplace settings. Notably, (Hoffman, Andrews & Feltovich 2012, p. 9) raised a question which was not well addressed in literature at the time of their study:

> Can the achievement of journeyman-level skill be accelerated? What might be the payoff if this problem were solved, say, by reducing the time to achieve journeyman

level skill by some significant amount (e.g., from 4 years to 2)?

6.2 ISSUES WITH TRAINING METHODS

Current methods of accelerating proficiency in the literature are primarily grounded in the domain of learning. Therefore, the role of training in accelerating proficiency is a topic of discussion.

Methods for effective skill acquisition training and learning interventions have continued to be the focus of researchers and organizations alike (Salas et al. 2012). For decades, the literature has positioned the value of training, learning and development interventions in improving the speed of learning, improving performance and acquiring skills required to do the job. As Lajoie (2003, p. 23) suggested '[t]he road to competence can be shortened if systematic studies of expertise lead to improvements in instruction and assessment'. Researchers have attempted to explore the mechanisms of accelerating proficiency or expertise from classical studies. However, there is a growing body of arguments over the past decade questioning the ability of traditional training models to develop and accelerate proficiency in complex domains. Hoffman et al. (2009, p. 19) appealed that 'traditional learning methods that focus on cursory exposure and short-term results might be insufficient to accelerate the achievement of proficiency'. Traditional, Instructor-led, classroom-based training posed some challenges to shorten time to proficiency due to several reasons. Some of the reasons are lengthy training programs required to develop complex skills (Andrews & Fitzgerald 2010); longer training design cycle (Arnold, Ringquist & Prien 1998); merely textbook problem-solving capabilities (Mayer 1986; Brown, Collins & Duguid 1989; Perkins & Soloman 1989); classroom methodologies disconnected from the workplace realities (Vaughan 2008); and the need to re-learn the same tasks in the workplace way (Bransford & Schwartz 2009).

More recently, Arnold & Collier (2013, p. 2) observed issues with traditional training methods: 'Traditional training methods, such as on-the-job training and expert-led lecture/discussion schemes, have shown little capability to accelerate this expertise development process'. For example, evidence showed that traditional pedagogies such as lecturing and demonstrating solutions to problems, very often result in students being capable of solving textbook problems but unable to apply the knowledge to solve real-life problems (Hung 2009).

To add to this challenge, the complexity in the workplace could influence how soon an employee reaches target proficiency and could be a determining factor that leads to variations in performance on the same task among several performers. Hoffman, Feltovich, et al. (2010, p. 17) pointed out that training notions need to be changed in view of increased complexity: 'The workers in sociotechnical systems must be trained to be adaptive, so that they can cope with the ever changing world and ever-changing workplace.... and workers must be trained faster'. Complexity raises the emphasis on adaptive expertise as a key component of accelerated proficiency, which allows an individual to be able to handle novel and unfamiliar problems (Hesketh & Ivancic 2002). However, traditional training methods did not appear to be helpful in developing adaptive expertise: 'Traditional methods are appropriate for training routine expertise and are designed to develop automatic behavioral responses to performance requirements that are familiar to the performer'.

Complexity brings another challenge to training development as well. According to Andrews & Fitzgerald (2010, p. 3) complexity may add time to learn by stating that, 'if the content to be learned is complex, we must allow considerable time, sometimes years, for the acquisition of that skill or knowledge, and we must spend considerable non-time resources'. Consequently, there is more content to be developed and the duration of such training programs tended to become long. Some studies to investigate methods to accelerate training development noted that 'what training departments need are sound methods for shortening the cycle time of the training development process, while not sacrificing validity and quality of the output' (Arnold, Ringquist & Prien 1998, p. 23). Sharing similar views, van Merriënboer, Clark & de Croock (2002, p. 39) made an appeal that training needed to focus on 'development of training programs for learner who need to learn and transfer highly complex cognitive skills or "competencies" to an increasingly varied set of real-world context and settings'.

Training is one of the several performance interventions (Stolovitch & Keeps 1999). Leading practitioners Pollock, Wick & Jefferson (2015, p. 41) asserted that performance is the result of the interaction of the worker, work, and workplace, but the '[t]raining impacts worker only'. Training is useful only if it focuses on developing performers to produce business results. However, most of the time training is just an event with the specific purpose to deliver necessary skills or behaviors, and usually, it has a specific assessment checkpoint that signals its end. Producing results or waiting till results are produced is usually not the goal of training interventions and is certainly not feasible.

Chevalier (2004; 2015), Soderstrom & Bjork (2015) and Stolovitch (2000) argued that performance during training interventions could be a misleading indicator of proficiency and long-term learning of behaviors that should persist in the workplace. Unless the performers are prepared to produce business outcomes in a shorter time, training may not contribute towards accelerating proficiency. While modern studies emphasize on aligning training objectives with business needs and goals (Hughes 2003; Saks, Haccoun & Belcourt 2010; Salas et al. 2012), preparing performers towards proficiency in shorter time appears to be beyond the reach of any instructional design models, just because instructional design models tend to focus on knowledge, skills, and behaviors. Baker (2017) argued that in modern organizations the assumption that a technically superior workforce is the key to organizational performance tended to gear all solutions to being skill-focused or training-focused. It is worth mentioning the observations made by Swanson & Holton III (2001) and Dean (2016) with regard to the need to use several non-linear interventions in addition to learning interventions to attain desired performance.

While modern studies emphasize aligning training objectives with business needs and goals (Hughes 2003; Saks, Haccoun & Belcourt 2010; Salas et al. 2012), preparing performers toward proficiency in a shorter time appears to be beyond the reach of any instructional design models, just because instructional design models tend to focus on knowledge, skills, and behaviors. In a study conducted by Attri (2018), almost all the project leaders unanimously advocated that while training helps with initial readiness and understanding the job, training is not a solution for developing or accelerating proficiency. Some researchers also argue that in general, training is just an event with a specific purpose to deliver the necessary skills or behaviors, and usually, it has a specific assessment checkpoint that signals its end. Producing results or waiting till results are produced is usually not the goal of training interventions and is indeed not feasible. Leading practitioners Pollock, Wick & Jefferson (2015, p. 41) asserted that performance is the result of the interaction of the worker, work, and workplace, but the '[t]raining impacts worker only.' Training is useful only if it focuses on developing performers to produce business results. In a comprehensive research report on speed to proficiency, it was noted that strategies to accelerated proficiency extend much beyond training or learning interventions (Attri 2019). Previous studies also positioned training as one of the several possible solutions to accelerate proficiency, rather than the total solution in itself. (Kang 2017; Marker et al. 2014; Pershing 2006; Van Tiem, Moseley & Dessinger 2012; Wallace 2006)

Admittedly, training is a critical part of most performance improvement interventions (Clark 2008; Kraiger 2014). There are cases in which desired proficiency can be attained in training settings, or training is the only a viable, practical option; for example, job roles in which life and safety matter (military, pilots, surgeons, firefighters, etc.) and failure is no option in real situations (Hintze 2008; Jenkins et al. 2016; Klein & Borders 2016; Kuchenbrod 2016). Alternatively, training may be more feasible solutions in the job roles that are not readily measured in terms of immediate on-the-job outcomes (e.g., roles related to business strategy), or job roles are governed by some licensing or other regulatory norms (e.g., oil and gas-related jobs). Such situations may necessitate training as a fail-safe mechanism or even a mandatory requirement (Crichton & Flin 2004).

Recognizing that traditional training methods, whether classroom-based or workplace-based do not appear to answer the challenge of accelerating proficiency, some studies have observed that training design for accelerating proficiency may require different methods. (Fadde 2007, p. 373) recognized in his studies that such methods may require 'instructional designers to create efficient instructional tasks'. This gap continues to persist, as evident by the concerns raised by Fadde (2016):

> The goal of accelerating expertise [proficiency] can leave researchers and trainers in human factors, naturalistic decision making, sports science, and expertise studies concerned about seemingly insufficient application of expert performance theories, findings and methods for training macrocognitive aspects of human performance (p. 1).... The theories, findings, and methods of expert performance research need to be translated into focused workplace training programs that meet the challenges of duration, curriculum development, resource optimization, and buy in from on-the-ground practitioners (p. 13).

There is no doubt that learning is an underlying process in all the endeavors undertaken by an individual in the workplace (Saks, Haccoun & Belcourt 2010; Salas et al. 2012).

While training and learning are the core mechanisms of professional development, skill acquisition and expertise development in organizations, a goal to strategically leverage training and learning efforts to shorten time to proficiency remains the prime concern of business leaders.

6.3 ISSUES WITH WORKPLACE METHODS

Most of the methods found in the literature are training methods for either classroom settings or simulation settings, and not all are transferable to workplace settings. Most are methods or techniques for addressing certain skill acquisition issues in specific contexts. Another school of thought have recognized the experience as a critical piece of proficiency and accelerating the same. The proficient person uses intuition, which comes out of his/her past experience (Dreyfus & Dreyfus 2005). This experience typically is acquired from real-world assignments and workplace tasks (Eraut 1994, 2004, 2007a, 2007b). Professionals normally learn and accelerate their skill acquisition while handling real assignments, challenging tasks and projects and practicing on their job (Eraut 1994, 2004, 2007a, 2007b). Learning at work is an expectation and a necessity, rather than a good-to-have protocol: 'Competent professionals are busy with everyday tasks. Thus, learning for journeymen mostly takes place by participating in projects' (Jung, Kim & Reigeluth 2016, p. 61). According to Sheckley & Keeton (1999, p. 28):

> Individuals develop proficiency by working in challenging and supportive environments, self-monitoring, engaging in deliberate practice, and solving ill-defined problems. The key becomes how to increase the learner's experience in the shortest amount of time yet ensure the learner ultimately attains domain mastery.

That experience generally comes through on-the-job assignments and tasks, through a training curriculum that is designed to incorporate this experience or using the workplace to deliver the training (Billett (2004). In preliminary findings, Attri & Wu (2015, p. 13) noted that 'rather than waiting for workplace to provide experiences, if designers can leverage day-to-day routine at workplace, systematically design experiences and pack those in a compressed timeframe, the time-to-proficiency could be accelerated.' However, workplace learning is subject to opportunities and may offer only routine situations. Lesgold (2001) cautioned about the lack of opportunities for practice on non-routine problems in the workplace: 'The real world mostly provides opportunities to do the routine. Expertise involving the non-routine is harder to get from everyday work experience because the right situations occur rarely ...' (Lesgold 2001, p. 967). This lack of opportunity to practice rare problems poses issues in accelerating proficiency. Conversely, simply doing the job may not accelerate proficiency unless there is certain deliberate planning associated with it. Hoffman, Andrews, et al. (2010) stated that working on the job is not enough to accelerate proficiency:

> Simply "working at a job" does not promote progression along the proficiency continuum. Unless there is continuous deliberate practice at difficult tasks, the only thing one can do "on the job" is forget and actually experience degradation of skill.

Klein (1998) reasoned that training is just a supplement to gain expertise and cannot be a substitute for real-world experience. Accepting that premise, Grossman, Spencer & Salas (2014, p. 315) also appealed that 'beyond the formal training settings, another important area in need of future research is how training opportunities can be extended into the work environment'. Thus, an important aspect of methods for accelerating proficiency appears to be extending training to the workplace. Hoffman et al. (2009) suggested that the training design should be such that '[t]he modes and means of training should engage real work practice–the job challenges, context, and duties to the greatest extent possible'. However, Lesgold (2001) cautioned about the lack of opportunities for practice on non-routine problems in the workplace:

> The real world mostly provides opportunities to do the routine. Expertise involving the non-routine is harder to get from everyday work experience because the right situations occur rarely and often are handled by established experts when they do occur, not by students (Lesgold 2001, p. 967).

Cross (2013) highlighted the importance of workplace learning:

> Companies that focus on shortening the time employees [sic] complete formal, explicit learning are looking at a drop in the bucket. Improving the effectiveness of experiential, tacit learning adds much more to the bottom line. [http://www.internetalliance.com]

While mainstream academic/scholarly literature showed insufficient coverage of workplace methods to accelerate proficiency in organizational settings, the practitioner literature, such as magazines, institutional reports, consulting blogs, industry awards and corporate white papers, continue to uphold several success stories and methods to reduce time to proficiency in business settings (Emily & Krob 2014; PetroSkills 2009; PTC 2005; Rosenbaum 2014; WalkMe 2013). Thus, it is understood that several organizations have pioneered certain methods and strategies to shorten time to proficiency, which unfortunately, has not seen its way into mainstream scholarly publications.

The literature appears to provide approaches favoring, as well as approaches rejecting workplace training methods. Thus, Wray & Wallace (2011, p. 243) appealed, 'A more realistic aspiration is to create conditions encouraging all individuals to proceed at the maximum pace possible for them, both in training settings and workplace practice.'

6.4 APPLYING LESSONS FROM THIS BOOK

The comprehensive study conducted by the author (Attri 2018) with 85 project leaders suggested that some of the methods suggested by the studies reviewed in this book indeed can work toward accelerating proficiency with appropriate orchestration of several resources, structure, systems and processes.

Clearly define proficiency in the target job role

A clear definition of proficiency leads to goal-orientation while aligning all the other elements of the organization towards that goal. One agreed definition of proficiency across the stakeholders might align the resources and efforts in the same direction. One should avoid the tendency to define performance in terms of activities and tasks. Rather, proficiency should be defined and measured in terms of business outcomes as much as possible. Historical data can be used to identify the current (baseline) time to proficiency of individuals in a given job role.

Conduct a detailed cognitive task analysis

A comprehensive task analysis can map inputs and factors that contribute positively or negatively towards developing and hampering proficiency. One can start from tasks and develop a large list of knowledge, skills, etc., required to do those tasks. Such an analysis allows identifying the skills required to perform a job so that curriculum can be designed correctly to target only those skills.

Conduct relevant cognitive work analysis

Performing a comprehensive work analysis may be helpful in certain cases. This allows outlining several things — what the performance measures of proficiency were, what tasks a performer was required to do to achieve those targeted outcomes, what s/he needed to know to do those tasks, what skills s/he needed to apply to complete the task and what behaviors s/he needed to exhibit to do the tasks effectively so as to attain desired outcomes, and what levers performers could maneuver to achieve outcomes effectively and efficiently. Such a work analysis may include workflow, procedure, responsibilities and ergonomics, whereas worker analysis includes knowledge, skills, capacity, motivation and expectations.

Modeling experts

By the law of averages, there are usually some exemplary performers in each team and in each job role who may be demonstrating shorter time to proficiency compared to the rest of the workforce. Such exemplary performers should be identified, and we should thoroughly understand, identify and benchmark the success behaviors of such exemplary performers. CTA techniques can come here handy to model experts how they perform certain tasks or achieve outcomes.

Time-compressed simulations and scenarios

Not all experiences can be attained on-the-job, however, because then one has to wait for those events to occur to experience them. For those low-frequency experiences, it is recommended that suitable time-compressed experiences are designed either through leveraging the job environment or otherwise. The key to such experiences is to expose the performers to a rapid cycle of multiple purposeful failures. Also, more failures one experiences at a rapid rate, more is the rate of acquisition of proficiency. Such failures can be easily recreated by using actual real-world cases that have occurred before, gamifying the scenarios with realistic challenges and deliberate errors the way it would unfold in real-life, and using representative simulation as close as possible to the real environment. Simulations could be on-the-equipment, simulators, operational mock-ups or role-playing the scenarios.

Emphasis on conceptual skills

Proficiency is about reproducible performance irrespective of the situation or problems. There will always be a limitation on the number of case scenarios or errors that can be incorporated into a given compressed training experience. To ensure consistent performance in novel situations, emphasis can be on developing employees with strong foundational conceptual skills, problem-solving and critical thinking skills that are principle-based, generic and transferable across unknown situations.

Sequencing learning and experiences

The normal tendency is to include every known aspect into some training program topic-by-topic hoping to position employees towards achieving proficiency. Instead, one needs to focus on designing a map of activities, opportunities, learning experiences and milestones representing the complete path of how one would reach desired proficiency in the desired time frame. It is recommended to classify the activities, tasks or events first, using data analytics, and then focus on the most frequent, critical and important activities that directly lead to producing outcomes. The key to shorter time to proficiency is sequencing these activities and seeing that the tasks are sequenced efficiently and organized in such a way to take the waste and non-value-added time out from the path by using process improvement philosophy.

Using workplace activities

The performers still need to acquire skills, knowledge and behaviors to perform the tasks required to do the job and actually acquire the experience to produce the real business outcomes that are the hallmark of attaining proficiency. As opposed to requiring massive content-heavy, instructor-centric training programs, practitioners are advised to assign performers onto authentic job activities and ongoing practical experiences in which they acquire the experience to produce the desired outcomes. Proficiency is greatly accelerated during the actual job due to pressures, consequences, stakes and contextual immersion of the job-specific tasks. It is strongly recommended that the focus should be placed on doing the job rather than learning. Learning will result from this doing. Consider how to provide experiences to the performers in the context of the overall job, particularly by interleaving training and work assignments and keeping the focus on the complete path to proficiency, i.e., leading to actually producing the outcomes defined as proficiency for the job rather than just some tasks in isolation.

Cognitive apprenticeship/structured workplace mentoring

Making someone learn to produce outcomes is a much faster approach than having him/her learn those things in the classroom. One needs to make sure a structured mentoring and coaching process exists in which new people can learn and practice under a qualified mentor. It is suggested that managers select the right mentors and then equip them with the right skills to mentor other people. Structured mentoring needs an outcome-driven focus so that people are put on the path that allows them to become proficient in producing desired outcomes.

Leveraging informal and social learning

Social learning is a powerful multiplier that fostered proficiency in a given job role at an accelerated rate. Employees work in teams and produced business results in the team. It is recommended that organizations pay attention to purpose-driven social connectivity where people work with each other, develop learning networks and develop connections with high performers. In addition, while informal learning is considered to be happening on-the-fly, ad hoc and unmanageable, leaders can create a structure for informal learning experiences so that those avenues are used to drive proficiency. For example, a person assigned to shadow a senior employee in the field should be given a checklist of things to observe, ask or perform, thus putting a structure around informal learning that happens on-the-job. Since managers manage the teams, they play an important role in fostering and developing such purpose-driven social connectivity.

Implementing technology-based support systems

Using the right performance support, such as knowledge repository, just-in-time information, checklists and technology-based tools, could eliminate the need for any formal training if orchestrated correctly. Implement a range of performance systems and leveraging institutionalized systems that improve how quickly people get support at the point of need.

6.5 FINAL WORDS

This booked reviewed several methods and approaches and also pointed out promises or potential each of it holds. Many of these methods can be used in training or workplace context in different shape and form.

However, to successfully accelerate proficiency, there needs to be a guiding theory, model or framework. The methods discussed in this book, while being innovative, do not necessarily evolve or converge into a consistent model. As such, there is no comprehensive theory or model to guide the acceleration of proficiency in the workplace. There is no compelling framework or model that could be applied to explain the concept of accelerated proficiency reasonably well in workplace settings or one which could actually be implemented to successfully accelerate workforce proficiency.

Hoffman, Feltovich, et al. (2010, p. 180) reiterated prevailing literature gaps on accelerated proficiency and appealed for researchers to address research questions such as:

> 1) How to quicken the training process while maintaining its effectiveness (*Rapidised Training*), ... 3) How to train and train quickly to higher levels of proficiency (*Accelerated Proficiency*). [emphasis in original]

Despite four decades of studies, organizations need methods and framework to 'Facilitating the achievement of high proficiency, especially accelerating across the apprentice to senior journeyman levels' (Hoffman et al. 2014, p. 173). In particular, two areas need further investigations:

(1) understanding the true nature of proficiency and accelerated proficiency in the workplace, including the understanding of market forces that drive such need in organizations; and

(2) workplace methods that are used to accelerate proficiency of the workforce in organizational settings and the pay-offs it may bring.

In an attempt to develop the first most framework and model of accelerated proficiency, Attri (2018, 2019b) conducted a large-scale study with 85 project leaders. It was found that proficiency can be accelerated only when the right conditions in the form of a total eco-system are ensured. It must be noted that attaining the consistent performance within the complexity of the workplace require not only skills, knowledge, and behaviors, but also requires several other support mechanisms and interventions. The focus should be on enabling learners on how to produce the business outcomes that mattered most to the organizations (Clark 2008; Swanson & Holton III 2001). The study by Attri (2018, 2019) showed that six business-level practices are required to work in close conjunction with each other to shorten time to proficiency of employees in various contexts. It was reported that organizations orchestrated these six business practices as an input-output-feedback system to reduce time to proficiency of the workforce. A conceptual model (*Accelerated Proficiency Model* or *S2Pro© model of speed to proficiency*) was developed representing interactions among six business-level practices/processes as a closed-loop system to explain the concept and process of accelerated proficiency in the workplace. These six business practices, as shown in figure 3, are:

(1) Defining business-driven proficiency measures in terms of expected business outcomes from a job role;
(2) Developing a proficiency reference map of all the inputs, conditions and roadblocks that determine or influence how required business outcomes are being produced in a job role;
(3) Sequencing an efficient proficiency path of activities and experiences ordered to produce the desired business outcomes in the shortest possible time;
(4) Manufacturing accelerated contextual experiences by leveraging on-the-job opportunities or training interventions in a compressed timeframe;

(5) Promoting an active emotional immersion through engagements, consequences, stakes, feedback and proficiency assessments; and

(6) Setting up a proficiency eco-system, providing timely support to performers while doing the job such as enabling job environment, highly involved manager, structured mentoring from experts, purposeful social connectivity with peers, leveraging subject matter experts and on-demand performance support systems.

It was seen that across the board, these practices were implemented through twenty-four strategies proven successful in various workplace contexts. The strategies employed were much beyond the boundaries of conventional training interventions, while the job itself acted as the primary mechanism to accelerate proficiency. A two-level hierarchical framework (*6/24 framework of strategies*) was also constructed in the form of a checklist consisting of six practices and twenty-four strategies for practitioners.

Overall findings and final model of accelerated proficiency are being published in the author's forthcoming books. The readers are highly encouraged to seek that book in order to learn proven methods, strategies and practices to shorten time to proficiency.

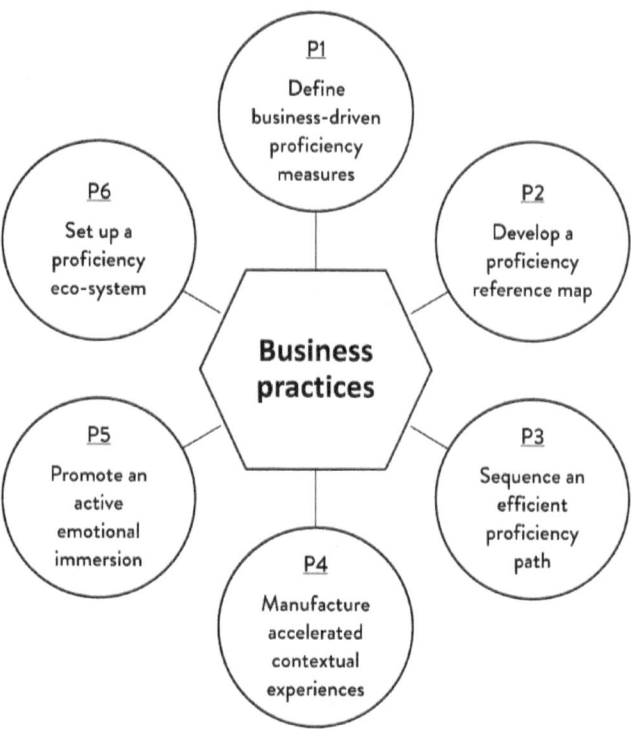

Figure 3: Six business practices to shorten time to proficiency in S2Pro© Model of Accelerated Proficiency

⊕ ⊕ ⊕ ⊕ ⊕

RELEVANT PUBLICATIONS

1. Attri, RK 2019a, *Models of Skill Acquisition and Expertise Development: A Quick Reference of Summaries*, Speed To Proficiency Research, Singapore.
2. Attri, RK 2019b, *Speed to Proficiency in Organizations: A Research Report on Model, Practices and Strategies to Shorten Time to Proficiency*, Speed To Proficiency Research, Singapore, viewed 26 Jun 2019 <https://www.amazon.com/gp/product/B07NYS81HQ/>.
3. Attri, RK 2019c, *Designing Training to Shorten Time to Proficiency: Online, Classroom and On-the-job Learning Strategies from Research*, Speed To Proficiency Research, Singapore, viewed 26 Jun 2019 <https://www.amazon.com/gp/product/9811406324>.Attri, RK 2018, *Accelerate your leadership development in training domain: Proven success strategies for new training & learning managers*, Speed To Proficiency Research: S2Pro©, Singapore, available at <https://www.amazon.com/dp/9811400660/>.
4. Attri, RK 2018, 'Modelling accelerated proficiency in organisations: practices and strategies to shorten time-to-proficiency of the workforce', PhD thesis, Southern Cross University, Lismore, Australia.
5. Attri, RK 2014, 'Rethinking professional skill development in competitive corporate world: accelerating time-to-expertise of employees at workplace', in J Latzo (ed.), *Proceedings of Conference on Education and Human Development in Asia*, Hiroshima, 2-4 March, PRESDA Foundation, Kitanagova, pp. 1–11, http://dx.doi.org/10.13140/RG.2.1.5125.7043.
6. Attri, RK & Wu, WS 2018, 'Model of accelerated proficiency in the workplace: six core concepts to shorten time-to-proficiency of employees', *Asia Pacific Journal of Advanced Business and Social Studies*, vol. 4, no. 1, http://dx.doi.org/10.25275/apjabssv4i1bus1.
7. Attri, RK & Wu, WS 2017, 'Model of accelerated proficiency in the workplace: six core concepts to shorten time-to-proficiency of employees', *First Australia and New Zealand Conference on Advanced Research*

(ANZCAR), Melbourne, Asia Pacific Institute of Advanced Research, Melbourne, 17-18 June, pp. 1-10, viewed 24 July 2017, <http://apiar.org.au/wp-content/uploads/2017/07/1_ANZCAR_2017_BRR713_Bus-1-10.pdf>.

8. Attri, RK & Wu, WS 2016a, 'Classroom-based instructional strategies to accelerate proficiency of employees in complex job skills', paper presented to the Asian American Conference for Education, Singapore, 15-16 January, viewed 24 June 2017, <https://www.researchgate.net/publication/303803099>.

9. Attri, RK & Wu, WS 2016b, 'E-learning strategies at workplace that support speed to proficiency in complex skills', in M Rozhan and N Zainuddin (eds.), *Proceedings of the 11th International Conference on E-Learning: ICEl2016*, Kuala Lampur, 2-3 June, Academic Conference and Publishing, Reading, pp. 176–184, viewed 24 June 2017, <https://www.researchgate.net/publication/303802961>.

10. Attri, R. K. & Wu, W. S. (2015). E-Learning Strategies to Accelerate Time-to-Proficiency in Acquiring Complex Skills: Preliminary Findings. Paper presented at *E-learning Forum Asia Conference*, Jun 2015. Singapore: SIM University, available at <https://www.researchgate.net/publication/282647943>.

11. Attri, RK & Wu, W 2015, 'Conceptual model of workplace training and learning strategies to shorten time-to-proficiency in complex skills: preliminary findings', paper presented to the *9th International Conference on Researching in Work and Learning (RWL)*, Singapore, 9-11 December, viewed 24 June 2017, <https://www.researchgate.net/publication/286623558>.

REFERENCES

Abston, KA & Rhodes, MK 2013, 'Experiential learning in accelerated human resource management courses', *Developments in Business Simulation and Experiential Learning*, vol. 40, pp. 68–73, viewed 24 June 2017, <https://absel-ojs-ttu.tdl.org/absel/index.php/absel/article/download/19/17>.

Accenture 2013, *Top-Five Focus Areas for Improving Sales Effectiveness Initiatives*, viewed 24 June 2017, <https://www.accenture.com/t20150523T052741__w__/us-en/_acnmedia/Accenture/Conversion-Assets/DotCom/Documents/Global/PDF/Strategy_4/Accenture-Top-Five-Improvements-Sales-Effectiveness.pdf>.

Ackerman, PL 1988, 'Determinants of individual differences during skill acquisition: cognitive abilities and information processing', *Journal of Experimental Psychology General*, vol. 117, no. 3, pp. 288–318, http://dx.doi.org/10.1037/0096-3445.117.3.288.

———— 1992, 'Predicting individual differences in complex skill acquisition: dynamics of ability determinants', *Journal of Applied Psychology*, vol. 77, no. 5, pp. 598–614, http://dx.doi.org/10.1037/0021-9010.77.5.598.

———— 2014, 'Nonsense, common sense, and science of expert performance: talent and individual differences', *Intelligence*, vol. 45, no. 4, pp. 6–17, http://dx.doi.org/10.1016/j.intell.2013.04.009.

Adams, BD, Karthaus, C & Rehak, LA 2011, *Accelerated Learning and Retention: Literature Review and Workshop Review*, Report No. CR 2011-105, Defernse R\&D Canada, Toronto, Canada, viewed 24 June 2017, <http://www.dtic.mil/cgi-bin/GetTRDoc?AD=ADA574124>.

Afiouni, F 2007, 'Human resource management and knowledge management: a road map toward improving organizational performance', *Journal of American Academy of Business*, vol. 11, no. 2, pp. 124–130, viewed 24 June 2017, <http://www.academia.edu/download/31163403/HR_and_KM.pdf>.

Albrecht, SL, Bakker, AB, Gruman, JA, Macey, WH & Saks, AM 2015, 'Employee engagement, human resource management practices and competitive advantage: an integrated approach', *Journal of Organizational Effectiveness: People and Performance*, vol. 2, no. 1, pp. 7–35, http://dx.doi.org/10.1108/JOEPP-08-2014-0042.

Alexander, PA 2003a, 'Can we get there from here?', *Educational Researcher*, vol. 32, no. 8, pp. 3–4, http://dx.doi.org/10.3102/0013189X032008003.

_____ 2003b, 'The development of expertise: the journey from acclimation to proficiency', *Educational Researcher*, vol. 32, no. 8, pp. 10–14, http://dx.doi.org/10.3102/0013189X032008010.

Allen, TD & Eby, LT 2007, *The Blackwell handbook of mentoring: a multiple perspectives approach*, Blackwell, Victoria, Australia, viewed 24 June 2017, <https://www.researchgate.net/publication/295660090>.

Allen, TD, Eby, LT, Poteet, ML, Lentz, E & Lima, L 2004, 'Career benefits associated with mentoring for protégés: a meta-analysis.', *Journal of Applied Psychology*, vol. 89, no. 1, p. 127, http://dx.doi.org/10.1037/0021-9010.89.1.127.

Alorica 2017, 'Think quick: increase speed to proficiency',, viewed 24 June 2018, <https://www.alorica.com/wp-content/uploads/2017/09/ebook_SpeedtoProficiency.pdf>.

Anderson, JR 1981, *Acquisition of Cognitive Skill*, Report No. 81-1, Carnegie-Mellon University, Pittsburgh, viewed 24 June 2017, <http://www.dtic.mil/cgi-bin/GetTRDoc?AD=ADA103283>.

_____ 1982, 'Acquisition of cognitive skill', *Psychological Review*, vol. 89, no. 4, pp. 369–406, http://dx.doi.org/10.1037/0033-295X.89.4.369.

_____ 2000, *Learning and memory*, John Wiley, New York.

Andresen, L, Boud, D & Cohen, R 2000, Experience-based learning, in G Foley (ed.), *Understanding Adult Education and Training*, Allen and Unwin, Crows Nest, pp. 225–239, viewed 24 June 2018, <http://complexworld.pbworks.com/f/Experience-based%20learning.pdf>.

Andrews, DH & Fitzgerald, P 2010, 'Accelerating learning of competence and increasing long-term learning retention', paper presented to the ITEC Conference, London, viewed 24 June 2017, <http://www.dtic.mil/cgi-bin/GetTRDoc?AD=ADA522088>.

Anitha, J 2014, 'Determinants of employee engagement and their impact on employee performance', *International Journal of Productivity and Performance Management*, vol. 63, no. 3, pp. 308–323, http://dx.doi.org/10.1108/IJPPM-01-2013-0008.

Arnold, DE, Ringquist, JJ & Prien, K 1998, 'Reducing the cycle time of training and development in organizations', *Journal of Cycle Time Research*, pp. 21–30, viewed

ACCELERATED PROFICIENCY FOR ACCELERATED TIMES

24 June 2017,
<http://citeseerx.ist.psu.edu/viewdoc/download?doi=10.1.1.508.9235&rep=rep1&type=pdf>.

Arnold, V & Collier, P 2013, 'Incase: simulating experience to accelerate expertise development by knowledge workers', *Intelligent Systems in Accounting and Financial Management*, vol. 20, no. 1, pp. 1–21, http://dx.doi.org/10.1002/isaf.

Ashoori, M & Burns, C 2013, 'Team cognitive work analysis: structure and control tasks', *Journal of Cognitive Engineering and Decision Making*, vol. 7, no. 2, pp. 123–140, http://dx.doi.org/10.1177/1555343412445577.

Attri, RK 2014, 'Rethinking professional skill development in competitive corporate world: accelerating time-to-expertise of employees at workplace', in J Latzo (ed.), *Proceedings of Conference on Education and Human Development in Asia*, Hiroshima, PRESDA Foundation, Kitanagova, pp. 1–11, http://dx.doi.org/10.13140/RG.2.1.5125.7043.

―――― 2018, 'Modelling accelerated proficiency in organisations: practices and strategies to shorten time-to-proficiency of the workforce', PhD thesis, Southern Cross University, Lismore, Australia.

―――― 2019, *Speed to Proficiency in Organizations: A Research Report on Model, Practices and Strategies to Shorten Time to Proficiency*, Speed To Proficiency Research, Singapore, viewed
<https://www.amazon.com/gp/product/B07NYS81HQ/>.

Attri, RK & Wu, W 2015, 'Conceptual model of workplace training and learning strategies to shorten time-to-proficiency in complex skills: preliminary findings', *9th International Conference on Researching in Work and Learning (RWL) Conference*, Singapore, Institute for Adult Learning, Singapore, viewed 24 June 2017, <http://www.rwl2015.com/papers/Paper100.pdf>.

Avolio, BJ, Waldman, DA & McDaniel, MA 1990, 'Age and work performance in nonmanagerial jobs: the effects of experience and occupational type', *Academy of Management Journal*, vol. 33, no. 2, pp. 407–422, http://dx.doi.org/10.2307/256331.

Bachlechner, D, Kohlegger, M, Maier, R & Waldhart, G 2010, 'Taking pressure off knowledge workers with the help of situational applications-improving time-to-proficiency in knowledge work settings', in A Fred & J Filipe (eds.), *Proceedings of the International Conference on Knowledge Management and Information Sharing (KMIS-2010)*, Valencia, SCITEPRESS Science and Technology, Setúbal, Portugal, pp. 378–381, http://dx.doi.org/10.5220/0003118203780381.

Backus, C, Keegan, K, Gluck, C & Gulick, LMV 2010, 'Accelerating leadership development via immersive learning and cognitive apprenticeship', *International Journal of Training and Development*, vol. 14, no. 2, pp. 144–148, http://dx.doi.org/10.1111/j.1468-2419.2010.00347.x.

Baker, T 2016, *The end of the job description: shifting from a job-focus to a performance-focus*, Palgrave MacMillan, London, http://dx.doi.org/10.1007/978-1-137-58146-4.

_____ 2017, Management myth# 7—a technically superior workforce is a pathway to a high-performing business, in *Performance Management for Agile Organizations*, Springer, Cham, pp. 159–173, http://dx.doi.org/10.1007/978-3-319-40153-9_10.

Bartel, AP 2000, 'Measuring the employer's return on investments in training: evidence from the literature', *Industrial Relations: A Journal of Economy and Society*, vol. 39, no. 3, pp. 502–524, viewed 24 June 2017, <http://sis.ashesi.edu.gh/courseware/cms/file.php/57/aaLIBRARY/Training_Development/Bartel_-_employer_s_ROI_from_training_devpt.pdf>.

Bates, R, Holton III, EF & Seyler, D 1997, 'Factors affecting transfer of training in an industrial setting', in R Torraco (ed.), *Proceedings of the Academy of Human Resource Development Annual Conference*, Atlanta, Academy of Human Resource Development, Baton Rouge, pp. 347–354.

Baxter, HC 2013, 'Transferring specialized knowledge: accelerating the expertise development cycle', *Interservice Industry Training, Simulation and Education Conference (I/ITSEC)*, Orlando, National Training and Simulation Association (NTSA), Arlington, pp. 1–9, viewed 24 June 2017, <http://ac.els-cdn.com/S2351978915003248/1-s2.0-S2351978915003248-main.pdf?_tid=cf441efa-6fc0-11e7-a40c-00000aab0f6b&acdnat=1500826136_7386e303f14ad6be5a585b89a0f44c22>.

_____ 2015, 'Specialized knowledge transfer: accelerating the expertise development cycle', *Procedia Manufacturing*, vol. 3, pp. 1465–1472, http://dx.doi.org/10.1016/j.promfg.2015.07.323.

Beattie, RS 2006, 'Line managers and workplace learning: learning from the voluntary sector', *Human Resource Development International*, vol. 9, no. 1, pp. 99–119, http://dx.doi.org/10.1080/13678860600563366.

Bedarkar, M & Pandita, D 2014, 'A study on the drivers of employee engagement impacting employee performance', *Procedia-Social and Behavioral Sciences*, vol. 133, pp. 106–115, http://dx.doi.org/10.1016/j.sbspro.2014.04.174.

Bedi, A 2003, 'Student profiling: the dreyfus model revisited', *Education for Primary Care*, vol. 14, no. 3, pp. 360–363, viewed 24 June 2017, <https://www.researchgate.net/publication/293527610>.

Behneman, A, Berka, C, Stevens, R, Villa, B, Tan, V, Galloway, T, Johnson, R & Raphael, G 2012, 'Neurotechnology to accelerate learning: during marksmanship training', *IEEE Pulse*, vol. 3, no. 1, pp. 60–63, http://dx.doi.org/10.1109/MPUL.2011.2175641.

Belling, PK, Sada, J & Ward, P 2015, 'Assessing hitting skill in baseball using simulated and representative tasks', *12th International Naturalistic Decision Making Conference*, McLean, The MITRE Corp, McLean, viewed 24 June 2017, <http://eprints.hud.ac.uk/24799/1/WardAssessing.pdf>.

Belling, PK, Suss, J & Ward, P 2014a, 'Advancing theory and application of cognitive research in sport: using representative tasks to explain and predict skilled anticipation, decision-making, and option-generation behavior', *Psychology of Sport and Exercise*, vol. 16, no. 1, pp. 45–59, http://dx.doi.org/10.1016/j.psychsport.2014.08.001.

———— 2014b, 'Cognitive processes supporting recognition in complex and dynamic tasks', *Proceedings of the Human Factors and Ergonomics Society 58th Annual Meeting*, Chicago, Sage, Thousand Oaks, pp. 290–294, http://dx.doi.org/10.1177/1541931214581060.

Benner, P 1984, *From novice to expert: excellence and power in clinical nursing practice*, Addison-Wesley, Palo Alto, http://dx.doi.org/10.1097/00000446-198412000-00025.

———— 2001, *From novice to expert: excellence and power in clinical nursing practice*, Commemorative. edn, Prentice Hall, London, http://dx.doi.org/10.1097/00000446-198412000-00025.

———— 2004, 'Using the dreyfus model of skill acquisition to describe and interpret skill acquisition and clinical judgment in nursing practice and education', *Bulletin of Science, Technology and Society*, vol. 24, no. 3, pp. 188–199, http://dx.doi.org/10.1177/0270467604265061.

Berka, C, Pojmani, N, Coyne, JJ, Cole, A & Denise, C 2010, Neurogaming: merging cognitive neuroscience \& virtual simulation in an interactive training platform, in T Marek, W Kawwowski & V Rice (eds.), *Advances in Understanding Human Performance: Neuroergonomics, Human Factors Design, and Special Populations*, CRC Press, Boca Raton, pp. 313–324, http://dx.doi.org/10.1201/ebk1439835012-33.

Bersin, J 2013, 'The end of a job as we know it',, viewed 24 June 2017, <http://blog.bersin.com/the-end-of-a-job-as-we-know-it/>.

Beta, G & Lidaka, A 2015, 'The aspect of proficiency in the theoretical overview of pedagogical practice of nurses', *Procedia-Social and Behavioral Sciences*, vol. 174, no. 2015, pp. 1957–1965, http://dx.doi.org/10.1016/j.sbspro.2015.01.861.

Billett, S 1996, 'Towards a model of workplace learning: the learning curriculum', *Studies in Continuing Education*, vol. 18, no. 1, pp. 43–58, http://dx.doi.org/10.1080/0158037960180103.

_____ 2002, 'Workplace pedagogic practices: a workplace study', *Lifelong Learning in Europe, VII*, vol. 2, pp. 94–103, viewed 24 June 2017, <http://citeseerx.ist.psu.edu/viewdoc/download?doi=10.1.1.603.7844&rep=rep1&type=pdf>.

_____ 2003, 'Workplace mentors: demands and benefits', *Journal of Workplace Learning*, vol. 15, no. 3, pp. 105–113, http://dx.doi.org/10.1102/13665620310468441.

_____ 2004, 'Workplace participatory practices: conceptualising workplaces as learning environments', *Journal of Workplace Learning*, vol. 16, no. 6, pp. 312–324, http://dx.doi.org/10.1108/13665620410550295.

_____ 2006, 'Constituting the workplace curriculum', *Journal of Curriculum Studies*, vol. 38, no. 1, pp. 31–48, http://dx.doi.org/10.1080/00220270500153781.

_____ 2010, The practices of learning through occupations, in S Billet (ed.), *Learning through practice*, Springer, Dordrecht, pp. 59–81, http://dx.doi.org/10.1007/978-90-481-3939-2_4.

_____ 2014, 'Mimesis: learning through everyday activities and interactions at work', *Human Resource Development Review*, vol. 13, no. 4, pp. 462–482, http://dx.doi.org/10.1177/1534484314548275.

Billett, S & Choy, S 2013, 'Learning through work: emerging perspectives and new challenges', *Journal of Workplace Learning*, vol. 25, no. 4, pp. 264–276, http://dx.doi.org/10.1108/13665621311316447.

Binder, C 2017, 'What it really means to be accomplishment based', *Performance Improvement*, vol. 56, no. 4, pp. 20–25, http://dx.doi.org/10.1002/pfi.21702.

Birnbaum, MS, Kornell, N, Bjork, EL & Bjork, R a 2013, 'Why interleaving enhances inductive learning: the roles of discrimination and retrieval', *Memory \& Cognition*, vol. 41, no. 3, pp. 392–402, http://dx.doi.org/10.3758/s13421-012-0272-7.

Bish, AJ & Kabanoff, B 2014, 'Star performers: task and contextual performance are components, but are they enough?', *Asia Pacific Journal of Human Resources*, vol. 52, no. 1, pp. 110–127, viewed 24 January 2017, <https://eprints.qut.edu.au/63849/3/Manuscript_Revised_changes_accepted_12-06-13_APHR.pdf>.

Bjork, RA 2009, Structuring the conditions of training to achieve elite performance: reflections on elite training programs and related themes in chapters 10-13, in K Ericsson (ed.), *Development of professional expertise: Toward measurement of expert performance and design of optimal learning environments*, Cambridge University Press, New York, pp. 312–329, http://dx.doi.org/10.1017/cbo9780511609817.017.

_____ 2013, Desirable difficulties perspective on learning, in H Pashler (ed.), *Encyclopedia of the mind*, SAGE, Thousand Oaks, pp. 243–245, http://dx.doi.org/10.4135/9781452257044.n88.

Boling, EC & Beatty, J 2010, 'Cognitive apprenticeship in computer-mediated feedback: creating a classroom environment to increase feedback and learning', *Journal of Educational Computing Research*, vol. 43, no. 1, pp. 47–65, http://dx.doi.org/10.2190/EC.43.1.d.

Bologa, R & Lupu, AR 2007, 'Accelerating the sharing of knowledge in order to speed up the process of enlarging software development teams - a practical example', in C Long, V Mladenov & Z Bojkovic (eds.), *Proceedings of the 6th WSEAS International Conference on Artificial Intelligence, Knowledge Engineering and Data Bases*, Corfu Island, Greece, World Scientific and Engineering Academy and Society, pp. 90–95, viewed 24 June 2017, <http://www.wseas.us/e-library/conferences/2007corfu/papers/540-225.pdf>.

Borders, J, Polander, N, Klein, G & Wright, C 2015, 'Shadowbox™: flexible training to impart the expert mindset" T Ahram, W Karwowski & D Schmorrow (eds.), *6th International Conference on Applied Human Factors and Ergonomics (AHFE 2015) and the Affiliated Conferences*, vol. 3, pp. 1574–1579, http://dx.doi.org/10.1016/j.promfg.2015.07.444.

Borman, WC & Motowidlo, SJ 1993, Expanding the criterion domain to include elements of contextual performance, in E Schmitt & W Borman (ed.), *Personnel Selection in Organizations*, Jossey-Bass, San Franscisco, pp. 71–98.

Borman, WC & Motowidlo, SJ (eds.) 1997, *Organizational citizenship behavior and contextual performance: a special issue of human performance*, Kindle. edn, Psychology Press, London, http://dx.doi.org/10.4324/9781315799254.

Borton, G 2007, 'Managing productivity: measuring the business impact of employee proficiency and the employee job life cycle', *Management Services*, no. 7, pp. 28–33, viewed 24 June 2017, <http://www.ims-productivity.com/user/custom/journal/2007/autumn/IMSaut07pg28-33.pdf>.

Van den Bosch, K, Helsdingen, AS & de Beer, MM 2004, 'Training critical thinking for tactical command', *The RTO Human Factors and Medicine Panel (HFM) Symposium: Advanced Technologies for Military Training*, Genoa, Research and Technology Organization (RTO) of North Atlantic Treaty Organization (NATO), Cedex, France, pp. 1–10, http://dx.doi.org/10.14339/RTO-MP-HFM-101.

Boshuizen, HPA 2003, Expertise development: how to bridge the gap between school and work, in P Boshuizen (ed.), *Expertise development: The transition between school and work*, Open University Netherlands, Heerlene, pp. 7–31, viewed 24 June 2017, <https://pure.tue.nl/ws/files/1776251/572181.pdf>.

Bott, JP, Svyantek, DJ, Goodman, SA & Bernal, DS 2003, 'Expanding the performance domain: who says nice guys finish last?', *The International Journal of Organizational*

Analysis, vol. 11, no. 2, pp. 137–152, http://dx.doi.org/10.1108/eb028967.

Boulton, L & Cole, J 2016, 'Adaptive flexibility: examining the role of expertise in the decision making of authorized firearms officers during armed confrontation', *Journal of Cognitive Engineering and Decision Making*, vol. 10, no. 3, pp. 291–308, http://dx.doi.org/10.1177/1555343416646684.

Bransford, JD, Brown, AL, Cocking, RR, Donovan, MS & Pellegrino, JW (eds.) 2004, *How people learn brain, mind, experience, and school*, Expanded.edn., National Academy Press, Washington, D.C., http://dx.doi.org/10.17226/6160.

Bransford, JD & Schwartz, DL 2009, It takes expertise to make expertise: some thoughts about why and how and reflections on the themes in chapters 15-18, in *Development of professional expertise: Toward measurement of expert performance and design of optimal learning environments*, Cambridge University Press, New York, pp. 432–448, http://dx.doi.org/10.1017/cbo9780511609817.023.

Brooker, R & Butler, J 1997, 'The learning context within the workplace: as perceived by apprentices and their workplace trainers', *Journal of Vocational Education and Training*, vol. 49, no. 4, pp. 487–510, http://dx.doi.org/10.1080/13636829700200028.

Bruck, B 2007, 'Speed to proficiency: strategically using training to drive profitability',, viewed 24 June 2017, <http://www.q2learning.com/docs/WP-S2P.pdf>.

_____ 2015, *Speed to proficiency: creating a sustainable competitive advantage*, CreateSpace, USA, viewed 24 June 2017, <http://www.readings.com.au/products/20647385/speed-to-proficiency-creating-a-sustainable-competitive-advantage>.

Brudnicki, D, Ethier, B & Chastain, K 2007, *Application of Advanced Technologies for Training the next Generation of Air Traffic Controllers*, Case No. 06-0978, MITRE Corporation, Bedford, viewed 24 June 2017, <https://www.mitre.org/sites/default/files/pdf/06_0978.pdf>.

Brundage, D, Lekowski, R, Carr, J, Finn, A, Hicks, P, Mehta, N & Perham, B 2014, 'Utilizing high signal simulation training to educate and ensure competency in high risk/low frequency skills in a pediatric pacu', *Journal of PeriAnesthesia Nursing*, vol. 29, no. 5, p. e27, http://dx.doi.org/10.1016/j.jopan.2014.08.092.

Brydges, R, Nair, P, Ma, I, Shanks, D & Hatala, R 2012, 'Directed self-regulated learning versus instructor-regulated learning in simulation training', *Medical Education*, vol. 46, no. 7, pp. 648–656, http://dx.doi.org/10.1111/j.1365-2923.2012.04268.x.

Buch, N & Wolff, T 2000, 'Classroom teaching through inquiry', *Journal of Professional Issues in Engineering Education and Practice*, vol. 126, no. 3, pp. 105–109, http://dx.doi.org/10.1061/(ASCE)1052-3928(2000)126:3(105).

Bunderson, CV 2011, 'Developing a domain theory defining and exemplifying a learning theory of progressive attainments.', *Journal of Applied Measurement*, vol. 12, no. 1, pp. 25–48, viewed 24 June 2017, <https://www.ncbi.nlm.nih.gov/pubmed/21512212>.

Butler, WM 2012, 'The impact of simulation-based learning in aircraft design on aerospace student preparedness for engineering practice: a mixed methods approach', PhD thesis, Virginia Polytechnic Institute and State University, Blacksburg, viewed <https://theses.lib.vt.edu/theses/available/etd-05082012-183206/unrestricted/Butler_WM_D_2012.pdf>.

Cagiltay, K 2006, 'Scaffolding strategies in electronic performance support systems: types and challenges', *Innovations in Education and Teaching International*, vol. 43, no. 1, pp. 93–103, http://dx.doi.org/10.1080/14703290500467673.

Campbell, J, Tirapelle, L, Yates, K, Clark, R, Inaba, K, Green, D, Plurad, D, Lam, L, Tang, A, Cestero, R & others 2011, 'The effectiveness of a cognitive task analysis informed curriculum to increase self-efficacy and improve performance for an open cricothyrotomy', *Journal of Surgical Education*, vol. 68, no. 5, pp. 403–407, http://dx.doi.org/10.1016/j.jsurg.2011.05.007.

Campbell, JP 1990, Modeling the performance prediction problem in industrial and organizational psychology, in M Dunnette & L Hough (eds.), *Handbook of industrial and organizational psychology, Vol. 1*, Consulting Psychologists Press, Palo Alto, pp. 687–732.

——— 1999, The definition and measurement of performance in the new age, in D Ilgen & E Pulakos (eds.), *The changing nature of performance: Implications for staffing, motivation, and development*, Jossey-Bass, San Francisco, pp. 399–429.

Campbell, JP, McCloy, RA, Oppler, SH & Sager, CE 1993, A theory of performance, in N Schmitt & W Borman (eds.), *Personnel selection in organizations*, Jossey-Bass, San Francisco, pp. 35–70.

Campbell, JP, McHenry, JJ & Wise, LL 1990, 'Modeling job performance in a population of jobs', *Personnel Psychology*, vol. 43, no. 2, pp. 313–575, http://dx.doi.org/10.1111/j.1744-6570.1990.tb01561.x.

Campbell, JP & Wiernik, BM 2015, 'The modeling and assessment of work performance', *Annual Review of Organizational Psychology and Organizational Behavior*, vol. 2, no. 1, pp. 47–74, http://dx.doi.org/10.1146/annurev-orgpsych-032414-111427.

Cannon-Bowers, JA & Bowers, CA 2008, Synthetic learning environments, in J Spector, M Merrill, J van Merrienboer & M Driscoll (eds.), *Handbook of research on educational communications and technology*, Lawrence Erlbaum Associates, New York, pp. 317–327, viewed 24 June 2017,

<http://www.aect.org/edtech/edition3/ER5849x_C027.fm.pdf>.

Cannon-Bowers, JA, Bowers, CA, Stout, R, Ricci, K & Hildabrand, A 2013, 'Using cognitive task analysis to develop simulation-based training for medical tasks.', *Military Medicine*, vol. 178, no. 10 Suppl, pp. 15–21, http://dx.doi.org/10.7205/MILMED-D-13-00211.

Carpenter, MA, Monaco, SJ, O'Mara, FE & Teachout, MS 1989, *Time to Job Proficiency: A Preliminary Investigation of the Effects of Aptitude and Experience on Productive Capacity*, Report No. AFHRK-TP-88-17, Air Force Systems Command, Brooks Air Force Base, San Antonio, viewed 24 June 2017, <https://www.researchgate.net/publication/235105070>.

Carter, TJ & Adkins, B 2017, Situated learning, communities of practice, and the social construction of knowledge, in V Wang (ed.), *Theory and Practice of Adult and Higher Education*, IAP, Charlotte, pp. 113–137.

Cash, JR, Behrmann, MB, Stadt, RW & Daniels, HM 1996, 'Effectiveness of cognitive apprenticeship instructional methods in college automotive technology classrooms', *Journal of Industrial Teacher's Education*, vol. 34, no. 2, pp. 29–49, viewed 24 June 2017, <http://scholar.lib.vt.edu/ejournals/JITE/v34n2/Cash.html>.

Ten Cate, O 2013, 'Nuts and bolts of entrustable professional activities', *Journal of Graduate Medical Education*, vol. 5, no. 1, pp. 157–158, http://dx.doi.org/10.4300/JGME-D-12-00380.1.

Chalofsky, N & Lincoln, C 1983, *Up the HRD ladder*, Addision-Wesley, Reading.

Chan, S 2013, 'Learning through apprenticeship: belonging to a workplace, becoming and being', *Vocations and Learning*, vol. 6, no. 3, pp. 367–383, http://dx.doi.org/10.1007/s12186-013-9100-x.

Charness, N & Tuffiash, M 2008, 'The role of expertise research and human factors in capturing, explaining, and producing superior performance', *Human Factors*, vol. 50, no. 3, pp. 427–32, http://dx.doi.org/10.1518/001872008X312206.

Chase, WG & Simon, HA 1973, 'Perception in chess', *Cognitive Psychology*, vol. 4, no. 1, pp. 55–81, http://dx.doi.org/10.1016/0010-0285(73)90004-2.

Chevalier, R 2003, 'Updating the behavior engineering model', *Performance Improvement*, vol. 42, no. 5, pp. 8–14, http://dx.doi.org/10.1002/pfi.4930420504.

―――― 2004, 'The link between learning and performance', *Performance Improvement*, vol. 43, no. 4, pp. 40–44, http://dx.doi.org/10.1002/pfi.4140430410.

Chi, MT 2006, Two approaches to the study of experts' characteristics, in R Hoffman, N Charness & P Feltovich (eds.), *The Cambridge Handbook of Expertise and Expert Performance*, Cambridge University Press, New York, pp. 21–30, http://dx.doi.org/10.1017/CBO9780511816796.002.

Chi, MT, Glaser, R & Farr, M (eds.) 1988, *The nature of expertise*, Lawrence Erlbaum, Hillsdale, http://dx.doi.org/10.4324/9781315799681.

Chi, MT, Glaser, R & Rees, E 1981, *Expertise in Problem Solving*, Technical Report No. 5, University of Pitsburg, Pittsburg, viewed 24 June 2017, <http://www.dtic.mil/cgi-bin/GetTRDoc?AD=ADA100138>.

_____ 1982, Expertise in problem solving, in R Sternberg (ed.), *Advances in psychology of human intelligence, Vol.1*, Erlbaum, Hillsdale, pp. 7–75, viewed 24 June 2017, <http://www.dtic.mil/cgi-bin/GetTRDoc?AD=ADA100138>.

Cho, Y & Yoon, SW 2010, 'Theory development and convergence of human resource fields: implications for human performance technology', *Performance Improvement Quarterly*, vol. 23, no. 3, pp. 39–56, http://dx.doi.org/10.1002/piq.20089.

Clark, RC 2008, *Building expertise: cognitive methods for training and performance improvement*, 3rd edn, Pfeiffer, San Francisco, http://dx.doi.org/10.1002/pfi.4140390213.

_____ 2009, 'Accelerating expertise with scenario-based learning', *T+D*, pp. 84–85, viewed 24 June 2017, <http://www.clarktraining.com/content/articles/ScenarioBasedLearning.pdf>.

Clark, RC & Mayer, RE 2013, *Scenario-based e-learning: evidence-based guidelines for online workforce learning*, Pfeiffer, San Francisco.

Clark, RE 2006, How much and what type of guidance is optimal for learning from instruction?, in S Tobias & T Duffy (eds.), *Constructivist Theory Applied to Instruction: Success or Failure*, Routledge, New York, pp. 158–183, viewed 24 June 2017, <http://www.anitacrawley.net/Articles/2009How%20much%20and%20what%20type%20of%20guidance%20is%20optimal%20for%20learning%20from%20instruction.pdf>.

_____ 2010, 'Recent neuroscience and cognitive research findings on cyber learning', paper presented to the AECT Annual Convention, Anaheim, viewed 24 June 2017, <http://www.cogtech.usc.edu/publications/clark_aect_oct_28_2010.pdf>.

_____ 2014, Cognitive task analysis for expert-based instruction in healthcare, in J Spector, M Merrill, J Elen & M Bishop (eds.), *Handbook of research on educational communications and technology*, Springer, New York, pp. 541–551, http://dx.doi.org/10.1007/978-1-4614-3185-5_42.

Clark, RE & Estes, F 1996, 'Cognitive task analysis for training', *International Journal of Education Research*, vol. 25, no. 5, pp. 403–417, http://dx.doi.org/10.1016/S0883-

0355(97)81235-9.

Clark, RE & Feldon, DF 2008, 'Gel, adaptable expertise and transfer of training',, viewed 24 June 2017, <http://www.cogtech.usc.edu/publications/gel_and_adaptability.pdf>.

Clark, RE, Feldon, DF, van Merriënboer, JJG, Yates, KA & Early, S 2008, Cognitive task analysis, in J Spector, M Merrill, J van Merriënboer & M Driscoll (eds.), *Handbook of research on educational communications and technology*, Lawrence Erlbaum, Mahwah, pp. 577–593, viewed 24 June 2017, <http://www.learnlab.org/research/wiki/images/0/0b/Clarketal2007-CTAchapter.pdf>.

Clark, RE, Feldon, DF & Yates, K 2011, 'Using cognitive task analysis to capture expert knowledge and skills for research and instructional design', *Annual Meeting of the American Educational Research Association*, New Orleans, American Educational Research Association, Washington, DC.

Clark, RE, Pugh, CM, Yates, K & Sullivan, M 2008, *The Use of Cognitive Task Analysis and Simulators for after Action Review of Medical Events in Iraq*, Center for Cognitive Technology, University of California, Los Angeles, viewed 24 June 2017, <http://www.dtic.mil/cgi-bin/GetTRDoc?AD=ADA466686>.

Clark, RE, Pugh, CM, Yates, KA, Inaba, K, Green, DJ & Sullivan, ME 2011, 'The use of cognitive task analysis to improve instructional descriptions of procedures.', *The Journal of Surgical Research*, vol. 173, no. 1, pp. e37–42, http://dx.doi.org/10.1016/j.jss.2011.09.003.

Clark, RE, Yates, K, Early, S, Moulton, K, Silber, K & Foshay, R 2010, An analysis of the failure of electronic media and discovery-based learning: evidence for the performance benefits of guided training methods, in K Silber & R Foshay (eds.), *Handbook of Training and Improving Workplace Performance, Volume I: Instructional Design and Training Delivery*, Pfeiffer, San Francisco, pp. 263–287, http://dx.doi.org/10.1002/9780470592663.ch8.

Clavarelli, A, Platte, WL & Powers, JJ 2009, 'Teaching and assessing complex skills in simulation with application to rifle marksmanship training', *Interservice Industry Training, Simulation and Education Conference (I/ITSEC)*, Orlando, National Training and Simulation Association (NTSA), Arlington, viewed 24 June 2017, <http://www.dtic.mil/cgi-bin/GetTRDoc?AD=ADA535072>.

Collins, A 1990, Cognitive apprenticeship and instructional technology, in B Jones & L Idol (eds.), *Dimensions of Thinking and Cognitive Instruction*, Lawrence Erlbaum, Hillsdale, pp. 121–138, viewed 24 June 2017, <http://files.eric.ed.gov/fulltext/ED331465.pdf>.

_____ 2002, Cogntive apprentice, in R Sawyer (ed.), *Cambridge Handbook of the Learning Sciences*, Cambridge University Press, New York, pp. 47–60, viewed 24 June 2017,

ACCELERATED PROFICIENCY FOR ACCELERATED TIMES

<http://ocw.metu.edu.tr/pluginfile.php/9108/mod_resource/content/1/Collins.pdf>.

Collins, A, Brown, JS & Newman, SE 1987, *Cognitive Apprenticeship: Teaching the Craft of Reading, Writing and Mathematics*, Technical Report No. 403, Center for the study of reading. University of Illinois, Urbana, Champaign, viewed 24 June 2017, <http://files.eric.ed.gov/fulltext/ED284181.pdf>.

Collins, A, Brown, JS & Newman, SE 1988, 'Cognitive apprenticeship: teaching the craft of reading, writing and mathematics', *Thinking: The Journal of Philosophy for Children*, vol. 8, no. 1, pp. 2–10, http://dx.doi.org/10.5840/thinking19888129.

_____ 1989, Cognitive apprenticeship: teaching the craft of reading, writing and mathematics, in L Resnick (ed.), *Knowing, learning, and instruction: Essays in honor of Robert Glaser*, Lawrence Erlbaum, Hillsdale, pp. 453–494, viewed 24 June 2017, <http://www.dtic.mil/cgi-bin/GetTRDoc?AD=ADA178530>.

Collins, H 2011, 'Three dimensions of expertise', *Phenomenology and the Cognitive Sciences*, vol. 12, no. 2, pp. 253–273, http://dx.doi.org/10.1007/s11097-011-9203-5.

Collins, H, Evans, R, Ribeiro, R & Hall, M 2006, 'Experiments with interactional expertise', *Studies in History and Philosophy of Science Part A*, vol. 37, no. 4, pp. 656–674, http://dx.doi.org/10.1016/j.shpsa.2006.09.005.

Cornford, I & Athanasou, J 1995, 'Developing expertise through training', *Industrial and Commercial Training*, vol. 27, no. 2, pp. 10–18, http://dx.doi.org/10.1108/00197859510082861.

Coulson, RL, Feltovich, PJ & Spiro, RJ 1997, 'Cognitive flexibility in medicine: an application to the recognition and understanding of hypertension', *Advances in Health Sciences Education*, vol. 2, no. 2, pp. 141–161, http://dx.doi.org/10.1023/A:1009780229455.

Crichton, M & Flin, R 2004, 'Identifying and training non-technical skills of nuclear emergency response teams', *Annals of Nuclear Energy*, vol. 31, no. 12, pp. 1317–1330, http://dx.doi.org/doi:10.1016/j.anucene.2004.03.011.

Cross, J 2013, 'How to shorten time-to-proficiency',, viewed <http://www.internettime.com/2013/02/how-to-shorten-time-to-proficiency/>.

Crossman, RM, Crossman, DC & Lovely, JE 2009, 'Human performance improvement', *Professional Safety*, vol. 54, no. 6, p. 63.

Cseh, M, Watkins, KE & Marsick, V 1999, 'Re-conceptualizing marsick and watkins' model of informal and incidental learning in the workplace', in K Kuchinke (ed.), *Proceedings of the Academy of Human Resource Development Conference*, Washington D.C., Academy of Human Resource Development, Baton Rouge, pp. 349–356.

Cummings, TG & Worley, CG 2001, *Essentials of organization development and change*, 7th edn, South-Western College Publishing, Cincinnati.

Dall'Alba, G & Sandberg, J 2006, 'Unveiling professional development: a critical review of stage models', *Review of Educational Research*, vol. 76, no. 3, pp. 383–412, http://dx.doi.org/10.3102/00346543076003383.

Darzi, M, Hosseini, M, Liaei, AA, Manesh, ZM & Asghari, H 2011, 'Accelerating growth in high tech mses through tacit knowledge sharing using case-based recommender systems',, viewed 24 June 2017, <http://old.ictrc.ir/Documents/Document0/Accelerating%20growth1.pdf>.

Day, J 2002, 'What is an expert?', *Radiography*, vol. 8, no. 2, pp. 63–70, viewed <http://www.blumehaiti.org/uploads/2/8/3/8/2838360/fallcelloday.pdf>.

Dean, PJ 2016, 'Tom gilbert: engineering performance with or without training', *Performance Improvement*, vol. 55, no. 2, pp. 30–38, http://dx.doi.org/10.1002/pfi.21556.

Deloitte 2017, *2017 Deloitte Global Human Capital Trends*, Deloitte University Press, viewed 24 June 2017, <https://www2.deloitte.com/us/en/pages/human-capital/articles/introduction-human-capital-trends.html>.

Demir, S, Abou-Jaoude, E & Kumral, M 2017, 'Cognitive work analysis to comprehend operations and organizations in the mining industry', *International Journal of Mining Science and Technology*, vol. 27, no. 4, pp. 605–609, http://dx.doi.org/10.1016/j.ijmst.2017.05.008.

Dennen, VP 2004, Cognitive apprenticeship in educational practice research on scaffolding, modeling, mentoring, and coaching as instructional strategies, in D Jonassen (ed.), *Handbook of research for educational communications and technology*, Lawrence Erlbaum, Mahwah, pp. 813–828, viewed 24 June 2017, <http://www.aect.org/edtech/ed1/31.pdf>.

Dennen, VP & Burner, KJ 2008, The cognitive apprenticeship model in educational practice, in J Spector, M Merrill, J van Merriënboer & M Driscoll (eds.), *Handbook of research on educational communications and technology*, Lawrence Erlbaum, Mahwah, pp. 425–439, viewed 24 June 2017, <http://www.aect.org/edtech/edition3/ER5849x_C034.fm.pdf>.

Deterline, WA & Rosenberg, MJ 1992, *Performance technology: Success stories*, International Society for Performance Improvement, Washington, D.C.

Deutscher, C, Gürtler, O, Prinz, J & Weimar, D 2017, 'The payoff to consistency in performance', *Economic Inquiry*, vol. 55, no. 2, pp. 1091–1103, http://dx.doi.org/10.1111/ecin.12415.

DiBello, L 1996, 'Providing multiple 'ways in' to expertise for learners with different backgrounds when it works and what it suggests about adult cognitive development', *Journal of Experimental & Theoretical Artificial Intelligence*, vol. 8, no. 3-4, pp. 229–257, http://dx.doi.org/10.1080/095281396147311.

DiBello, L & Missildine, W 2008, 'Information technologies and intuitive expertise: a method for implementing complex organizational change among new yorkcity transit authority's bus maintainers', *Cognition, Technology and Work*, vol. 12, no. 1, pp. 61–75, http://dx.doi.org/10.1007/s10111-008-0126-z.

―――― 2011, 'Future of immersive instructional design for the global knowledge economy: a case study of an ibm project management training in virtual worlds', *International Journal of Web Based Learning and Teaching Technologies*, vol. 6, no. 3, pp. 14–34, http://dx.doi.org/10.4018/jwltt,2011070102.

DiBello, L, Missildine, W & Struttman, M 2009, 'Intuitive expertise and empowerment: the long-term impact of simulation training on changing accountabilities in a biotech firm', *Mind, Culture, and Activity*, vol. 16, no. 1, pp. 11–31, http://dx.doi.org/10.1080/10749030802363863.

Doane, SM, Alderton, DL, Sohn, YW & Pellegrino, JW 1996, 'Acquisition and transfer of skilled performance: are visual discrimination skills stimulus specific?', *Journal of Experimental Psychology: Human Perception and Performance*, vol. 22, no. 5, pp. 1218–1248, http://dx.doi.org/10.1037/0096-1523.22.5.1218.

Dodd, L 2009, 'Valuing investment in military command and control training: can we use intermediate decision-based measures?', *14th International Command and Control Research and Technology Symposium*, Washington, D.C., Department of Defense, USA, viewed 24 June 2017, <https://pdfs.semanticscholar.org/681c/d5102b91fbbee2c7c8f586c432f781ca2b9a.pdf>.

Donderi, D, Niall, KK, Fish, K & Goldstein, B 2012, 'Above-real-time training (artt) improves transfer to a simulated flight control task', *Human Factors: The Journal of the Human Factors and Ergonomics Society*, vol. 54, no. 3, pp. 469–479, http://dx.doi.org/10.1177/0018720812439711.

Dörfler, V, Baracskai, Z & Velencei, J 2009, 'Knowledge levels: 3-d model of the levels of expertise', paper presented to the 68th Annual Meeting of the Academy of Management, Chicago, viewed 24 June 2017, <http://www.viktordorfler.com/webdav/papers/KnowledgeLevels.pdf>.

Dreyfus, HL & Dreyfus, SE 1986, *Mind over machine: the power of human intuition and expertise in the era of the computer*, The Free Press, New York, http://dx.doi.org/10.1109/mex.1987.4307079.

―――― 2004, 'The ethical implications of the five-stage skill-acquisition model', *Bulletin of Science, Technology and Society*, vol. 24, no. 3, pp. 251–264, http://dx.doi.org/10.1177/0270467604265023.

_____ 2005, 'Peripheral vision: expertise in real world contexts', *Organization Studies*, vol. 26, no. 5, pp. 779–792, http://dx.doi.org/10.1177/0170840605053102.

Dreyfus, SE 2004, 'The five-stage model of adult skill acquisition', *Bulletin of Science, Technology \& Society*, vol. 24, no. 3, pp. 177–181, http://dx.doi.org/10.1177/0270467604264992.

Dror, IE 2011, The paradox of human expertise: why experts get it wrong, in N Kapur (ed.), *The paradoxical brain*, Cambridge University Press, New York, pp. 177–188, http://dx.doi.org/10.1017/cbo9780511978098.011.

Druckman, D & Bjork, RA 1991, *In the mind's eye: enhancing human performance*, D Druckman & R Bjork (eds.), National Academies Press, Washington, D.C., http://dx.doi.org/10.17226/1580.

Dumas, A & Hanchane, S 2010, 'How does job-training increase firm performance? the case of morocco', *International Journal of Manpower*, vol. 31, no. 5, pp. 585–602, http://dx.doi.org/10.1108/01437721011066371.

Emily, D & Krob, A 2014, 'Partnering to improve time to competency and proficiency', *Talent Development*, vol. 68, no. 8, pp. 40–44.

Enos, MD, Kehrhahn, MT & Bell, A 2003, 'Informal learning and the transfer of learning: how managers develop proficiency', *Human Resource Development Quarterly*, vol. 14, no. 4, pp. 369–387, http://dx.doi.org/10.1002/hrdq.1074.

Eraut, M 1994, *Developing professional knowledge and competence*, Routledge, London, http://dx.doi.org/10.4324/9780203486016.

_____ 2004, 'Informal learning in the workplace', *Studies in Continuing Education*, vol. 26, no. 2, pp. 247–273, http://dx.doi.org/10.1080/158037042000225245.

_____ 2007a, 'Learning from other people in the workplace', *Oxford Review of Education*, vol. 33, no. 4, pp. 403–422, http://dx.doi.org/10.1080/03054980701425706.

_____ 2007b, How professionals learn through work, in N Jackson (ed.), *Learning to be Professional through a Higher Education E-BOOK*, Surrey Centre of Excellence in Professional Training and Education, University of Surrey, Surrey, pp. 1–28, viewed 24 June 2017, <http://learningtobeprofessional.pbworks.com/f/CHAPTER+A2+MICHAEL+ERAUT.pdf>.

Ericsson, K, Charness, N, Feltovich, P & Hoffman, R (eds.) 2006, *Cambridge handbook of expertise and expert performance*, Cambridge University Press, New York.

ACCELERATED PROFICIENCY FOR ACCELERATED TIMES

Ericsson, KA 2000, 'Expertise in interpreting: an expert-performance perspective', *Interpreting*, vol. 5, no. 2, pp. 187–220, http://dx.doi.org/10.1075/intp.5.2.08eri.

_____ 2002, Attaining excellence through deliberate practice: insights from the study of expert performance, in M Ferrari (ed.), *The Pursuit of Excellence Through Education*, Lawrence Erlbaum, Mahwah, pp. 21–55, http://dx.doi.org/10.1002/9780470690048.ch1.

_____ 2003, Development of elite performance and deliberate practice: an update from the perspective of the expert performance approach, in J Starkes & K Ericsson (eds.), *Expert Performance in Sports: Advances in Research on Sport Expertise*, Human Kinetics, Champaign, pp. 53–83, viewed 24 June 2017, <http://drjj5hc4fteph.cloudfront.net/Articles/2003%20Starkes%20and%20Ericsson%20Chapt%203.pdf>.

_____ 2004, 'Deliberate practice and the acquisition and maintenance of expert performance in medicine and related domains', *Academic Medicine*, vol. 79, no. 10, pp. 70–81, http://dx.doi.org/10.1097/00001888-200410001-00022.

_____ 2006, The influence of experience and deliberate practice on the development of superior expert performance, in K Ericsson, N Charness, P Feltovich & R Hoffman (eds.), *The Cambridge Handbook of Expertise and Expert Performance*, Cambridge University Press, New York, pp. 683–704, http://dx.doi.org/10.1017/CBO9780511816796.038.

_____ 2007, 'Deliberate practice and the modifiability of body and mind: toward a science of the structure and acquisition of expert and elite performance', *International Journal of Sport Psychology*, vol. 38, no. 1, pp. 4–34, viewed 24 June 2017, <http://drjj5hc4fteph.cloudfront.net/Articles/2007 IJSP - Ericsson - Deliberate Practice target art.pdf>.

_____ 2008, 'Deliberate practice and acquisition of expert performance: a general overview', *Academic Emergency Medicine*, vol. 15, no. 11, pp. 988–94, http://dx.doi.org/10.1111/j.1553-2712.2008.00227.x.

_____ 2009a, *Enhancing the development of professional performance: implications from the study of deliberate practice*, EDITED (ed.), Cambridge University Press, New York.

_____ 2009b, 'Discovering deliberate practice activities that overcome plateaus and limits on improvement of performance', in A Willamon, S Pretty & R Buck (eds.), *International Symposium on Performance Science*, Auckland, European Association of Conservatoires (AEC), Utrecht, The Netherlands, pp. 11–21, viewed 24 June 2017, <http://www.performancescience.org/ISPS2009/Proceedings/Rows/003Ericsson.pdf>

_____ 2009c, Enhancing the development of professional performance: implications from the study of deliberate practice, in K Ericsson (ed.), *Development of professional expertise: Toward measurement of expert performance and design of optimal learning environments*, Cambridge University Press, New York, pp. 405–431, http://dx.doi.org/10.1017/cbo9780511609817.022.

———— 2014, 'Why expert performance is special and cannot be extrapolated from studies of performance in the general population: a response to criticisms', *Intelligence*, vol. 45, no. 4, pp. 81–103, http://dx.doi.org/10.1016/j.intell.2013.12.001.

Ericsson, KA & Charness, N 1994, 'Expert performance: its structure and acquisition', *American Psychologist*, vol. 49, no. 8, pp. 725–747, http://dx.doi.org/10.1037/0003-066X.49.8.725.

Ericsson, KA, Krampe, RTR, Tesch-romer, C, Ashworth, C, Carey, G, Grassia, J, Hastie, R, Heizmann, S, Kellogg, R, Levin, R, Lewis, C, Oliver, W, Poison, P, Rehder, R, Schlesinger, K, Schneider, V & Tesch-Römer, C 1993, 'The role of deliberate practice in the acquisition of expert performance', *Psychological Review*, vol. 100, no. 3, pp. 363–406, http://dx.doi.org/10.1037/0033-295X.100.3.363.

Ericsson, KA, Prietula, MJ & Cokely, ET 2007, 'The making of an expert', *Harvard Business Review*, vol. 85, no. 7-8, pp. 114–121, 193, viewed 24 June 2017, <https://www.researchgate.net/publication/6196703>.

Ericsson, KA & Ward, P 2007, 'Capturing the naturally occurring superior performance of experts in the laboratory: toward a science of expert and exceptional performance', *Current Directions in Psychological Science*, vol. 16, no. 6, pp. 346–350, http://dx.doi.org/10.1111/j.1467-8721.2007.00533.x.

Evers, AT, Kreijns, K, Heijden, BIJMVD & Gerrichhauzen, JTG 2011, 'An organizational and task perspective model aimed at enhancing teachers' professional development and occupational expertise', *Human Resource Development Review*, vol. 10, no. 2, pp. 151–179, http://dx.doi.org/10.1177/1534484310397852.

Fadde, P & Sullivan, P 2013, 'Using interactive video to develop preservice teachers' classroom awareness', *Contemporary Issues in Technology and Teacher Education*, vol. 13, no. 2, pp. 156–174, viewed 24 October 2018, <http://www.citejournal.org/volume-13/issue-2-13/general/using-interactive-video-to-develop-preservice-teachers-classroom-awareness/>.

Fadde, PJ 2007, 'Instructional design for advanced learners: training recognition skills to hasten expertise', *Educational Technology Research and Development*, vol. 57, no. 3, pp. 359–376, http://dx.doi.org/10.1007/s11423-007-9046-5.

———— 2009a, Training complex psychomotor performance skills: a part-task approach, in K Silber & W Foshay (eds.), *Handbook of Training and Improving Workplace Performance, Volume I: Instructional Design and Training Delivery*, Pfeiffer, San Francisco, pp. 468–507, http://dx.doi.org/10.1002/9780470587089.ch14.

_____ 2009b, 'Training of expertise and expert performance', *Technology, Instructional, Cognition and Learning*, vol. 7, no. 2, pp. 77–81, viewed 24 June 2017, <http://web.coehs.siu.edu/Units/CI/Faculty/PFadde/Research/xbtintro.pdf>.

_____ 2009c, 'Expertise-based training: getting more learners over the bar in less time', *Technology, Instructional, Cognition and Learning*, vol. 7, no. 2, pp. 171–197, viewed 24 June 2017, <http://web.coehs.siu.edu/units/ci/faculty/pfadde/Research/xbttraining.pdf>.

_____ 2010, 'Look'ma, no hands: part-task training of perceptual-cognitive skills to accelerate psychomotor expertise', *The Interservice Industry Training, Simulation and Education Conference (I/ITSEC)*, Orlando, National Training and Simulation Association (NTSA), Arlington, pp. 1–10, viewed 24 June 2017, <http://ntsa.metapress.com/index/A4018183135VJ842.pdf>.

_____ 2012, 'What's wrong with this picture? video-annotation with expert-model feedback as a method of accelerating novices' situation awareness', *The Interservice Industry Training, Simulation and Education Conference (I/ITSEC)*, London, National Training and Simulation Association (NTSA), Arlington, viewed 24 June 2017, <http://www.peterfadde.com/Research/iitsec12.pdf>.

_____ 2013, 'Accelerating the acquisition of intuitive decision-making through expertise-based training (xbt)', *The Interservice Industry Training, Simulation and Education Conference (I/ITSEC)*, Orlando, National Training and Simulation Association (NTSA), Arlington, pp. 1–11, viewed 24 June 2017, <http://peterfadde.com/Research/iitsec13.pdf>.

_____ 2016, 'Instructional design for accelerated macrocognitive expertise in the baseball workplace', *Frontiers in Psychology*, vol. 7, no. 292, pp. 1–16, http://dx.doi.org/10.3389/fpsyg.2016.00292.

Fadde, PJ & Klein, G 2010, 'Deliberate performance: accelerating expertise in natural settings', *Performance Improvement*, vol. 49, no. 9, pp. 5–14, http://dx.doi.org/10.1002/pfi.

_____ 2012, 'Accelerating expertise using action learning activities', *Cognitive Technology*, vol. 17, no. 1, pp. 11–18, viewed 24 June 2017, <http://peterfadde.com/Research/cognitivetechnology12.pdf>.

Faneuff, RS, and Stone, BM, Curry, GL & Hageman, DC 1990, *Extending the Time to Proficiency Model for Simultaneous Application to Multiple Jobs*, Report No. AFHRL-TP-90-42, Air Force Systems Command Brooks Air Force Base, San Antonio, viewed 24 June 2017, <http://www.dtic.mil/docs/citations/ADA224759>.

Farnsworth, V, Kleanthous, I & Wenger-Trayner, E 2016, 'Communities of practice as a social theory of learning: a conversation with etienne wenger', *British Journal of Educational Studies*, vol. 64, no. 2, pp. 139–160, http://dx.doi.org/10.1080/00071005.2015.1133799.

Farrington-Darby, T & Wilson, JR 2006, 'The nature of expertise: a review', *Applied Ergonomics*, vol. 37, no. 1, pp. 17–32, http://dx.doi.org/10.1016/j.apergo.2005.09.001.

Feldon, DF 2006, 'The implications of research on expertise for curriculum and pedagogy', *Educational Psychology Review*, vol. 19, no. 2, pp. 91–110, http://dx.doi.org/10.1007/s10648-006-9009-0.

Feltovich, PJ, Spiro, RJ & Coulson, RL 1997, Issues of expert flexibility in contexts characterized by complexity and change, in P Feltovich, K Ford & R Hoffman (eds.), *Expertise in context: Human and machine*, MIT Press, Cambridge, pp. 125–146, viewed 24 June 2017, <http://www.academia.edu/download/29334639/Issues_of_Expert_Flexibility.pdf>.

Fiorella, L, Vogel-Walcutt, JJ & Fiore, S 2012, 'Differential impact of two types of metacognitive prompting provided during simulation-based training', *Computers in Human Behavior*, vol. 28, no. 2, pp. 696–702, http://dx.doi.org/10.1016/j.chb.2011.11.017.

Fitts, P & Posner, M 1967, *Learning and skilled performance in human performance*, Brock-Cole, Belmont.

Fitts, PM 1964, Perceptual-motor skill learning, in A Melton (ed.), *Categories of human learning*, Academic Press, New York, pp. 243–285, viewed 24 June 2017, <http://www.sciencedirect.com/science/article/pii/B9781483231457500169>.

Fletcher, J 2010, *Phase 1 Iwar Test Results*, IDA Document No. D-4047, Institute for Defense Analyses, Alexandria, Virginia, viewed 24 June 2017, <http://www.dtic.mil/dtic/tr/fulltext/u2/a518737.pdf>.

Fred, CL 2002, *Breakaway: deliver value to your customers-fast!*, Jossey-Bass, San Francisco, viewed 24 June 2017, <http://www.wiley.com/WileyCDA/WileyTitle/productCd-0787961647.html>.

Furterer, SL (ed.) 2009, *Lean Six Sigma in service: applications and case studies*, CRC Press, Boca Raton.

Gagne, RM & Briggs, LJ 1974, *Principles of instructional design.*, Holt, Rinehart \& Winston.

Gal, E, Meishar-tal, H, Non, RB, Ben-Basat, A & Paikin, L 2017, 'Applying tablet-based performance support application for technicians' training at the israeli air force: a case study', *Performance Improvement Quarterly*, vol. 30, no. 2, pp. 121–136, http://dx.doi.org/10.1002/piq.21243.

Gannan, T 2002, 'Train them less; support them more- the case for integrating online learning with business process guidance', in E McKay (ed.), *E-Learning Conference on Design and Development 2002: International Best Practice to Enhance Corporate Performance*, Melboune, RMIT Publishing, Melbourne, pp. 1–8, viewed 24 June 2017, <http://search.informit.org/documentSummary;dn=747615798730397;res=IELBUS>.

Garrick, J 1998, *Informal learning in the workplace: unmasking human resource development*, Routledge, London, http://dx.doi.org/10.4324/9780203028926.

Ge, X & Hardré, PL 2010, 'Self-processes and learning environment as influences in the development of expertise in instructional design', *Learning Environments Research*, vol. 13, no. 1, pp. 23–41, http://dx.doi.org/10.1007/s10984-009-9064-9.

Geissler, N, Hoffmeier, A, Kotzsch, S, Trapp, S, Riemenschneider, N & Korb, W 2012, Cognitive task analysis-a relevant method for the development of simulation training in surgery, in D de Waard, N Merat, A Jamson, Y Barnard & O Carsten (eds.), *Human Factors of Systems and Technology*, Shaker Publishing, Maastricht, The Netherlands, pp. 307–315, http://dx.doi.org/10.7205/MILMED-D-13-00211.

Gilbert, TF 1978, 'Human competence—engineering worthy performance', *Performance Improvement*, vol. 17, no. 9, pp. 19–27, http://dx.doi.org/10.1002/pfi.4180170915.

———— 2013, *Human competence: engineering worthy performance*, Tribute. edn, Pfeiffer, San Francisco.

Gilley, J, England, S & Wesley, A 1998, *Principles of Human Resource Management*, Perseus Publishing.

Glaser, R & Chi, MTH 1988, Overview, in Chi, Michelene TH and Glaser, Robert and Farr, MJ (eds.), *The nature of expertise*, Lawrence Erlbaum, Mahwah, pp. xv–xxviii.

Gobet, F 2013, 'Expertise vs. talent', *Talent Development & Excellence*, vol. 5, no. 1, pp. 75–86, viewed <http://citeseerx.ist.psu.edu/viewdoc/download?doi=10.1.1.297.2267&rep=rep1&type=pdf>.

Gok, A & Law, M 2017, 'Performance improvement in the literature', *Performance Improvement*, vol. 56, no. 1, pp. 14–20, http://dx.doi.org/10.1002/pfi.21675.

Gott, SP 1988, *Rediscovering Learning: Acquiring Expertise in Real World Problem Solving Tasks*, Report No. AL/HR-TR-1997-0009, United States Air Force Armstrong Laboratory, Brooks, viewed 24 June 2017, <http://www.dtic.mil/dtic/tr/fulltext/u2/a345016.pdf>.

Gott, SP, Lesgold, A & Kane, RS 1996, Tutoring for transfer of technical competence, in B Wilson (ed.), *Constructivist learning environments: Case studies in instructional design*, Education Technology, Englewood Cliffs, pp. 33–48, http://dx.doi.org/10.1037/e447862004-001.

Gott, SP & Lesgold, AM 2000, Competence in the workplace: how cognitive performance models and situated instruction can accelerate skill acquisition, in R Glaser (ed.), *Advances in instructional psychology: Educational design and cognitive science, Vol. 5*, Lawrence Erlbaum, Mahwah, pp. 239–327.

Gottfredson, C & Mosher, B 2011, *Innovative performance support: Strategies and practices for learning in the workflow*, McGraw Hill.

Government Publishing Office 2013, *Pilot Certification and Qualification Requirements for Air Carrier*, No. 78, Government Publishing Office, USA.

Graesser, AC, McNamara, DS & VanLehn, K 2005, 'Scaffolding deep comprehension strategies through point&query, autotutor, and istart', *Educational Psychologist*, vol. 40, no. 4, pp. 225–234, viewed 24 June 2017, <http://www.learnlab.org/uploads/mypslc/publications/graesser%20mcnamara%20vanlehn%20ep%2005.pdf>.

Gratton, L 2016, 'Rethinking the manager's role', *MIT Sloan Management Review*, vol. 58, no. 1, p. 8, viewed 24 June 2017, <http://sloanreview.mit.edu/article/technology-and-the-end-of-management/>.

Grenier, RS & Kehrhahn, M 2008, 'Toward an integrated model of expertise redevelopment and its implications for hrd', *Human Resource Development Review*, vol. 7, no. 2, pp. 198–217, http://dx.doi.org/10.1177/1534484308316653.

Griffin, MA, Neal, A & Parker, SK 2007, 'A new model of work role performance: positive behavior in uncertain and interdependent contexts', *Academy of Management Journal*, vol. 50, no. 2, pp. 327–347, http://dx.doi.org/10.5465/amj.2007.24634438.

De Groot, A 1965, *Thought and choice in chess (translated from the dutch original, 1946)*, Reprinted. edn, G Baylor (ed.), Ishi Press, New York.

De Groot, A 1966, Perception and memory versus thought: some old ideas and recent findings, in B Kleinmuntz (ed.), *Problem solving*, John Wiley, New York, pp. 19–50.

Grossman, R, Salas, E, Pavlas, D & Rosen, MA 2013, 'Using instructional features to enhance demonstration-based training in management education', *Academy of Management Learning \& Education*, vol. 12, no. 2, pp. 219–243, http://dx.doi.org/10.5465/amle.2011.0527.

Grossman, R, Spencer, JM & Salas, E 2014, Enhancing naturalistic decision making and accelerating expertise in the workplace: training strategies that work, in S Highhouse, R Dalal & E Salas (eds.), *Judgment and decision making at work*, Routledge, New York, pp. 277–325.

Guckenberger, D, Uliano, KC & Lane, NE 1993, *Teaching High-Performance Skills Using above-Real-Time Training*, Contract Report No. 4528, National Aeronautics and Space Administration, Edwards, viewed 24 June 2017, <http://ntrs.nasa.gov/archive/nasa/casi.ntrs.nasa.gov/19940007155.pdf>.

Guerra-Lopez, I 2016, 'Setting clear direction and ensuring alignment', *Performance Improvement Quarterly*, vol. 28, no. 4, pp. 3–5, http://dx.doi.org/10.1002/piq.21212.

Güss, CD, Devore Edelstein, H, Badibanga, A & Bartow, S 2017, 'Comparing business experts and novices in complex problem solving', *Journal of Intelligence*, vol. 5, no. 2, p. 20, http://dx.doi.org/10.3390/jintelligence5020020.

Hager, P 1998, Understanding workplace learning: general perspectives, in D Boud (ed.), *Current issues and new agendas in workplace learning*, NCVER, Adelaide, Australia, pp. 30–42, viewed 24 June 2017, <https://pdfs.semanticscholar.org/431b/4773d7fc8bb616ba50ea4acddbb0d5a56e43.pdf#page=30>.

Hambrick, DZ, Altmann, EM, Oswald, FL, Meinz, EJ, Gobet, F & Campitelli, G 2014, 'Accounting for expert performance: the devil is in the details', *Intelligence*, vol. 45, no. 4, pp. 112–114, http://dx.doi.org/10.1016/j.intell.2014.01.007.

Hambrick, DZ, Oswald, FL, Altmann, EM, Meinz, EJ, Gobet, F & Campitelli, G 2014, 'Deliberate practice: is that all it takes to become an expert?', *Intelligence*, vol. 45, no. 4, pp. 34–45, http://dx.doi.org/10.1016/j.intell.2013.04.001.

Harris, KR, Eccles, DW, Freeman, C & Ward, P 2017, '"gun! gun! gun!": an exploration of law enforcement officers' decision-making and coping under stress during actual events', *Ergonomics*, vol. 60, no. 8, pp. 1112–1122, http://dx.doi.org/10.1080/00140139.2016.1260165.

Harris-Thompson, D, Malek, D & Wiggins, S 2010, Shortening the expertise curve: identifying and developing cognitive skills in board operators, in D Kaber & G Boy (eds.), *Advances in Cognitive Ergonomics*, Advances in Human Factors and Ergonomics Series, CRC Press, Boca Raton, pp. 774–783, http://dx.doi.org/10.1201/ebk1439834916-c77.

Hartt, D, Quiram, T & Marken, JA 2016, 'Where the performance issues are and are not: a meta-analytic examination', *Performance Improvement Quarterly*, vol. 29, no. 1, pp. 35–49, http://dx.doi.org/10.1002/piq.21213.

Harward, D 2017, 'Controlling variation in time to performance', *Training Industry Magazine*, vol. 10, no. 3, p. 55, viewed 24 June 2017, <http://www.nxtbook.com/nxtbooks/trainingindustry/tiq_20170506/index.php?startid=55#/54>.

Hatano, G & Inagaki, K 1986, Two courses of expertise, in H Stevenson, H Azuma & K Hakuta (eds.), *Children development and education in Japan*, Freeman, New York, pp. 262–272, viewed 24 June 2017, <https://eprints.lib.hokudai.ac.jp/dspace/bitstream/2115/25206/1/6_P27-36.pdf>.

Hausmann, RG, van de Sande, B & VanLehn, K 2008, Shall we explain? augmenting learning from intelligent tutoring systems and peer collaboration, in B Woolf et al. (eds.), *Intelligent tutoring systems*, Springer-Verlag, Berlin Heidelberg, Germany, pp. 636–645, http://dx.doi.org/10.1007/978-3-540-69132-7_66.

Hayes, JR 1989, *The complete problem solver*, 2nd edn, Erlbaum, Hillsdale.

Healy, A 2007, Transfer: specificity and generality, in H Roediger, Y Dudai & S Fitzpatrick (eds.), *Science of memory: Concepts*, Oxford University Press, New York, pp. 271–275.

Van der Heijden, BI 2002, 'Individual career initiatives and their influence upon professional expertise development throughout the career', *International Journal of Training and Development*, vol. 6, no. 2, pp. 54–79, http://dx.doi.org/10.1111/1468-2419.00150.

Hesketh, B & Ivancic, K 2002, Enhancing performance through training, in S Sonnentag (ed.), *Psychological management of individual performance*, John Wiley, San Francisco, pp. 249–265, http://dx.doi.org/10.1002/0470013419.ch12.

Hesketh, B & Neal, A 1999, Technology and performance, in D Ilgen & E Pulakos (eds.), *The changing nature of performance: Implications for staffing, motivation, and development*, Jossey-Bass, San Francisco, pp. 21–55.

Higgins, N 2015, *Gamification: Accelerating Learning*, KBR Kellogg Brown and Root Pty Ltd, Kingston, ACT, Australia.

Hintze, NR 2008, 'First responder problem solving and decision making in today's asymmetrical environment', Naval Postgraduate School, Monterey, viewed 24 June 2017, <http://www.dtic.mil/cgi-bin/GetTRDoc?AD=ADA479926>.

Hoffman, R, Feltovich, PJ, Fiore, S, Klein, G & Moon, B 2008, *Program on Technology Innovation: Accelerating the Achievement of Mission-Critical Expertise: A Research Roadmap*, Report No. 1016710, Electric Power Research Institute (EPRI), Palo Alto, viewed 24 June 2017, <http://perigeantechnologies.com/publications/AcceleratingAchievementofExpertise.pdf>.

Hoffman, RR 1998, How can expertise be defined? implications of research from cognitive psychology, in R Williams, W Faulkner & J Fleck (eds.), *Exploring expertise*, Palgrave Macmillan, Edinburgh, Scotland, pp. 81–100, http://dx.doi.org/10.1007/978-1-349-13693-3_4.

_____ 2012, *Expertise out of context*, Psychology Press.

Hoffman, RR & Andrews, DH 2012, 'Cognition and cognitive technology for research on accelerated learning and developing expertise', *Cognitive Technology*, vol. 17, no. 1, pp. 5–6, viewed 24 June 2017, <http://cmapsinternal.ihmc.us/rid=1LM7CN14D-1335H6-1B3K/CogTech%20for%20Accelerated%20Learning-2013.pdf>.

Hoffman, RR, Andrews, DH & Feltovich, PJ 2012, 'What is 'accelerated learning'?', *Cognitive Technology*, vol. 17, no. 1, pp. 7–10.

Hoffman, RR, Andrews, DH, Fiore, SM, Goldberg, S, Andre, T, Freeman, J, Fletcher, JD & Klein, G 2010, 'Accelerated learning: prospects, issues and applications', *Proceedings of the Human Factors and Ergonomics Society 54th Annual Meeting*, San Francisco, Sage, Thousand Oaks, pp. 399–402, http://dx.doi.org/10.1177/154193121005400427.

Hoffman, RR, Feltovich, PJ, Fiore, SM & Klein, G 2010, *Accelerated Proficiency and Facilitated Retention: Recommendations Based on an Integration of Research and Findings from a Working Meeting*, Report No. AFRL-RH-AZ-TR-2011-0001, Air Force Research Laboratory, Mesa, http://dx.doi.org/10.21236/ada536308.

Hoffman, RR, Feltovich, PJ, Fiore, SM, Klein, G & Ziebell, D 2009, 'Accelerated learning (?)', *IEEE Intelligent Systems*, vol. 24, no. 2, pp. 18–22, http://dx.doi.org/10.1109/MIS.2009.21.

Hoffman, RR & Lintern, G 2006, Eliciting and representing the knowledge of experts, in K Ericsson, N Charness, P Feltovich & R Hoffman (eds.), *Cambridge handbook of expertise and expert performance*, Cambridge University Press, New York, pp. 203–222, http://dx.doi.org/10.1017/CBO9780511816796.012.

Hoffman, RR, Ward, P, Feltovich, PJ, DiBello, L, Fiore, SM & Andrews, DH 2014, *Accelerated Expertise: Training for high proficiency in a complex world*, Expertise: Research and Applications Series, Psychology Press, New York, http://dx.doi.org/10.4324/9780203797327.

Holt, D, Mackay, D & Smith, R 2004, 'Developing professional expertise in the knowledge economy: integrating industry-based learning with the academic curriculum in the field of information technology', *Asia-Pacific Journal of Cooperative Education*, vol. 5, no. 2, pp. 1–11, viewed 24 June 2017, <http://dro.deakin.edu.au/eserv/DU:30002681/holt-developingprofessionalexpertise-2004.pdf>.

Holton, EFI, Bates, RA & Ruona, WE 2000, 'Development of a generalized learning transfer system inventory', *Human Resource Development Quarterly*, vol. 11, no. 4, pp. 333–360, viewed 24 June 2018, <http://www.nakahara-lab.net/temp/jyugyo/holton.pdf>.

Holton III, EF 1999, 'An integrated model of performance domains: bounding the theory and practice', *Performance Improvement Quarterly*, vol. 12, no. 3, pp. 95–118, http://dx.doi.org/10.1111/j.1937-8327.1999.tb00140.x.

Hong, CM, Chen, CM, Chang, MH & Chen, SC 2007, 'Intelligent web-based tutoring system with personalized learning path guidance', in J Spector, D Sampson, T Okamoto, Kinshuk, S Cerri, M Ueno & A Kashihara (eds.), *Seventh IEEE International Conference on Advanced Learning Technologies (ICALT 2007)*, Tokyo, IEEE, Los Alamitos, pp. 512–516, http://dx.doi.org/10.1109/ICALT.2007.167.

Houger, VP 2006, 'Trends of employee performance collaborative effort between managers and employees', *Performance Improvement*, vol. 45, no. 5, pp. 26–31, http://dx.doi.org/10.1002/pfi.2006.4930450508.

Hsieh, TC & Wang, TI 2010, 'A mining-based approach on discovering courses pattern for constructing suitable learning path', *Expert Systems with Applications*, vol. 37, no. 6, pp. 4156–4167, http://dx.doi.org/10.1016/j.eswa.2009.11.007.

Hug, T 2015, Microlearning and mobile learning, in Z Yan (ed.), *Encyclopedia of Mobile Phone Behavior*, IGI Global, Hersey, pp. 490–505, http://dx.doi.org/10.4018/978-1-4666-8239-9.ch041.

Hug, T, Lindner, M & Bruck, PA (eds.) 2006, *Micromedia & E-Learning 2.0: Gaining the Big Picture: Proceedings of Microlearning Conference 2006*, PLACE, Innsbruck University Press, Innsbruck, Austria, viewed 24 June 2017, <https://www.uibk.ac.at/iup/buch_pdfs/microlearning2006-druck.pdf>.

Hughes, BD 2003, 'Performance-based instruction: training that works', , no. August, pp. 1–38.

Hughes, C 2004, 'The supervisor's influence on workplace learning', *Studies in Continuing Education*, vol. 26, no. 2, pp. 275–287, http://dx.doi.org/10.1080/158037042000225254.

Humphress, R & Berge, ZL 2006, 'Justifying human performance improvement interventions', *Performance Improvement*, vol. 45, no. 7, pp. 13–22, http://dx.doi.org/DOI: 10.1002/pfi.2006.4930450704.

Hung, W 2009, 'The 9-step problem design process for problem-based learning: application of the 3c3r model', *Educational Research Review*, vol. 4, no. 2, pp. 118–141, http://dx.doi.org/10.1016/j.edurev.2008.12.001.

Hunter, JE 1986, 'Cognitive ability, cognitive aptitudes, job knowledge, and job performance', *Journal of Vocational Behavior*, vol. 29, no. 3, pp. 340–362, http://dx.doi.org/10.1016/0001-8791(86)90013-8.

Huselid, MA & Becker, BE 2011, 'Bridging micro and macro domains: workforce differentiation and strategic human resource management', *Journal of Management*, vol. 37, no. 2, pp. 421–428, http://dx.doi.org/10.1177/0149206310373400.

Imel, S 2002, 'Accelerated learning in adult education and training and development', *Trends and Issue Alerts No. 33*, pp. 1–2, viewed 24 June 2017, <http://www.calpro-online.org/ERIC/docs/tia00101.pdf>.

Jacobs, R 2001, Managing employee competence and human intelligence in global organizations, in F Richter (ed.), *Maximizing human intelligence in Asia business: The sixth generation project.* New York: Prentice-Hall, Prentice-Hall, New York, pp. 44–54.

Jacobs, R & Washington, C 2003, 'Employee development and organizational performance: a review of literature and directions for future research', *Human Resource Development International*, vol. 6, no. 3, pp. 343–354, http://dx.doi.org/10.1080/1367886011009621l.

Jacobs, RL 1989, System theory applied to human resource development, in D Gradous (ed.), *System Theory Applied to Human Resource Development*, ASTD, Alexendria, pp. 27–60, http://dx.doi.org/10.1002/hrdq.3920010413.

_____ 1997, 'A taxonomy of employee development: toward an organizational culture of expertise', *Proceedings of the Academy of Human Resource Development*, PLACE, Academy of Human Resource Development, Baton Rouge, pp. 278–283.

_____ 2003, *Structured on-the-job training: Unleashing employee expertise in the workplace*, 2nd edn, Berrett-Koehler, San Francisco.

_____ 2014a, System theory and hrd, in N Chalofsky and T Rocco and M Morris (eds.), *Handbook of human resource development*, Wiley Online Library, Hoboken, pp. 21–39, http://dx.doi.org/10.1002/9781118839881.ch2.

_____ 2014b, Structured on-the-job training, in R Poell, T Rocco & G Roth (eds.), *The Routledge Companion to Human Resource Development*, Routledge, Oxon, pp. 272–284.

Jacobs, RL & Jones, MJ 1995, *Structured on-the-job training: Unleashing employee expertise in the workplace*, Berrett-Koehler, San Francisco.

Jacobs, RL & Bu-Rahmah, MJ 2012, 'Developing employee expertise through structured on-the-job training (s-ojt): an introduction to this training approach and the knpc experience', *Industrial and Commercial Training*, vol. 44, no. 2, pp. 75–84, http://dx.doi.org/10.1108/00197851211202902.

Janssen, J, Berlanga, AJ & Koper, R 2010, 'Evaluation of the learning path specification: lifelong learners' information needs', *Educational Technology \& Society*, vol. 14, no. 3, pp. 218–230, viewed 24 June 2017, <http://www.ifets.info/journals/14_3/18.pdf>.

Jenkins, JT, Currie, A, Sala, S & Kennedy, RH 2016, 'A multi-modal approach to training in laparoscopic colorectal surgery accelerates proficiency gain', *Surgical Endoscopy*, vol. 30, no. 7, pp. 3007–3013, http://dx.doi.org/10.1007/s00464-015-

4591-1.

Jin, W & Corbett, A 2011, 'Effectiveness of cognitive apprenticeship learning (cal) and cognitive tutors (ct) for problem solving using fundamental programming concepts', *Proceedings of the 42nd ACM Technical Symposium on Computer Science Education*, Dallas, ACM, New York, pp. 305–310, http://dx.doi.org/10.1145/1953163.1953254.

Jipp, M 2016, 'Expertise development with different types of automation a function of different cognitive abilities', *Human Factors: The Journal of the Human Factors and Ergonomics Society*, vol. 58, no. 1, pp. 92–106, http://dx.doi.org/10.1177/0018720815604441.

Jonassen, DH 1992, Cognitive flexibility theory and its implications for designing cbi, in S Dijkstra, H Krammer & J van Merrienboer (eds.), *Instructional models in computer-based learning environments*, Springer, Berlin Heidelberg, pp. 385–403, http://dx.doi.org/10.1007/978-3-662-02840-7_23.

Jonassen, DH, Dyer, D, Peters, K, Robinson, T, Harvey, D, King, M & Loughner, P 1997, Cognitive flexibility hypertexts on the web: engaging learners in meaning making, in B Khan (ed.), *Web-based instruction*, Education Technology, Englewood Cliffs, pp. 119–133, viewed 24 June 2017, <http://www.academia.edu/download/6676532/36489.pdf>.

Jonassen, DH & Hernandez-Serrano, J 2002, 'Case-based reasoning and instructional design: using stories to support problem solving', *Educational Technology Research and Development*, vol. 50, no. 2, pp. 65–77, http://dx.doi.org/10.1007/BF02504994.

Jonassen, DH & Hung, W 2008, 'All problems are not equal: implications for problem-based learning', *Interdisciplinary Journal of Problem Solving*, vol. 2, no. 2, pp. 10–13, http://dx.doi.org/10.7771/1541-5015.1080.

Jung, E, Kim, M & Reigeluth, CM 2016, 'Learning in action: how competent professionals learn', *Performance Improvement Quarterly*, vol. 28, no. 4, pp. 55–69, http://dx.doi.org/10.1002/piq.21209.

Kaiser, S & Holton III, E 1998, 'The learning organization as a performance improvement strategy', in R Torraco (ed.), *Proceedings of the Academy of Human Resource Development Conference*, Oak Brook, Academy of Human Resource Development, Baton Rouge, pp. 75–82.

Kalyuga, S, Ayres, P, Chandler, P & Sweller, J 2003, 'The expertise reversal effect', *Educational Psychologist*, vol. 38, no. 1, pp. 23–31.

Kanfer, R & Kantrowitz, TM 2002, Ability and non-ability predictors of job performance, in S Sonnentag (ed.), *Psychological management of individual performance*, John Wiley, pp. 27–50, http://dx.doi.org/10.1002/0470013419.ch2.

Kang, S "Pil" 2017, 'What do hpt consultants do for performance analysis?', *TechTrends*, vol. 61, no. 1, pp. 32–45, http://dx.doi.org/10.1007/s11528-016-0129-1.

Karatepe, OM 2013, 'High-performance work practices and hotel employee performance: the mediation of work engagement', *International Journal of Hospitality Management*, vol. 32, pp. 132–140, http://dx.doi.org/DOI: 10.1016/j.ijhm.2012.05.003.

Karoly, LA 2007, *Forces Shaping the Future Us Workforce and Workplace: Implications for 21st Century Work*, Report No. CT-273, Rand Corporation, Santa Monica, viewed 24 June 2017, <http://www.rand.org/content/dam/rand/pubs/testimonies/2007/RAND_CT273.pdf>.

Karpicke, JD & Bauernschmidt, A 2011, 'Spaced retrieval: absolute spacing enhances learning regardless of relative spacing', *Journal of Experimental Psychology, Learning, Memory, and Cognition*, vol. 37, no. 5, pp. 1250–1257, http://dx.doi.org/10.1037/a0023436.

Katz, SN, Hall, E & Lesgold, A 1997, *Cognitive Task Analysis and Intelligent Computer-Based Training Systems: Lessons Learned from Coached Practice Environments in Air Force Avionics*, Report No. TM 027360, University of Pittsburgh, Pittsburg, PA, viewed 24 June 2017, <https://archive.org/details/ERIC_ED411309>.

Kaufman, SB & Kaufman, JC 2007, 'Ten years to expertise, many more to greatness: an investigation of modern writers', *The Journal of Creative Behavior*, vol. 41, no. 2, pp. 114–124, http://dx.doi.org/10.1002/j.2162-6057.2007.tb01284.x.

Khan, K & Ramachandran, S 2012, 'Conceptual framework for performance assessment: competency, competence and performance in the context of assessments in healthcare-deciphering the terminology', *Medical Teacher*, vol. 34, no. 11, pp. 920–928, http://dx.doi.org/10.3109/0142159X.2012.722707.

Khan, RAG, Khan, FA & Khan, MA 2011, 'Impact of training and development on organizational performance', *Global Journal of Management and Business Research*, vol. 11, no. 7, pp. 63–67, viewed 24 June 2017, <https://globaljournals.org/GJMBR_Volume11/8-Impact-of-Training-and-Development-on-Organizational-Performance.pdf>.

Kim, MK 2012, 'Theoretically grounded guidelines for assessing learning progress: cognitive changes in ill-structured complex problem-solving contexts', *Educational Technology Research and Development*, vol. 60, no. 4, pp. 601–622, http://dx.doi.org/10.1007/s11423-012-9247-4.

—— 2015, 'Models of learning progress in solving complex problems: expertise development in teaching and learning', *Contemporary Educational Psychology*, vol. 42, no. 3, pp. 1–16, http://dx.doi.org/10.1016/j.cedpsych.2015.03.005.

King Jr, CL & Cennamo, K 2016, 'The use of gilbert's behavior engineering model to identify barriers to technology integration in a public school', in G Chamblee and L Langub (eds.), *Society for Information Technology & Teacher Education International Conference*, Savannah, Association for the Advancement of Computing in Education (AACE), Waynesville, pp. 1224–1228, viewed 24 June 2017, <https://www.learntechlib.org/d/171844>.

Kirkman, MA 2013, 'Deliberate practice, domain-specific expertise, and implications for surgical education in current climes', *Journal of Surgical Education*, vol. 70, no. 3, pp. 309–317, http://dx.doi.org/10.1016/j.jsurg.2012.11.011.

Kirkpatrick, DL & Kirkpatrick, JD 2009, *Transferring Learning to Behavior: Using the Four Levels to Improve Performance*, Berrett-Koehler.

Kirschenbaum, SS, McInnis, SL & Correll, KP 2009, Contrasting submarine speciality training: sonar and fire control, in K Ericsson (ed.), *Development of professional expertise*, Cambridge University Press, New York, pp. 271–285, http://dx.doi.org/10.1017/cbo9780511609817.015.

Klein, G 1997, 'Developing expertise in decision making', *Thinking \& Reasoning*, vol. 3, no. 4, pp. 337–352, http://dx.doi.org/10.1080/135467897394329.

Klein, GA 1993, A recognition-primed decision (rpd) model of rapid decision making, in G Klein, J Orasanu, R Calderwood & C Zsambok (eds.), *Decision Making in Action*, Norwood, Ablex, pp. 138–147, viewed 24 June 2017, <https://pdfs.semanticscholar.org/0672/092ecc507fb41d81e82d2986cf86c4bff14f.pdf>.

_____ 1998, *Sources of power: how people make decisions*, MIT Press, Cambridge.

_____ 2003, *Intuition at work: why developing your gut instinct will make you better at what you do*, Currency Doubleday, New York.

Klein, GA & Baxter, HC 2009, Cognitive transformation theory: contrasting cognitive and behavioral learning, in D Schmorrow, J Cohn & D Nicholson (eds.), *The PSI handbook of virtual environment for training and education: Developments for the military and beyond, Volume 1, Education: Learning, requirements and metrics*, Praeger Security International, Santa Barbara, pp. 50–65, viewed 24 June 2017, <https://pdfs.semanticscholar.org/99f0/b9bdbce6432c3232fdeffeae0fddea7bcebd.pdf>.

Klein, GA & Borders, J 2016, 'The shadowbox approach to cognitive skills training an empirical evaluation', *Journal of Cognitive Engineering and Decision Making*, vol. 10, no. 3, pp. 268–280, http://dx.doi.org/10.1177/1555343416636515.

Klein, GA, Hintze, N & Saab, D 2013, 'Thinking inside the box: the shadowbox method for cognitive skill development', in H Chaudet, L Pellegrin & N Bonnardel (eds.), *Proceedings of the 11th International Conference on Naturalistic Decision Making*,

ACCELERATED PROFICIENCY FOR ACCELERATED TIMES

Marseille, Aepege Science Publishing, Paris, pp. 121–124, viewed 24 June 2017, <http://arpege-recherche.org/ndm11/papers/ndm11-121.pdf>.

Klein, GA, McCloskey, M, Pliske, R & Schmitt, J 1997, 'Decision skills training', *Proceedings of the Human Factors and Ergonomics Society 41st Annual Meeting*, Albuquerque, SAGE, Los Angeles, pp. 182–185, http://dx.doi.org/10.1177/107118139704100142.

Kolb, D 1984, *Experiential learning as the science of learning and development*, Prentice Hall, Englewood Cliffs.

Kooken, J, Ley, T & De Hoog, R 2007, How do people learn at the workplace? investigating four workplace learning assumptions, in E Durval, R Lamma & M Wolpers (eds.), *Creating new learning experiences on a global scale: Proceedings of Second European Conference on Technology Enhanced Learning*, Springer Verlag, Berlin Heidelberg, pp. 158–171, http://dx.doi.org/10.1007/978-3-540-75195-3_12.

Koopmans, L, Bernaards, CM, Hildebrandt, VH, Schaufeli, WB, de Vet Henrica, C & van der Beek, AJ 2011, 'Conceptual frameworks of individual work performance: a systematic review', *Journal of Occupational and Environmental Medicine*, vol. 53, no. 8, pp. 856–866, http://dx.doi.org/10.1097/JOM.0b013e318226a763.

Korotov, K 2007, Accelerated development of organizational talent, in V Vaiman & C Vance (eds.), *Smart Talent Management: Building Knowledge Assets for Competitive Advantage*, Dward Elgar, Cheltenham, pp. 139–157, http://dx.doi.org/10.4337/9781848442986.00015.

Koubek, RJ, Clarkston, TP & Calvez, V 1994, 'The training of knowledge structures for manufacturing tasks: an empirical study', *Ergonomics*, vol. 37, no. 4, pp. 765–780, http://dx.doi.org/10.1080/00140139408963687.

Kraiger, K 2014, 'Looking back and looking forward: trends in training and development research', *Human Resource Development Quarterly*, vol. 25, no. 4, pp. 401–408, http://dx.doi.org/10.1002/hrdq.21203.

Kraiger, K, Passmore, J & Rebelo, N 2014, The psychology of training, development, and performance improvement, in K Kraiger, J Passmore, N Santos & S Malvezzi (eds.), *The Wiley Blackwell Handbook of the Psychology of Training, Development, and Performance Improvement*, John Wiley, San Fransisco, pp. 535–544, http://dx.doi.org/10.1002/9781118736982.ch1.

Kreutzer, C, Marks, M, Bowers, C & Murphy, C 2016, 'Enhancing surgical team performance with game-based training', *International Journal of Serious Games*, vol. 3, no. 1, http://dx.doi.org/10.17083/ijsg.v3i1.103.

Kuchenbrod, R 2016, 'Accelerating expertise to facilitate decision making in high-risk professions using the dacum system', PhD thesis, Eastern Illinois University, Charleston, viewed 24 June 2017,

<http://thekeep.eiu.edu/cgi/viewcontent.cgi?article=3462&context=theses>.

Kulasegaram, KM, Grierson, LEM & Norman, GR 2013, 'The roles of deliberate practice and innate ability in developing expertise: evidence and implications', *Medical Education*, vol. 47, no. 10, pp. 979–989, http://dx.doi.org/10.1111/medu.12260.

Kuo, F-R, Hwang, G-J, Chen, S-C & Chen, SY 2012, 'A cognitive apprenticeship approach to facilitating web-based collaborative problem solving.', *Journal of Educational Technology \& Society*, vol. 15, no. 4, pp. 319–331, viewed 24 June 2017, <http://www.ifets.info/others/download_pdf.php?j_id=57&a_id=1305>.

Lajoie, SP 2003, 'Transitions and trajectories for studies of expertise', *Educational Researcher*, vol. 32, no. 8, pp. 21–25, http://dx.doi.org/10.3102/0013189X032008021.

―――― 2009, Developing professional expertise with a cognitive apprenticeship model: examples from avionics and medicine, in K Ericsson (ed.), *Development of professional expertise: Toward measurement of expert performance and design of optimal learning environments*, Cambridge University Press, New York, pp. 61–83, http://dx.doi.org/10.1017/cbo9780511609817.004.

Lajoie, SP & Lesgold, A 1992, 'Dynamic assessment of proficiency for solving procedural knowledge tasks', *Educational Psychologist*, vol. 27, no. 3, pp. 365–384, http://dx.doi.org/10.1207/s15326985ep2703_6.

Langan-Fox, J, Armstrong, K, Balvin, N & Anglim, J 2002, 'Process in skill acquisition: motivation, interruptions, memory, affective states, and metacognition', *Australian Psychologist*, vol. 37, no. 2, pp. 104–117, http://dx.doi.org/10.1080/00050060210001706746.

Langerak, F, Hultink, EJ & Griffin, A 2008, 'Exploring mediating and moderating influences on the links among cycle time, proficiency in entry timing, and new product profitability', *Journal of Product Innovation Management*, vol. 25, no. 4, pp. 370–385, http://dx.doi.org/10.1111/j.1540-5885.2008.00307.x.

Lazzara, EH, Dietz, AS, Weaver, SJ, Pavlas, D, Heyne, K, Salas, E & Ramachandran, S 2010, 'Guidelines for training adaptive expertise', *Proceedings of the Human Factors and Ergonomics Society 54th Annual Meeting*, San Francisco, SAGE, pp. 2294–2298, http://dx.doi.org/10.1518/107118110X12829370266400.

Lee, PWY 2011, 'Structured proficiency based progression phacoemulsification training curriculum using virtual reality simulator technology', Masters thesis, Royal College of Surgeons in Ireland, Dublin, Ireland, viewed 24 June 2017, <http://epubs.rcsi.ie/cgi/viewcontent.cgi?article=1007&context=mchrestheses>.

Lee, RL 2004, 'The impact of cognitive task analysis on performance: a meta-analysis of comparative studies', PhD thesis, University of Southern California, Los Angeles.

Lesgold, AM 1991, *Methodological Foundations for Designing Intelligent Computer-Based Training*, Research Report No. N00014-89-J-1168, Office of Naval Research, Arlington, viewed 24 June 2017, <http://www.dtic.mil/dtic/tr/fulltext/u2/a257925.pdf>.

—— 2001, 'The nature and methods of learning by doing', *American Psychologist*, vol. 56, no. 11, pp. 961–973, http://dx.doi.org/10.1037/0003-066X.56.11.964.

Lesgold, AM, Lajoie, S, Bunzo, M & Eggan, G 1988, *Sherlock: A Coached Practice Environment for an Electronics Troubleshooting Job*, Report No. AD-A201-748, University of Pittsburg, Pittsburg, PA, viewed 24 June 2017, <http://eric.ed.gov/?id=ED299450>.

Lesgold, AM & Nahemow, M 2001, Tools to assist learning by doing: achieving and assessing efficient technology for learning, in S Carver & D Klahr (eds.), *Cognition and instruction: Twenty-five years of progress*, Lawrence Erlbaum, Mahwah, pp. 307–345.

Li, X, Wang, J & Ferguson, MK 2014, 'Competence versus mastery: the time course for developing proficiency in video-assisted thoracoscopic lobectomy', *The Journal of Thoracic and Cardiovascular Surgery*, vol. 147, no. 4, pp. 1150–4, http://dx.doi.org/10.1016/j.jtcvs.2013.11.036.

Liu, X & Batt, R 2007, 'The economic pay-offs to informal training: evidence from routine service work', *Industrial and Labor Relations Review*, vol. 61, no. 1, pp. 75–89, http://dx.doi.org/10.1177/001979390706100104.

Logan, GD 1988, 'Toward an instance theory of automatization', *Psychological Review*, vol. 95, no. 4, pp. 492–527, http://dx.doi.org/10.1037//0033-295x.95.4.492.

Lombardo, MP & Deaner, RO 2014, 'You can't teach speed: sprinters falsify the deliberate practice model of expertise', *PeerJ*, vol. 2: e445, pp. 1–31, http://dx.doi.org/10.7717/peerj.445.

London, M & Mone, EM 1999, Continuous learning, in D Ilgen & E Pulakos (eds.), *The changing nature of performance: Implications for staffing, motivation, and development*, Jossey-Bass, San Francisco, pp. 119–153.

Lynn, G & Kalay, F 2015, 'The effect of vision and role clarity on team performance', *Journal of Business Economics and Finance*, vol. 4, no. 3, pp. 473–499, http://dx.doi.org/10.17261/Pressacademia.2015313067.

Lynn, GS, Akgün, AE & Keskin, H 2003, 'Accelerated learning in new product development teams', *European Journal of Innovation Management*, vol. 6, no. 4, pp. 201–212, http://dx.doi.org/10.1108/14601060310500922.

Lynn, GS, Skov, RB & Abel, KD 1999, 'Practices that support team learning and their impact on speed to market and new product success', *Journal of Product Innovation*

Management, vol. 16, no. 5, pp. 439–454, http://dx.doi.org/10.1111/1540-5885.1650439.

Macdonald, RL 2014, 'See one, simulate fifty, then do one?', *Journal of Neurosurgery*, vol. 121, no. 2, pp. 225–227, http://dx.doi.org/10.3171/2014.3.JNS132591.

Macmillan, PJ 2015, 'Thinking like an expert lawyer: measuring specialist legal expertise through think-aloud problem solving and verbal protocol analysis', PhD thesis, BOND UNIVERSITY, Robina, Australia, viewed 24 June 2017, <http://epublications.bond.edu.au/cgi/viewcontent.cgi?article=1167&context=theses>.

Marker, A, Villachica, SW, Stepich, D, Allen, D & Stanton, L 2014, 'An updated framework for human performance improvement in the workplace: the spiral hpi framework', *Performance Improvement*, vol. 53, no. 1, pp. 10–23, http://dx.doi.org/10.1002/pfi.21389.

Marquardt, MJ 1996, *Building the learning organization*, McGraw Hill, New York.

Marsick, VJ & Volpe, M 1999, The nature and need for informal learning, in *Advances in developing human resources*, Sage, Thousand Oaks, pp. 1–9, http://dx.doi.org/10.1177/152342239900100302.

Marsick, VJ & Watkins, K 1997, Lessons from informal and incidental learning, in J Burgoyne & M Reynolds (eds.), *Management learning: integrating perspectives in theory and practice*, Sage, London, http://dx.doi.org/10.4135/9781446250488.n18.

―――― 2015, *Informal and incidental learning in the workplace*, Routledge Revivals. edn, Routledge, New York.

Marsick, VJ & Watkins, KE 2001, 'Informal and incidental learning', *New Directions for Adult and Continuing Education*, vol. 2001, no. 89, pp. 25–34, viewed 24 June 2017, <http://gcc.upb.de/www/WI/WI2/wi2_lit.nsf/d2f7ed56380ef2fdc125683100441206/6f9731f184cd7b3dc12570c3006303ed/$FILE/Informal+workplace+learning_Marsick.pdf>.

Marsick, VJ, Watkins, KE, Scully-Russ, E & Nicolaides, A 2017, 'Rethinking informal and incidental learning in terms of complexity and the social context', *Journal of Adult Learning, Knowledge and Innovation*, vol. 1, no. 1, pp. 27–34, http://dx.doi.org/10.1556/2059.01.2016.003.

Matthews, P 1999, 'Workplace learning: developing an holistic model', *The Learning Organization*, vol. 6, no. 1, pp. 18–29, http://dx.doi.org/10.1108/09696479910255684.

McDaniel, MA, Schmidt, FL & Hunter, JE 1988, 'Job experience correlates of job performance', *Journal of Applied Psychology*, vol. 73, no. 2, p. 327, http://dx.doi.org/10.1037/0021-9010.73.2.327.

McKinley, RA, McIntire, L, Bridges, N & Goodyear, C 2013, 'Acceleration of image analyst training with transcranial direct current stimulation', *Behavioral Neuroscience*, vol. 127, no. 6, pp. 936–946, http://dx.doi.org/10.1037/a0034975.

McLagan, PA 1989a, *Model for HRD Practice*, American Society for Training and Development, Alexandria.

―――― 1989b, 'Models for hrd practice', *Training \& Development Journal*, vol. 43, no. 9, pp. 49–60.

McLaughlin, MF 2016, 'Managers coaching employees to improve performance: supports and barriers', PhD thesis, ProQuest, Ann Arbor, viewed <https://search.proquest.com/openview/f84533858510deea42fb2b4d4052a28c/1?pq-origsite=gscholar&cbl=18750&diss=y>.

McQueen, RJ & Chen, J 2010, 'Building script-based tacit knowledge in call centre trainees', *Knowledge Management Research \& Practice*, vol. 8, no. 3, pp. 240–255, viewed 24 June 2017, <https://www.researchgate.net/profile/Jihong_Chen2/publication/47354229>.

McQueen, RJ & Janson, A 2016, 'Accelerating tacit knowledge building of client-facing consultants: can organizations better support these learning processes?', *The Learning Organization*, vol. 23, no. 4, pp. 202–217, http://dx.doi.org/10.1108/TLO-07-2015-0035.

Meier, D 2000, *The accelerated learning handbook: a creative guide to designing and delivering faster, more effective training programs*, McGraw-Hill, New York.

Merkelbach, EJHM & Schraagen, JMC 1994, *A Framework for the Analysis of Cognitive Tasks*, Report No. TNO-TM 1994 B-13, TNO Human Factors Research, Soesterberg, The Netherlands, viewed 24 June 2017, <http://www.dtic.mil/docs/citations/ADA285345>.

Van Merriënboer, JJ & Kester, L 2008, Whole-task models in education, in J Spector, M Merrill, J van Merriënboer & M Driscoll (eds.), *Handbook of research on educational communications and technology*, Erlbaum/Routledge, Mahwah, pp. 441–456, viewed 24 June 2017, <https://www.researchgate.net/publication/268000667>.

Van Merriënboer, JJG, Clark, RE & de Croock, MBM 2002, 'Blueprints for complex learning: the 4c/id-model', *Educational Technology Research and Development*, vol. 50, no. 2, pp. 39–61, http://dx.doi.org/10.1007/BF02504993.

Merrill, MD 2006, Hypothesized performance on complex tasks as a function of scaled instructional strategies, in J Enen & R Clark (eds.), *Handling complexity in learning environments: Research and theory*, Elsevier, Amsterdam, pp. 265–282, viewed 24 June 2017,

<http://www.mdavidmerrill.com/Papers/Scaled_Instructional_Strategies.pdf>.

Mieg, HA 2009, 'Two factors of expertise? excellence and professionalism of environmental experts', *High Ability Studies*, vol. 20, no. 1, pp. 91–115, http://dx.doi.org/10.1080/13598130902860432.

Miller, P 2003, 'Workplace learning by action learning: a practical example', *Journal of Workplace Learning*, vol. 15, no. 1, pp. 14–23, http://dx.doi.org/10.1108/13665620310458785.

Millington, R 2018, 10.10: measuring time-to-full productivity, in *How to Calculate the ROI of online Communities*, FeverBee Ltd, London, viewed 24 October 2018, <https://www.feverbee.com/roi/measuring-time-to-full-productivity/>.

Mills, N 2011, 'Situated learning through social networking communities: the development of joint enterprise, mutual engagement, and a shared repertoire', *Calico Journal*, vol. 28, no. 2, pp. 345–368, http://dx.doi.org/10.1080/00071005.2015.1133799.

Mitchell, MD 2014, 'Effectiveness of electronic performance support system and training in a higher education setting', PhD thesis, ProQuest, Ann Arbor, viewed <https://search.proquest.com/openview/b8fd77082542d8496fb06aa33e883c4a/1.pdf?pq-origsite=gscholar&cbl=18750&diss=y>.

Mitrovic, A, Ohlsson, S & Barrow, D 2013, 'The effect of positive feedback in a constraint-based intelligent tutoring system', *Computers \& Education*, vol. 60, no. 1, pp. 264–272, http://dx.doi.org/10.1016/j.compedu.2012.07.002.

Moon, YK, Kim, EJ & You, Y-M 2013, 'Study on expertise development process based on arête', *International Journal of Information and Education Technology*, vol. 3, no. 2, pp. 226–230, http://dx.doi.org/10.7763/IJIET.2013.V3.269.

Morf, M 1986, *Optimizing work performance: a look beyond the bottom line*, Praeger, New York.

Morris, C & Blaney, D 2010, Work-based learning, in T Swanwick (ed.), *Understanding medical education: Evidence, theory and practice*, Wiley-Blackwell, Hoboken, pp. 69–82, http://dx.doi.org/10.1002/9781444320282.ch5.

Mostafavi, B & Barnes, T 2016, 'Exploring the impact of data-driven tutoring methods on students' demonstrative knowledge in logic problem solving', in T Barnes, M Chi & M Feng (eds.), *Proceedings of the 9th International Conference on Educational Data Mining*, Raleigh, International Educational Data Mining Society (IEDMS), pp. 460–465, viewed 24 June 2017, <http://www.educationaldatamining.org/EDM2016/proceedings/paper_125.pdf>.

Mostafavi, B, Liu, Z & Barnes, T 2015, 'Data-driven proficiency profiling', *Proceedings of the 8th International Conference on Educational Data Mining*, Madrid,

International Educational Data Mining Society, pp. 335–341, viewed 24 June 2017, <http://files.eric.ed.gov/fulltext/ED560536.pdf>.

Motowidlo, SJ, Borman, WC & Schmit, MJ 1997, 'A theory of individual differences in task and contextual performance', *Human Performance*, vol. 10, no. 2, pp. 71–83, http://dx.doi.org/10.1207/s15327043hup1002_1.

Motowidlo, SJ & Van Scotter, JR 1994, 'Evidence that task performance should be distinguished from contextual performance', *Journal of Applied Psychology*, vol. 79, no. 4, pp. 475–480, http://dx.doi.org/10.1037//0021-9010.79.4.475.

Mott, V 2000, 'The development of professional expertise in the workplace', *New Directions for Adult and Continuing Education*, vol. 2000, no. 86, pp. 23–31, http://dx.doi.org/10.1002/ace.8603.

Muhammad, A, Zhou, Q, Beydoun, G, Xu, D & Shen, J 2016, 'Learning path adaptation in online learning systems', *2016 IEEE 20th International Conference on Computer Supported Cooperative Work in Design (CSCWD)*, Nanchang, IEEE, Piscataway, pp. 421–426, http://dx.doi.org/10.1109/cscwd.2016.7566026.

Müller, S & Abernethy, B 2014, 'An expertise approach to training anticipation using temporal occlusion in a natural skill setting', *Technology, Instruction, Cognition and Learning*, vol. 9, no. 4, pp. 295–312, viewed 24 June 2017, <https://espace.library.uq.edu.au/view/UQ:353646/UQ353646_OA.pdf>.

Munro, A & Clark, RE 2013, 'Cognitive task analysis-based design and authoring software for simulation training.', *Military Medicine*, vol. 178, no. 10 Suppl, pp. 7–14, http://dx.doi.org/10.7205/MILMED-D-13-00265.

Murphy, KR 1989, 'Is the relationship between cognitive ability and job performance stable over time?', *Human Performance*, vol. 2, no. 3, pp. 183–200, http://dx.doi.org/10.1207/s15327043hup0203_3.

Nadler, L, Wiggs, GD & Smith, S 1988, 'Managing human resource development', *R&D Management*, vol. 18, no. 3, pp. 289–289.

Naikar, N 2011, *Cognitive Work Analysis: Foundations, Extensions, and Challenges*, Report No. DSTO-GD-0680, Defence Science and Technology Organization (DTSO), Fisherman's Bend, VIC, Australia, viewed 24 June 2017, <http://www.dtic.mil/dtic/tr/fulltext/u2/a564221.pdf>.

—————— 2017, 'Cognitive work analysis: an influential legacy extending beyond human factors and engineering', *Applied Ergonomics*, vol. 59, pp. 528–540, http://dx.doi.org/10.1016/j.apergo.2016.06.001.

Naikar, N, Lintern, G & Sanderson, P 2002, Cognitive work analysis for air defense applications in australia, in M McNeese & M Vidulich (eds.), *Cognitive Systems Engineering in Military Aviation Environments: Avoiding Cogminutia Fragmentosa!*,

Human Systems Information Analysis Center, Dayton, pp. 169–200, viewed 24 June 2017, <https://www.researchgate.net/profile/Gavan_Lintern2/publication/242410104>.

Nguyen, F 2006, 'What you already know does matter: expertise and electronic performance support systems', *Performance Improvement*, vol. 45, no. 4, pp. 9–12, http://dx.doi.org/10.1002/pfi.2006.4930450404.

Nguyen, F, Klein, JD & Sullivan, H 2005, 'A comparative study of electronic performance support systems', *Performance Improvement Quarterly*, vol. 18, no. 4, pp. 71–86, http://dx.doi.org/10.1111/j.1937-8327.2005.tb00351.x.

Niazi, BRAS 2011, 'Training and development strategy and its role in organizational performance', *Journal of Public Administration and Governance*, vol. 1, no. 2, pp. 42–57, http://dx.doi.org/10.5296/jpag.v1i2.862.

Novak, D 2011, *The systematic development of expertise*, CreateSpace Independent Publishing Platform, USA.

Oliver, RL & Anderson, E 1994, 'An empirical test of the consequences of behavior-and outcome-based sales control systems', *The Journal of Marketing*, vol. 58, no. 4, pp. 53–67, http://dx.doi.org/10.2307/1251916.

Ong, J & Ramachandran, S 2003, *Intelligent Tutoring Systems: Using Ai to Improve Training Performance and ROI*, Stotler Henke Associate, Inc., San Mateo, viewed 24 June 2017, <http://stage.shai.com/wp-content/uploads/2014/12/ITS_using_AI_to_improve_training_performance_and_ROI.pdf>.

Oyewole, S a, Farde, AM, Haight, JM & Okareh, OT 2011, 'Evaluation of complex and dynamic safety tasks in human learning using the act-r and soar skill acquisition theories', *Computers in Human Behavior*, vol. 27, no. 5, pp. 1984–1995, http://dx.doi.org/10.1016/j.chb.2011.05.005.

Paas, F & van Gog, T 2009, Principles for designing effective and efficient training of complex cognitive skills, in F Durso (ed.), *Reviews of Human Factors and Ergonomics*, SAGE, Thousand Oaks, pp. 166–194, http://dx.doi.org/10.1518/155723409X448053.

Pandy, MG, Petrosino, AJ, Austin, B a & Barr, RE 2004, 'Assessing adaptive expertise in undergraduate biomechanics', *Journal of Engineering Education*, vol. 93, no. 3, pp. 211–222, http://dx.doi.org/10.1002/j.2168-9830.2004.tb00808.x.

Parker, SK & Turner, N 2002, Work design and individual work performance: research findings and an agenda for future inquiry, in S Sonnentag (ed.), *Psychological management of individual performance*, John Wiley, San Francisco, pp. 69–93, http://dx.doi.org/10.1002/0470013419.ch4.

Patchan, MM, Schunn, CD, Sieg, W & McLaughlin, D 2015, 'The effect of blended instruction on accelerated learning', *Technology, Pedagogy and Education*, vol. 25, no. 3, pp. 1–18, http://dx.doi.org/10.1080/1475939X.2015.1013977.

Patterson, M, Militello, LG, Taylor, R, Bunger, A, Wheeler, D, Klein, G & Geis, G 2013, 'Acceleration to expertise in healthcare: leveraging the critical decision method and simulation-based training', in H Chaudet and L Pellegrin and N Bonnardel (eds.), *Proceedings of the 11th International Conference on Naturalistic Decision Making (NDM 2013)*, Marseille, France, Arpege Science Publishing, Paris, France, pp. 233–236, viewed 24 June 2017, <http://arpege-recherche.org/ndm11/papers/ndm11-233.pdf>.

Pedler, M 2011, *Action learning in practice*, 4th edn, Gower Publishing, Burlington.

Peña, A 2010, 'The dreyfus model of clinical problem-solving skills acquisition: a critical perspective', *Medical Education Online*, vol. 15, no. 1, pp. 1–11, http://dx.doi.org/10.3402/meo.v15i0.4846.

Pershing, JA (ed.) 2006, *Handbook of human performance technology: principles, practices, and potential*, 3rd edn, Pfeiffer, San Francisco.

Pershing, JA, Abaci, S & Symonette, S 2016, 'A treatise on the field of human performance technology: the need for a scholars' guild', *Performance Improvement*, vol. 55, no. 7, pp. 6–14, http://dx.doi.org/10.1002/pfi.21604.

Pershing, JA, Lee, J-E & Cheng, J 2008, 'Current status, future trends, and issues in human performance technology, part 2: models, influential disciplines, and research and development', *Performance Improvement*, vol. 47, no. 2, pp. 7–15, http://dx.doi.org/10.1002/pfi.182.

PetroSkills 2009, 'Accelerating time to competence through accelerated development programs', , pp. 1–4, viewed 24 June 2017, <https://www.yumpu.com/en/document/view/8813692/accelerating-time-to-competence-through-accelerated-petroskills>.

Phillips, JJ 2012, *Return on investment in training and performance improvement programs*, Routledge, New York.

Piercy, NF, Cravens, DW & Morgan, NA 1998, 'Salesforce performance and behaviour-based management processes in business-to-business sales organizations', *European Journal of Marketing*, vol. 32, no. 1/2, pp. 79–100, viewed <http://neil-a-morgan.com/wp-content/uploads/2016/01/Piercy-Cravens-Morgan-EJM-1998.pdf>.

———— 1999, 'Relationships between sales management control, territory design, salesforce performance and sales organization effectiveness', *British Journal of Management*, vol. 10, no. 2, pp. 95–111, http://dx.doi.org/10.1111/1467-8551.00113.

Pinder, CC & Schroeder, KG 1987, 'Time to proficiency following job transfers', *Academy of Management Journal*, vol. 30, no. 2, pp. 336–353, http://dx.doi.org/10.2307/256278.

Piskurich, GM 1993, *Self-directed learning: A practical guide to design, development, and implementation*, Jossey-Bass, San Francisco.

Pollock, RV, Wick, CW & Jefferson, A 2015, *The six disciplines of breakthrough learning: how to turn training and development into business results*, 3rd edn, John Wiley, San Francisco.

PTC 2005, 'Precision learning programs: personalized curriculums that accelerate adoption, boost productivity', , pp. 1–2, viewed 24 June 2017, <http://www.singlesourcing.com/products/arbortext/elearning/32047en_file1.pdf>.

Quartey, SH 2012, 'Effect of employee training on the perceived organisational performance: a case study of the print-media industry in ghana', *Human Resource Management (HRM)*, vol. 4, no. 15, viewed 24 June 2017, <https://www.academia.edu/6817560/>.

Qui'nones, MA, Ford, JK & Teachout, MS 1995, 'The relationship between work experience and job performance: a conceptual and meta-analytic review', *Personnel Psychology*, vol. 48, no. 4, pp. 887–910, http://dx.doi.org/10.1111/j.1744-6570.1995.tb01785.x.

Radler, D & Bocianu, I 2017, 'Accelerated teaching and learning: roles and challenges for learners and tutors', *The International Scientific Conference eLearning and Software for Education*, Bucharest, ProQuest, Ann Arbor, pp. 601–608, http://dx.doi.org/10.12753/2066-026X-17-170.

Ramaswami, A & Dreher, GF 2007, The benefits associated with workplace mentoring relationships, in T Allen & L Eby (eds.), *The Blackwell handbook of mentoring: a multiple perspectives approach*, Blackwell, Victoria, Australia, pp. 211–232, http://dx.doi.org/10.1111/b.9781405133739.2007.00013.x.

Ramsburg, L 2010, 'An initial investigation of the applicability of the dreyfus skill acquisition model to the professional development of nurse educators', PhD thesis, Marshall University Graduate College, Huntington, viewed 24 June 2017, <http://mds.marshall.edu/cgi/viewcontent.cgi?article=1371&context=etd>.

Raphael, G, Berka, C, Popovic, D, Chung, GKWK, Nagashima, SO, Behneman, A, Davis, G & Johnson, R 2009, 'Adaptive performance trainer (apt): interactive neuro-educational technology to increase the pace and efficiency of rifle marksmanship training', in S Constantine (ed.), *Proceedings of the 13th International Conference on Human-Computer Interaction*, San Diego, Springer-Verlag, Berlin Heidelberg, Germany, viewed 24 June 2017,
<http://www.researchgate.net/profile/Chris_Berka2/publication/236660610>.

Rasmussen, J, Pejtersen, AM & Goodstein, L 1994, *Cognitive systems engineering*, John Wiley, New York.

Razer, A, Blair, L & Fadde, P 2015, 'Accelerating expert noticing in classroom teaching, nursing, and academic coaching', paper presented to the Annual Convention of Association for Educational Communications and Technology Conference, Indianapolis.

Revans, R 1982, *The Origins and Evolution of Action Learning*, Chartwell-Bratt, Bromley.

Robinson, DG & Robinson, JC 1995, *Performance consulting: Moving beyond training*, Berrett-Koehler Publishers, San Francisco.

Robinson, W & Pennotti, M 2013, 'Accelerating experience with live simulation of designing complex systems', paper presented to the ASEE International Forum, Atlanta, Georgia, viewed 24 June 2017, <https://peer.asee.org/accelerating-experience-with-live-simulation-of-designing-complex-systems.pdf>.

Rose, C 2000, *Master it faster: how to learn faster, make good decisions \& think creatively*, Accelerated Learning Systems, Las Vegas, viewed 24 June 2017, <http://www.goodreads.com/book/show/1026903.Master_it_Faster>.

Rosenbaum, S 2014, How we bring employees up to speed in record time using leaning path methodology, in R Pollock, C Wick & A Jefferson (eds.), *The field guide to the 6Ds*, Wiley & Sons, San Francisco, pp. 345–351.

Rosenbaum, S 2018, *Up to Speed: Secrets of Reducing Time to Proficiency*, BookBaby, US.

Rosenbaum, S & Pollock, R 2015, 'Creating a conducive talent development and learning culture', paper presented to the ATD International Conference and Exposition, Orlando.

Rosenbaum, S & Williams, J 2004, *Learning paths: increase profits by reducing the time it takes employees to get up to speed*, Jossey-Bass, San Francisco, viewed 24 June 2017, <http://www.wiley.com/WileyCDA/WileyTitle/productCd-0787975346.html>.

Roth, E & O'Hara, J 2014, 'Discussion panel: how to recognize a "good" cognitive task analysis?', *Proceedings of the Human Factors and Ergonomics Society 58th Annual Meeting*, Chicago, SAGE, Thousand Oaks, pp. 320–324, http://dx.doi.org/10.1177/1541931214581066.

Roth, R 2009, 'Acquiring and maintaining expert ability',, viewed 24 June 2017, <http://www.r2research.com/Research_files/ExpertAbility_Roth_2009.pdf>.

Rothwell, WJ, Brock, MC, Dean, PJ & Rosenberg, MJ 2000, *ASTD models for human performance improvement: roles, competencies, and outputs*, 2nd edn, W Rothwell (ed.), American Society for Training and Development (ASTD), Alexandria.

Rothwell, WJ & Kazanas, HC 2004, *Improving on-the-job training: How to establish and operate a comprehensive OJT program*, John Wiley & Sons, San Francisco.

Rothwell, WJ & Sullivan, RL 2005, *Practicing organization development: A guide for consultants*, 2nd edn, W Rothwell & R Sullivan (eds.), Jossey-Bass/Pfeiffer, San Francisco.

Rummler, GA & Brache, AP 1995, *Improving performance: How to manage the white space on the organization chart*, 2nd edn, Jossey-Bass, San Francisco.

Saks, A, Haccoun, R & Belcourt, M 2010, *Managing performance through training and development*, 5th ed., Nelson Education, Canada, viewed 24 June 2017, <https://www.amazon.com/Managing-Performance-Through-Training-Development/dp/0176507337>.

Salas, E, Rosen, MA, Weaver, SJ, Held, JD & Weissmuller, JJ 2009, 'Research on sbt leads to the development of guidelines applicable to diverse training scenarios', *Ergonomics in Design: The Quarterly of Human Factors Applications*, vol. 17, no. 4, pp. 12–18, http://dx.doi.org/10.1518/106480409X12587548298009.

Salas, E, Tannenbaum, SI, Kraiger, K & Smith-Jentsch, K a 2012, 'The science of training and development in organizations: what matters in practice', *Psychological Science in the Public Interest*, vol. 13, no. 2, pp. 74–101, http://dx.doi.org/10.1177/1529100612436661.

Sancar-Tokmak, H 2013, 'Effects of video-supported expertise-based training (xbt) on preservice science teachers' self-efficacy beliefs', *Eurasia Journal of Mathematics, Science \& Technology Education*, vol. 9, no. 2, pp. 131–141, http://dx.doi.org/10.12973/eurasia.2013.924a.

Schaafstal, AA, Schraagen, JM, van Berlo, M & van Berlo, M 2000, 'Cognitive task analysis and innovation of training: the case of structured troubleshooting', *Human Factors*, vol. 42, no. 1, pp. 75–86, http://dx.doi.org/10.1518/001872000779656570.

Schaffer, SP 2000, 'A review of organizational and human performance frameworks', *Performance Improvement Quarterly*, vol. 13, no. 3, pp. 220–243, http://dx.doi.org/10.1111/j.1937-8327.2000.tb00183.x.

Van Schaik, P, Pearson, R & Barker, P 2002, 'Designing electronic performance support systems to facilitate learning', *Innovations in Education and Teaching International*, vol. 39, no. 4, pp. 289–306, http://dx.doi.org/10.1080/13558000210161043.

Schmitt, J 1996, 'Designing good tdgs', *Marine Corps Gazette*, vol. 80, no. 5, pp. 96–97.

Schmutz, J & Manser, T do 2013, 'Do team processes really have an effect on clinical performance? a systematic literature review', *British Journal of Anaesthesia*, vol. 110, no. 4, pp. 529–544, http://dx.doi.org/10.1093/bja/aes513.

Schneider, W 1993, Acquiring expertise: determinants of exceptional performance., in K Heller, F Mönks & A Passow (eds.), *International handbook of research and development of giftedness and talent*, Pergamon Press, Elmsford, NY, pp. 311–324, viewed 24 October 2018, <https://opus.bibliothek.uni-wuerzburg.de/frontdoor/deliver/index/docId/7140/file/Schneider_W_OPUS_7140.pdf >.

Schraagen, JM 1993, 'How experts solve a novel problem in experimental design', *Cognitive Science*, vol. 17, no. 2, pp. 285–309, http://dx.doi.org/10.1207/s15516709cog1702_4.

Schreiber, BT, Bennett Jr, W, Colegrove, CM, Portrey, AM, Greschke, DA & Bell, HH 2009, Evaluating pilot performance, in K Ericsson (ed.), *Development of professional expertise*, Cambridge University Press, New York, pp. 247–270, http://dx.doi.org/10.1017/cbo9780511609817.014.

Schulz, M & Roßnagel, CS 2010, 'Informal workplace learning: an exploration of age differences in learning competence', *Learning and Instruction*, vol. 20, no. 5, pp. 383–399, http://dx.doi.org/10.1016/j.learninstruc.2009.03.003.

Schwartz, DL, Bransford, JD & Sears, D 2005, Efficiency and innovation in transfer, in J Mestre (ed.), *Transfer of learning from a modern multidisciplinary perspective*, Information Age, Greenwich, pp. 1–51.

Scobey, BW 2006, 'The journey to expertise: pathways to expert knowledge traveled by texas juvenile probation officers', PhD thesis, Texas State University, San Marcos, viewed 24 June 2017, <https://digital.library.txstate.edu/bitstream/handle/10877/4267/fulltext.pdf?sequence=1>.

Senge, PM 1994a, *The fifth discipline fieldbook. New York: Transformation thinking*, Berkley Publishing Group, New York.

———— 1994b, Building learning organizations, in *The training and development sourcebook*, Prentice Hall, Englewood Cliffs, pp. 3.67–3.74.

Senge, PM, Kleiner, A, Roberts, C, Ross, RB & Smith, BJ 1994, *The fifth discipline fieldbook: Strategies and tools for building a learning organization*, Crown Business, New York.

Seow, C, Hughes, J, Moon, S, Birchall, D, Williams, S & Vrasidas, C 2005, 'Developing design principles for an e-learning programme for sme managers to support accelerated learning at the workplace', *Journal of Workplace Learning*, vol. 17, no. 5/6, pp. 370–384, http://dx.doi.org/10.1108/13665620510606788.

Seto, AH & Kern, MJ 2016, 'Simulator training: the bridge between 'primum non nocere' and 'learning by doing,''' *Catheterization and Cardiovascular Interventions*, vol. 87, no. 3, pp. 381–382, http://dx.doi.org/10.1002/ccd.26432.

Shadrick, SB & Lussier, JW 2009, Training complex cognitive skills: a theme-based approach to the development of battlefield skills, in K Ericsson (ed.), *Development of professional expertise: Toward measurement of expert performance and design of optimal learning environments*, Cambridge University Press, New York, pp. 286–311, http://dx.doi.org/10.1017/cbo9780511609817.016.

Shadrick, SB, Lussier, JW & Fultz, C 2007, *Accelerating the Development of Adaptive Performance: Validating the Think like a Commander Training*, Research Report No. 1868, U.S. Army Research Institute for the Behavioral and Social Sciences, Arlington, http://dx.doi.org/10.21236/ada464668.

Sheckley, B & Keeton, M 1999, *Ecologies that support and enhance adult learning*, College Park: University of Maryland College.

Shiffrin, RM & Schneider, W 1977, 'Controlled and automatic human information processing: perceptual learning, automatic attending and a general theory', *Psychological Review*, vol. 84, no. 2, pp. 127–190, viewed 24 June 2017, <http://www.bryanburnham.net/wp-content/uploads/2014/01/Shiffrin-1977-Psychological-Review.pdf>.

Shuell, TJ 1986, 'Individual differences: changing conceptions in research and practice', *American Journal of Education*, vol. 94, no. 3, pp. 356–377, http://dx.doi.org/10.1086/443854.

Simonton, DK 1997, 'Creative productivity: a predictive and explanatory model of career trajectories and landmarks.', *Psychological Review*, vol. 104, no. 1, pp. 66–89, viewed 24 June 2017, <https://pdfs.semanticscholar.org/abb5/02a8b01b50790a44cf5438f01f9f5ac9bf42.pdf>.

Slootmaker, A, Kurvers, H, Hummel, H & Koper, R 2014, 'Developing scenario-based serious games for complex cognitive skills acquisition: design, development and evaluation of the emergo platform', *Journal of Universal Computer Science*, vol. 20, no. 4, pp. 561–582, http://dx.doi.org/10.3217/jucs-020-04-0561.

Smeds, R 2003, 'Simulation for accelerated learning and development in industrial management', *Production Planning \& Control*, vol. 14, no. 2, pp. 107–110, http://dx.doi.org/10.1080/0953728031000107707.

Smith, A & Call, N 1999, *The alps approach: accelerated learning in primary schools: brain-based methods for accelerating motivation and achievement*, Network Educational Press, Stafford, viewed 24 June 2017, <http://capitadiscovery.co.uk/brighton-ac/items/1253656>.

Smith, EM, Ford, JK, Kozlowski & Quiñones, SWJ 1997, Building adaptive expertise: implications for training design strategies, in A Miguel & A Ehrenstein (eds.), *Training for a rapidly changing workplace: Applications of psychological research*, American Psychological Association, Washington, D.C., pp. 89–118, http://dx.doi.org/10.1037/10260-004.

Sobel, HS, Cepeda, NJ & Kapler, IV 2011, 'Spacing effects in real-world classroom vocabulary learning', *Applied Cognitive Psychology*, vol. 25, no. 5, pp. 763–767, http://dx.doi.org/10.1002/acp.1747.

Soderstrom, NC & Bjork, RA 2015, 'Learning versus performance: an integrative review', *Perspectives on Psychological Science*, vol. 10, no. 2, pp. 176–199, http://dx.doi.org/10.1177/1745691615569000.

Sonnentag, S & Frese, M 2002, Performance concepts and performance theory, in S Sonnentag (ed.), *Psychological management of individual performance*, John Wiley, New York, pp. 3–25, http://dx.doi.org/10.1002/0470013419.ch1.

Sonnentag, S & Kleine, BM 2000, 'Deliberate practice at work: a study with insurance agents', *Journal of Occupational and Organizational Psychology*, vol. 73, no. 1, pp. 87–102, http://dx.doi.org/10.1348/096317900166895.

Sottilare, R & Goldberg, B 2012, 'Designing adaptive computer-based tutoring systems to accelerate learning and facilitate retention', *Cognitive Technology*, vol. 17, no. 1, pp. 19–33, viewed 24 June 2017, <http://www.researchgate.net/profile/Bob_Sottilare/publication/267037687>.

Soule, RT 2016, 'The learning experience of tough cases: a descriptive case study', PhD thesis, The George Washington University, Ann Harbor, MI, viewed 24 June 2017, <http://pqdtopen.proquest.com/doc/1751007250.html?FMT=AI>.

Souza, MIF, Torres, T, de Carvalho, J, Evangelista, S & do Amaral, S 2015, 'Non-formal education for technology transfer in embrapa: microlearning, microtraining and microcontent by mobile devices', *Proceedings of the 7th International Conference on Education and New Learning Technologies (EDULEARN15)*, Barcelona, IATED, Valencia, pp. 5728–5736, viewed 24 June 2017, <https://www.researchgate.net/publication/280091194>.

Spiro, RJ, Collins, BP, Thota, JJ & Feltovich, PJ 2003, 'Cognitive flexibility theory: hypermedia for complex learning, adaptive knowledge application, and experience acceleration', *Educational Technology*, vol. 43, no. 5, pp. 5–10.

Spiro, RJ, Coulson, RL, Feitovich, PJ & Anderson, DK 1988, *Cognitive Flexibility Theory: Advanced Knowledge Acquisition in Ill-Structured Domains*, Technical Report No. 441, University of Illinois, Champaign, viewed 24 June 2017, <http://files.eric.ed.gov/fulltext/ED302821.pdf>.

Spiro, RJ, Feltovich, PJ, Coulson, RL, Jacobson, M, Durgunoglu, A, Ravlin, S & Jehng, J-C 1992, *Knowledge Acquisition for Application: Cognitive Flexibility and Transfer of Training in Iii-Structured Domains*, ARI Research Note No. 92-21, United States Army Research Institute for the Behaviorai and Social Sciences, Alexandria, viewed 24 June 2017, <http://www.dtic.mil/dtic/tr/fulltext/u2/a250147.pdf>.

Spiro, RJ & Jehng, J-C 1990, Cognitive flexibility and hypertext: theory and technology for the nonlinear and multidimensional traversal of complex subject matter, in D Nix & R Spiro (eds.), *Cognition, education, and multimedia: Exploring ideas in high technology*, Erlbaum, Hilldale, pp. 163–205.

Spiro, RJ, Vispoel, WP, J G Schmitz, Samarapungavan, A & Boerger, AE 1987, *Knowledge Acquisition for Application: Cognitive Flexibility and Transfer in Complex Content Domains*, Report No. 409, University of Illinois, Champaign, viewed 24 June 2017, <http://files.eric.ed.gov/fulltext/ED287155.pdf>.

Spruit, EN, Band, GP & Hamming, JF 2015, 'Increasing efficiency of surgical training: effects of spacing practice on skill acquisition and retention in laparoscopy training', *Surgical Endoscopy*, vol. 29, no. 8, pp. 2235–2243, http://dx.doi.org/10.1007/s00464-014-3931-x.

Squires, A, Wade, J, Dominick, P & Gelosh, D 2011, *Building a Competency Taxonomy to Guide Experience Acceleration of Lead Program Systems Engineers*, ERIC No. ADA589178, Stevens Institute of Technology, Hoboken, viewed 24 June 2017, <http://www.dtic.mil/cgi-bin/GetTRDoc?AD=ADA589178>.

Stalmeijer, RE, Dolmans, DH, Snellen-Balendong, HA, van Santen-Hoeufft, M, Wolfhagen, IH & Scherpbier, AJ 2013, 'Clinical teaching based on principles of cognitive apprenticeship: views of experienced clinical teachers', *Academic Medicine*, vol. 88, no. 6, pp. 861–865, http://dx.doi.org/10.1097/ACM.0b013e31828fff12.

Starkes, JL & Lindley, S 1994, 'Can we hasten expertise by video simulations?', *Quest*, vol. 46, no. 2, pp. 211–222, http://dx.doi.org/10.1080/00336297.1994.10484122.

Sternberg, RJ 1999, 'Intelligence as developing expertise.', *Contemporary Educational Psychology*, vol. 24, no. 4, pp. 359–375, http://dx.doi.org/10.1006/ceps.1998.0998.

Stolovitch, H 2007, The development and evolution of human performance improvement, in R Reiser & L Dempsey (eds.), *Trends and issues in instructional design and technology*, Pearson, Upper Saddle River, pp. 134–146.

Stolovitch, HD 2000, 'Human performance technology: research and theory to practice', *Performance Improvement*, vol. 39, no. 4, pp. 7–16, http://dx.doi.org/10.1002/pfi.4140390407.

Stolovitch, HD & Keeps, EJ 1992, What is human performance technology?, in H Stolovich & E Keeps (eds.), *Handbook of human performance technology: A comprehensive guide for analyzing and solving performance problems in organizations*, Pfeiffer, San Francisco.

―――― 1999, What is performance technology?, in H Stolovitch & E Keeps (eds.), *Handbook of human performance technology. Improving individual and organizational performance worldwide.*, Jossey-Bass/Pfeiffer, San Francisco, pp. 3–23.

Sudnickas, T 2016, 'Different levels of performance evaluation-individual versus organizational', *Viesoji Politika Ir Administravimas*, vol. 15, no. 2, http://dx.doi.org/10.13165/VPA-16-15-2-01.

Sullivan, ME, Yates, KA, Inaba, K, Lam, L & Clark, RE 2014, 'The use of cognitive task analysis to reveal the instructional limitations of experts in the teaching of procedural skills', *Academic Medicine*, vol. 89, no. 5, pp. 811–816, http://dx.doi.org/10.1097/ACM.0000000000000224.

Sullivan, R, Brechin, S & Lacoste, M 1999, Structured on-the-job training: innovations in international health training, in R Jacobs (ed.), *Linking HRD Programs with Organizational Strategy*, American Society for Training and Development (ASTD), Washinton, D.C., pp. 155–179, viewed 24 June 2017, <http://reprolineplus.org/system/files/resources/astd_ojt.pdf>.

Swanson, RA 1994, *Analysis for improving performance: tools for diagnosing organizations and documenting workplace expertise*, Berrett-Koehler, Oakland.

―――― 1995, 'Human resource development: performance is the key', *Human Resource Development Quarterly*, vol. 6, no. 2, pp. 207–213, viewed 24 June 2018, <http://www.richardswanson.com/publications/Swanson(1995)HRDPerform.pdf>.

―――― 1999, The foundations of performance improvement and implications for practice, in R Torraco (ed.), *The theory and practice of performance improvement*, Berrett-Koehler, San Francisco, pp. 1–25, http://dx.doi.org/10.1177/152342239900100102.

―――― 2001, 'Human resource development and its underlying theory', *Human Resource Development International*, vol. 4, no. 3, pp. 299–312, http://dx.doi.org/10.1080/13678860126440.

―――― 2007, *Analysis for improving performance: tools for diagnosing organizations and documenting workplace expertise*, 2nd ed., Berrett-Koehler, Oakland, viewed 24 June 2017, <http://www.bkconnection.com/static/Analysis-For-Improving-Performance_EXCERPT.pdf>.

Swanson, RA & Arnold, DE 1996, 'Part one: what is the purpose of human resource development? the purpose of human resource development is to improve organizational performance', *New Directions for Adult and Continuing Education*, vol. 1996, no. 72, pp. 13–19, http://dx.doi.org/10.1002/ace.36719967204.

Swanson, RA & Holton III, EF 2001, *Foundations of human resource development*, Berrett-Koehler, Oakland, viewed 24 June 2017, <https://www.bkconnection.com/static/Foundations_of_Human_Resource_Development_EXCERPT.pdf>.

Taghizadeh, F & Daneshfar, A 2014, 'Sequencing skills in teaching table tennis: inter-task transfer of learning', *International Journal of Sport Studies*, vol. 4, no. 1, pp. 631–634, viewed 24 June 2017, <http://ijssjournal.com/fulltext/paper-09012016125242.pdf>.

Tam, V, Lam, EY & Fung, S 2014, 'A new framework of concept clustering and learning path optimization to develop the next-generation e-learning systems', *Journal of Computers in Education*, vol. 1, no. 4, pp. 335–352, http://dx.doi.org/10.1007/s40692-014-0016-8.

Thomas, A, Thomas, A, Antony, J, Antony, J, Haven-Tang, C, Haven-Tang, C, Francis, M, Francis, M, Fisher, R & Fisher, R 2017, 'Implementing lean six sigma into curriculum design and delivery-a case study in higher education', *International Journal of Productivity and Performance Management*, vol. 66, no. 5, pp. 577–597, http://dx.doi.org/10.1108/IJPPM-08-2016-0176.

Thompson, KS 2017, Training's impact on time-to-proficiency for new bankers in a financial services organization, in S Frasard & P Frederick (eds.), *Training Initiatives and Strategies for the Modern Workforce*, IGI Global, Hershey, pp. 169–185, http://dx.doi.org/10.4018/978-1-5225-1808-2.ch009.

Thomsen, BC, Renaud, CC, Savory, SJ, Romans, EJ, Mitrofanov, O, Rio, M, Day, SE, Kenyon, AJ & Mitchell, JE 2010, 'Introducing scenario based learning: experiences from an undergraduate electronic and electrical engineering course', *IEEE Education Engineering Conference EDUCON 2010*, Madrid, IEEE, Piscataway, pp. 953–958, http://dx.doi.org/10.1109/EDUCON.2010.5492474.

Van Tiem, D, Moseley, JL & Dessinger, JC 2012, *Fundamentals of performance improvement: optimizing results through people, process, and organizations*, 3rd edn, Pfeiffer, San Francisco.

Van Tiem, DM, Moseley, JL & Dessinger, JC 2004, *Fundamentals of performance technology: a guide to improving people process and performance*, International Society for Performance Improvement, Washington DC, http://dx.doi.org/10.1002/pfi.4140400313.

Tims, M, Bakker, AB, Derks, D & van Rhenen, W 2013, 'Job crafting at the team and individual level: implications for work engagement and performance', *Group \& Organization Management*, vol. 38, no. 4, pp. 427–454, http://dx.doi.org/10.1177/1059601113492421.

Tjiam, IM, Schout, BMA, Hendrikx, AJM, Scherpbier, AJJM, Witjes, JA & van Merriënboer, JJG 2012, 'Designing simulator-based training: an approach integrating cognitive task analysis and four-component instructional design.', *Medical Teacher*, vol. 34, no. 10, pp. e698–707, http://dx.doi.org/10.3109/0142159X.2012.687480.

Tofel-Grehl, C & Feldon, DF 2013, 'Cognitive task analysis-based training: a meta-analysis of studies', *Journal of Cognitive Engineering and Decision Making*, vol. 7, no. 3, pp. 293–304, http://dx.doi.org/10.1177/1555343412474821.

Tokmak, HS, Baturay, HM & Fadde, P 2013, 'Applying the context, input, process, product evaluation model for evaluation, research, and redesign of an online master's program', *The International Review of Research in Open and Distributed Learning*, vol. 14, no. 3, pp. 273–293, http://dx.doi.org/10.19173/irrodl.v14i3.1485.

Trekles, AM & Sims, R 2013, 'Designing instruction for speed: qualitative insights into instructional design for accelerated online graduate coursework', *Online Journal of Distance Learning Administration*, vol. 16, no. 3, viewed 24 June 2017, <http://www.westga.edu/~distance/ojdla/winter164/trekles_sims164.html>.

Vandergriff, DE 2012, *Raising the bar: creating and nurturing adaptability to deal with the changing face of war*, Center for Defense Information, Washington, D.C.

VanLehn, K & Chi, M 2012, Adaptive expertise as acceleration of future learning, in P Durlach & A Tresgold (eds.), *Adaptive technologies for training and education*, Cambridge University Press, New York, pp. 28–46, http://dx.doi.org/10.1017/cbo9781139049580.005.

Vaughan, K 2008, *Workplace Learning: A Literature Review*, The New Zealand Engineering Food \& Manufacturing Industry Training Organisation Incorporated, Auckland, viewed 24 June 2017, <https://www.akoaotearoa.ac.nz/download/ng/file/group-189/n1575-workplace-learning-a-literature-review.pdf>.

Velmahos, GC, Toutouzas, KG, Sillin, LF, Chan, L, Clark, RE, Theodorou, D & Maupin, F 2004, 'Cognitive task analysis for teaching technical skills in an inanimate surgical skills laboratory', *The American Journal of Surgery*, vol. 187, no. 1, pp. 114–119, http://dx.doi.org/10.1016/j.amjsurg.2002.12.005.

Vidulich, M, Yeh, Y-Y & Schneider, W 1983, 'Time-compressed components for air-intercept control skills', *Proceedings of the Human Factors Society Annual Meeting*, vol. 27, no. 2, pp. 161–164, http://dx.doi.org/10.1177/154193128302700211.

Vihavainen, A, Paksula, M & Luukkainen, M 2011, 'Extreme apprenticeship method in teaching programming for beginners', *Proceedings of the 42nd ACM Technical Symposium on Computer Science Education*, Dallas, ACM, New York, pp. 93–98, viewed 24 June 2017, <http://moodle2.beitberl.ac.il/pluginfile.php/136972/mod_forum/attachment/55467/p93.pdf>.

Villachica, SW, Stone, DL & Endicott, J 2006, Performance support systems, in J Pershing (ed.), *Handbook of human performance technology: Principles, practices, and potential*, Pfeiffer, San Fransisco, pp. 539–566.

Viswesvaran, C 1993, *Modeling Job Performance: Is There a General Factor?*, University of Iowa, Iowa, viewed 24 June 2017, <http://www.dtic.mil/dtic/tr/fulltext/u2/a294282.pdf>.

Viswesvaran, C & Ones, DS 2000, 'Perspectives on models of job performance', *International Journal of Selection and Assessment*, vol. 8, no. 4, pp. 216–226, viewed 24 June 2017, <https://www.researchgate.net/profile/Deniz_Ones/publication/229645528>.

Vygotsky, LS 1978, *Mind in society: the development of higher mental process*, Harvard University Press, Cambridge.

WalkMe 2013, 'Express train: how to accelerate employee time to competence',, viewed 24 June 2017, <http://trainingstation.walkme.com/wp-content/uploads/2013/05/Express-Train.pdf>.

Wallace, GW 2006, Modeling mastery performance and systematically deriving the enablers for performance improvement, in J Pershing (ed.), *Handbook of human performance technology: Principles, practices, and potential*, Pfeiffer, San Francisco, viewed 24 June 2017, <http://widyo.staff.gunadarma.ac.id/Downloads/files/20372/HANDBOOK+OF+HPT_THIRD+EDITION.pdf#page=284>.

Wang, Z, Zhou, R & Shah, P 2014, 'Spaced cognitive training promotes training transfer', *Frontiers in Human Neuroscience*, vol. 8, pp. 1–8, http://dx.doi.org/10.3389/fnhum.2014.00217.

Ward, P, Hodges, NJ, Starkes, JL & Williams, AM 2007, 'The road to excellence: deliberate practice and the development of expertise', *High Ability Studies*, vol. 18, no. 2, pp. 119–153, http://dx.doi.org/10.1080/13598130701709715.

Ward, P, Williams, AM & Hancock, PA 2006, Simulation for performance and training, in K Ericsson, N Charness, P Feltovich & R Hoffman (eds.), *Development of expertise and expert performance*, Cambridge University Press, New York, pp. 243–262, http://dx.doi.org/10.1017/cbo9780511816796.014.

Watkins, K 1989, Five metaphors: alternative theories for human resource development, in D Gradous (ed.), *Systems theory applied to human resource development*, ASTD Press, Alexandria, pp. 167–184.

Watkins, KE & Marsick, VJ 1992, 'Towards a theory of informal and incidental learning in organizations', *International Journal of Lifelong Education*, vol. 11, no. 4, pp. 287–300, http://dx.doi.org/10.1080/0260137920110403.

_____ 1993, *Sculpting the learning organization: Lessons in the art and science of systemic change*, Jossey-Bass, San Francisco.

Welch, SK 2008, 'A metasynthesis of the transition from novice to expert: can instructional interventions shorten the process?', PhD thesis, ProQuest, Ann Arbor, viewed 24 June 2017, <https://search.proquest.com/docview/304821165>.

Wenger, E 2000, 'Communities of practice and social learning systems', *Organization*, vol. 7, no. 2, pp. 225–246, http://dx.doi.org/10.1177/135050840072002.

Werner, J & DeSimone, R 2009, Organization development and change, in J Werner & R DeSimone (eds.), *Human resource development*, Cengage, Mason, pp. 462–500.

Van de Wiel, MWJ & Van den Bossche, P 2013, 'Deliberate practice in medicine: the motivation to engage in work-related learning and its contribution to expertise', *Vocations and Learning*, vol. 6, no. 1, pp. 135–158, http://dx.doi.org/10.1007/s12186-012-9085-x.

Williams, AM, Ward, P, Knowles, JM & Smeeton, NJ 2002, 'Anticipation skill in a real-world task: measurement, training, and transfer in tennis', *Journal of Experimental Psychology: Applied*, vol. 8, no. 4, pp. 259–270, http://dx.doi.org/10.1037/1076-898X.8.4.259.

Williams, R, Faulkner, W & Fleck, J 1998, *Exploring expertise: issues and perspectives*, Palgrave Macmillan, Basingstoke, http://dx.doi.org/10.1007/978-1-349-13693-3_1.

Woodall, J 2000, 'Corporate support for work-based management development', *Human Resource Management Journal*, vol. 10, no. 1, pp. 18–32, http://dx.doi.org/10.1111/j.1748-8583.2000.tb00011.x .

Wooderson, JR, Cuskelly, M & Meyer, KA 2017, 'Evaluating the performance improvement preferences of disability service managers: an exploratory study using gilbert's behavior engineering model', *Journal of Applied Research in Intellectual Disabilities*, vol. 30, no. 4, pp. 661–671, http://dx.doi.org/10.1111/jar.12260.

Woolley, NN & Jarvis, Y 2007, 'Situated cognition and cognitive apprenticeship: a model for teaching and learning clinical skills in a technologically rich and authentic learning environment', *Nurse Education Today*, vol. 27, no. 1, pp. 73–9, http://dx.doi.org/10.1016/j.nedt.2006.02.010.

Wray, A & Wallace, M 2011, 'Accelerating the development of expertise: a step-change in social science research capacity building', *British Journal of Educational Studies*, vol. 59, no. 3, pp. 241–264, http://dx.doi.org/10.1080/00071005.2011.599790.

Wright, PM & McMahan, GC 2011, 'Exploring human capital: putting 'human' back into strategic human resource management', *Human Resource Management Journal*, vol. 21, no. 2, pp. 93–104, http://dx.doi.org/10.1111/j.1748-8583.2010.00165.x.

Yang, F, Li, FW & Lau, RW 2014, 'A fine-grained outcome-based learning path model', *IEEE Transactions on Systems, Man, and Cybernetics: Systems*, vol. 44, no. 2, pp. 235–245, http://dx.doi.org/10.1109/TSMCC.2013.2263133.

Yates, K, Sullivan, M & Clark, R 2012, 'Integrated studies on the use of cognitive task analysis to capture surgical expertise for central venous catheter placement and open cricothyrotomy', *The American Journal of Surgery*, vol. 203, no. 1, pp. 76–80, http://dx.doi.org/10.1016/j.amjsurg.2011.07.011.

Yawson, RM 2013, 'Systems theory and thinking as a foundational theory in human resource development—a myth or reality?', *Human Resource Development Review*, vol. 12, no. 1, pp. 53–85, http://dx.doi.org/10.1177/1534484312461634.

Yen, M, Trede, F & Patterson, C 2016, 'Learning in the workplace: the role of nurse managers', *Australian Health Review*, vol. 40, no. 3, pp. 286–291, http://dx.doi.org/10.1071/AH15022.

Zachary, W, Hoffman, R, Crandall, B, Miller, T & Nemeth, C 2012, '"Rapidized" cognitive task analysis', *IEEE Intelligent Systems*, vol. 27, no. 2, pp. 61–66, http://dx.doi.org/10.1109/mis.2012.29.

Zhamanov, A & Zhamapor, M 2013, 'Computer networks teaching by microlearning principles', *Journal of Physics: Conference Series*, vol. 423, no. 1, p. 012028, http://dx.doi.org/10.1088/1742-6596/423/1/012028.

Zhao, C & Wan, L 2006, 'A shortest learning path selection algorithm in e-learning', *Proceedings of the 6th International Conference on Advanced Learning Technologies (ICALT'06)*, Kerkrade, The Netherlands, IEEE, pp. 94–95, http://dx.doi.org/10.1109/ICALT.2006.33.

INDEX

Abilities, ix, 27
Accelerated proficiency, 91, 97, 103, 144
Accelerated Proficiency, xi, xiii, xiv, 109, 110, 112, 114, 194, 195, 197, 224
Accelerating learning, 201
Accelerating proficiency, 91
Action learning, 238
Anderson, ix, 3, 21, 33, 34, 35, 37, 39, 40, 42, 43, 46, 75, 77, 109, 122, 201, 237, 244
Behavioral performance, 18
BEM, 8, 9, 10
CFT, xi, 110, 112, 113, 114, 145, 149, 168
Cognitive task analysis, xi, 119, 121, 210, 211, 220, 236, 241, 248
Competence, 42, 221, 232
Competent, 53, 185
Conceptual skills, xi, 147
CTA, xi, 43, 119, 121, 122, 123, 124, 125, 126, 127, 128, 129, 131, 134, 135, 159, 169, 189
CTT, xi, 110, 111, 114, 145, 149, 168

Deliberate performance, xii, 163, 218
Deliberate practice, x, xii, 79, 80, 162, 163, 216, 222, 229, 244, 250
Desirable difficulties, xi, 142, 205
Experiential learning, 153, 200, 230
Expert, x, xi, xii, 32, 42, 43, 45, 54, 60, 73, 84, 122, 132, 167, 209, 216, 217, 219, 225
Expert performance, 217
Expert vs Proficient, x, 84
Expert-based systems, xii, 167
Expertise, xv, 32, 42, 43, 49, 73, 74, 84, 186, 187, 198, 206, 209, 210, 216, 218, 219, 220, 223, 224, 227
Fitts and Posner, ix, 33, 34, 35, 37, 78
Games, 230
Gamification, xi, 134, 223
HPT, 7, 10, 11, 12, 13, 249
Human performance, 212, 245
Human Performance Technology, 10
Human resource development, ix, 3, 246, 250
Individual performance, 24
Informal learning, 152, 215, 220
Job performance, ix, 14, 15, 17, 26

Knowledge capture, xii, 169
Langan-Fox, x, 33, 39, 40, 41, 42, 43, 56, 231
Learning, ix, xi, xii, xv, 5, 27, 29, 30, 42, 43, 67, 100, 107, 134, 164, 173, 185, 191, 198, 199, 200, 201, 202, 205, 209, 211, 214, 215, 218, 219, 220, 221, 223, 225, 227, 228, 229, 230, 233, 234, 235, 236, 240, 242, 244, 248, 250, 251, 258
Learning organizations, xii, 164
Learning paradigm, ix, 5
Model, xv, 8, 42, 43, 107, 195, 197, 198, 202, 218, 234, 259
Novice to expert, x, 46, 49
Novice to expert transition, x, 49
Operational simulation, xi, 138
Outcome performance, 20
Part-task, xi, 119, 120, 149
Part-task based methods, 119, 120
Performance improvement, 7, 220
Performance paradigm, ix, 6
Personalised learning, xii, 170
Proficiency, 4, x, xi, xii, xiii, xiv, xv, 1, 42, 50, 57, 59, 63, 66, 67, 69, 71, 73, 89, 91, 92, 95, 100, 107, 109, 110, 112, 114, 177, 190, 191, 194, 195, 197, 198, 199, 202, 209, 218, 224, 240, 259
Proficiency scaling, 59
Proficient, x, 54, 64, 84, 94
Role of proficiency, x, 64
Scenario-based training, xi, 119, 120, 141
Simulation, 119, 200, 203, 211, 218, 243, 249
Simulation-based training methods, 119
Social learning, 192
Stages, x, 50
Task performance, 27
Technology-based methods, xii, 119, 167
Time compression, xi, 130
Time to expertise, x, 81
Time to proficiency, 93, 239
Tough case, xi, 131, 143
Tutoring systems, xii, 167
Workplace, xi, xii, 41, 119, 120, 152, 185, 205, 211, 217, 228, 233, 235, 242, 248
Workplace activities, 120

THE AUTHOR

Dr. Raman K Attri is a speaker, author, and an expert on expertise, learning, and performance. He writes, speaks and appeals about the need for speed in today's business and provides directions on how to do so. An accomplished researcher, he specializes in competitive strategies to speed up professional and organizational performance. Awarded with several certified designations, his experience spans over 25 years in several cross-functional & interdisciplinary areas like systems engineering, management, and training. Most recently, he has served as a senior global training and learning manager at a $25bn corporation, named as Top 10 training organizations in the world. An accomplished practice researcher, he holds a Doctorate from SCU Australia in workforce performance and has developed a range of models, strategies, and techniques for personal, professional and organizational performance improvement. He has authored over 15 books in different genres and he holds several journal publications.

LinkedIn https://www.linkedin.com/in/rkattri
Facebook https://www.facebook.com/DrRamanKAttri
YouTube https://www.youtube.com/RamanKAttri
Research https://www.researchgate/profile/RamanKattri
Website http://ramankattri.com
Contact rkattri@ramankattri.com

FURTHER READINGS

DESIGNING TRAINING TO SHORTEN TIME TO PROFICIENCY: Online, Classroom and On-the-Job Learning Strategies from Research

ISBN: 978-981-14-0633-1 (e-book)
ISBN: 978-981-14-0632-4 (paperback)
ISBN: 978-981-14-0645-4 (hardcover)

Available with major retailers, distributors and market places

ACCELERATE YOUR LEADERSHIP DEVELOPMENT IN TRAINING DOMAIN: Proven Success Strategies for New Training & Learning Managers

ISBN: 978-981-11-8991-3 (e-book)
ISBN: 978-981-14-0066-7 (paperback)

Available with major retailers, distributors and market places

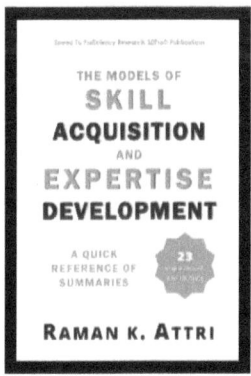

THE MODELS OF SKILL ACQUISITION AND EXPERTISE DEVELOPMENT: A Quick Reference of Summaries

SBN: 978-981-11-8988-3 (e-book)
ISBN: 978-981-14-1122-9 (paperback)
ISBN: 978-981-14-1130-4 (hardcover)

Available with major retailers, distributors and market places

TRAINING EFFECTIVENESS MEASUREMENT FOR LARGE SCALE PROGRAMS: DEMYSTIFIED! A 4-Tier Practical Model for Technical Training Managers

ISBN: 978-981-11-8990-6 (e-book)
ISBN: 978-981-11-417672 (paperback)

Available with major retailers, distributors and market places

ACCELERATING COMPLEX PROBLEM-SOLVING SKILLS: Problem-Centered Training Design Methods

ISBN: 978-981-11-8991-2 (e-book)
ISBN: 978-981-14-1766-5 (paperback)

Available with major retailers, distributors and market places

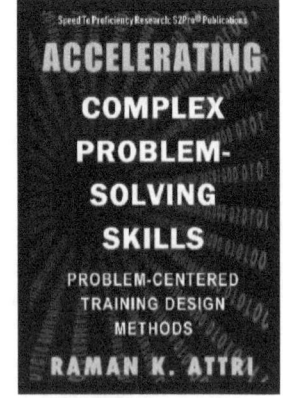

SPEED TO PROFICIENCY IN ORGANIZATIONS: Model, Practices and Strategies to Shorten Time To Proficiency

ISBN 978-981-14-0753-6 (e-book)

Available with major retailers, distributors and market places

www.ingramcontent.com/pod-product-compliance
Lightning Source LLC
LaVergne TN
LVHW091548070526
838199LV00029B/608/J